Cybersecurity & Personal Data Protection

Safeguarding Your Digital Life in a Vulnerable World

By Laura Lee

Lauxon Publishing, LLC

A Practical Guide to Protecting Your Data, Identity, and Privacy from Cyber Threats and Breaches in the Modern Digital Landscape.

Published by Lauxon Publishing, LLC

For permission requests, please contact:
Email: info@Lauxonpublishing.com
Website: www.Lauxonpublishing.com

Author Note:

Writing this book has been a journey of discovery, both for the reader and for me. I began with questions: How do we protect what is deeply personal in a world designed to share everything? How can we reclaim control over our digital selves without fear or overwhelm? Through research, reflection, and conversations with cybersecurity experts, I realized that the solutions are both practical and profoundly human.

This book is written for anyone navigating the digital world—from beginners to seasoned users, from families to professionals. Its purpose is to provide not just knowledge, but confidence. You do not need to be a technical expert to protect yourself; you need intention, understanding, and consistent habits. I hope these pages empower you to take control, make informed decisions, and live securely in the digital age.

TABLE OF CONTENTS:

Chapter 17: Understanding the Role of Data Privacy Laws
How Legislation, Such as GDPR and CCPA, Helps Protect Your Personal Information.

Chapter 18: Cybersecurity in the Cloud: Safeguarding Your Files
How to Securely Store, Share, and Access Your Files in Cloud Storage Platforms.

Chapter 19: Securing Your Email: The Digital Gateway to Your Identity
How to Protect Your Email Accounts from Being Hacked and Used for Fraud.

Chapter 20: The Risks of Data Breaches and How to Respond
What to Do When Your Personal Information Has Been Compromised in a Data Breach.

Chapter 21: The Role of Artificial Intelligence in Cybersecurity
How AI Is Revolutionizing the Field of Cyber Defense and Enhancing Personal Data Protection.

Chapter 22: Navigating Internet of Things (IoT) Security
How to Safeguard Your Smart Devices and Ensure They Don't Become a Gateway for Cybercriminals.

Chapter 23: What to Know About Digital Footprints and Tracking
How Your Online Activity Leaves Traces and How to Minimize Its Impact on Your Privacy.

Chapter 24: Protecting Your Data During Remote Work
Essential Security Measures for Telecommuters to Safeguard Personal and Corporate Data.

Chapter 25: The Dangers of Data Collection and How to Opt-Out
How Companies Collect and Use Your Data, and How to Limit or Refuse Their Access.

PROLOGUE:

In today's world, our lives are deeply entwined with the digital landscape. Every click, message, and transaction leaves traces that are both useful and vulnerable. What was once a private, physical existence now exists in the cloud, on servers, and across networks we may never see. The convenience of technology comes with a hidden cost: exposure to threats that can compromise our identity, finances, and even our freedom. This book is a roadmap, a guide, and a toolkit designed to empower you to navigate the digital age with confidence. Together, we will explore not only the mechanics of cybersecurity but the mindset, habits, and strategies needed to safeguard your most valuable digital assets.

The goal of this book is simple: to give you the awareness, understanding, and practical tools to take control of your online life. Cybersecurity is often presented as a technical, intimidating field—but at its heart, it is about awareness, responsibility, and proactive choices. The chapters that follow will demystify digital threats, provide actionable strategies, and help you build a personal plan that protects your data, devices, and identity. This is your invitation to take ownership, strengthen your defenses, and reclaim peace of mind in a world that never stops connecting.

Chapter .1

Introduction to Cybersecurity & Personal Data Protection

Understanding the Growing Threats in Our Digital Lives and Why Data Protection Matters More Than Ever.

In today's hyper-connected world, cybersecurity and personal data protection have become more critical than ever. The digital landscape is rapidly evolving, and so are the threats that accompany it. Every day, millions of people worldwide interact with technology, whether through social media, shopping online, or simply sending emails. With each action, a small but significant piece of personal information is often shared. Unfortunately, not everyone uses the internet responsibly, and malicious actors are continuously exploiting vulnerabilities for financial gain or to cause harm. The time to understand and act on cybersecurity principles is now—before it's too late.

The idea of personal data protection is not a new concept, but its importance has grown exponentially. Personal information, such as bank details, medical records, and even personal preferences, is now stored digitally. This data can easily be manipulated, stolen, or sold on the black market, often with devastating consequences for individuals. Cybersecurity isn't just about securing your computer from viruses; it's about safeguarding your identity, your assets, and your peace of mind. As more data becomes digital, the risk of cybercrime increases, making cybersecurity an essential part of our daily lives. Without proper protection, the threat of identity theft, fraud, and cyberattacks looms larger than ever.

For many, cybersecurity is an abstract and complex field filled with jargon and technical terms. However, cybersecurity is much simpler when approached from a personal perspective. Think of your personal data as valuable as your home or car—things that need locks, alarms, and protection. With just a few simple precautions, you can create a barrier between your personal information and cybercriminals. By learning about common threats, like phishing, ransomware, and hacking, you can better understand how to guard your digital assets. This chapter will serve as an introduction to the importance of cybersecurity and personal data protection in a digital world that increasingly requires vigilance and awareness.

Unfortunately, many individuals and businesses do not prioritize cybersecurity until they become victims of a cybercrime. It's a sad reality that many only take action after their data has been compromised, resulting in financial loss, reputation damage, or worse. Prevention, however, is far better than dealing with the aftermath of an attack. By making cybersecurity and data protection a top priority, you can mitigate the risks and safeguard your digital life. This chapter aims to provide an overview of the key elements involved in protecting your data and identity online. It's about shifting from a reactive to a proactive mindset, where you understand the risks and actively defend against them.

The importance of cybersecurity will only continue to grow in the coming years. As technology evolves, so do the tactics of cybercriminals, making it essential for everyone to stay informed about emerging threats. Many people mistakenly believe that cybersecurity is something only big businesses need to worry about, but the reality is that everyone, from individuals to large corporations, is a potential target. Whether you're a high-profile individual, a small business owner, or just someone who enjoys browsing the web, cybersecurity should be top of mind. As we proceed through this book, we will explore the steps you can take to secure your digital presence and ensure that your data remains protected. By understanding the threats and the solutions available, you'll be better equipped to navigate the digital world securely.

The digital world operates on trust, yet that trust is frequently tested by unseen threats. Every login, transaction, or message assumes that systems are secure and that personal data will remain private. Unfortunately, this assumption is often misplaced, as attackers actively search for weaknesses to exploit. Many cyber incidents occur not because technology fails, but because awareness is lacking. A single careless click or overshared detail can open the door to serious consequences. Understanding this reality is the first step toward building a safer digital life.

Cybersecurity is no longer a concern reserved for technology professionals or large corporations. Individuals now manage more digital assets than ever before, including personal photos, financial records, and sensitive communications. These assets hold real value, both emotionally and economically. When compromised, they can lead to identity theft, financial loss, and long-term stress. The emotional toll of a cyber incident is often underestimated, yet it can be just as damaging as the financial impact. Recognizing personal data as something worth protecting is a crucial mindset shift.

Personal data protection is deeply connected to everyday behavior. The choices we make online, such as which apps we trust or what permissions we grant, directly affect our security. Many digital services are designed for convenience, not safety, which places the burden of protection on the user. Without clear guidance, people often prioritize ease of use over security. This imbalance creates opportunities for cybercriminals to take advantage of human habits. Learning to balance convenience with caution is essential for long-term protection.

Another challenge in cybersecurity is the false sense of anonymity many people feel online. The internet can create the illusion that our actions are invisible or disconnected from our real lives. In reality, most online activity is tracked, logged, and stored in some form. Data brokers, advertisers, and malicious actors alike can piece together information from multiple sources. What seems like harmless data in isolation can become dangerous when combined. Awareness of this interconnectedness helps explain why personal data protection matters so deeply.

Education is one of the most powerful defenses against cyber threats. While no system can be made completely immune to attack, informed users are far less likely to become victims. Understanding basic concepts such as secure passwords, data privacy, and online scams dramatically reduces risk. This book is designed to demystify cybersecurity and make it accessible to everyone. You do not need to be a technical expert to protect yourself effectively. What you need is awareness, consistency, and a willingness to adapt.

The responsibility for cybersecurity is shared between technology providers and users. Companies must design secure systems, but individuals must use them wisely. Blaming technology alone ignores the human factor that plays a role in most breaches. By taking ownership of our digital behavior, we become active participants in our own protection. This sense of responsibility is empowering rather than limiting. It allows us to navigate the digital world with confidence instead of fear.

As digital threats continue to evolve, so must our understanding of them. Cybersecurity is not a one-time action, but an ongoing process of learning and adjustment. New technologies introduce new vulnerabilities, and attackers are quick to exploit them. Staying informed is no longer optional; it is a necessity. This chapter sets the foundation for that ongoing learning process. The chapters that follow will build practical skills and strategies to help you stay secure in an ever-changing digital environment.

Ultimately, cybersecurity is about preserving freedom and trust in the digital age. Without adequate protection, innovation slows and fear takes its place. Personal data protection ensures that individuals can participate in digital life without constant worry. It safeguards not only information, but dignity and autonomy as well.

By understanding the risks and solutions, we reclaim control over our digital identities. This journey begins with awareness, and awareness begins here.

Modern life is deeply intertwined with digital systems that operate quietly in the background. From navigation apps to online banking, these systems handle sensitive data every second. Most users rarely see how their information is processed, stored, or shared. This invisibility can create complacency, making risks easier to ignore. Cybercriminals thrive in this gap between usage and understanding. Closing that gap is essential to meaningful personal data protection.

One reason cybersecurity feels overwhelming is the speed at which technology evolves. New platforms, devices, and services appear constantly, each with unique risks. Users are often expected to adapt instantly, with little guidance or education. This rapid change creates security blind spots that attackers exploit. Staying secure does not require mastering every new technology, but it does require a foundational understanding of risk. Once that foundation is built, adapting becomes far easier.

Another critical issue is the normalization of data sharing. Many services require personal information as the price of entry, conditioning users to give up data without question. Over time, this erodes caution and weakens privacy boundaries. People may share birthdays, locations, or contact lists without considering how that data could be misused. Cybersecurity begins with questioning what is being asked and why. Thoughtful resistance to unnecessary data sharing is a powerful protective act.

The impact of weak cybersecurity extends beyond individuals to families and communities. A compromised account can be used to scam friends, spread malware, or steal from others. In this way, one person's vulnerability can affect many. Cybersecurity is therefore not just personal, but collective. Protecting your own data helps protect the people connected to you. This interconnected reality makes personal responsibility even more important.

Trust is a fragile element in the digital ecosystem. When data breaches and cyber scams become common, trust in technology erodes. People become hesitant to use digital tools that once improved their lives. This hesitation can slow progress and widen the digital divide. Strong cybersecurity practices help rebuild and maintain trust. They ensure that digital innovation remains a force for good rather than a source of harm.

Fear-based narratives around cybersecurity can be counterproductive. While threats are real, constant alarm can lead to avoidance rather than action. Effective cybersecurity education focuses on empowerment, not panic. Understanding risks should lead to confidence, not paralysis. This book is designed to replace fear with clarity and confusion with practical guidance. Confidence is one of the strongest defenses against cyber threats.

Cybersecurity also intersects with ethics and personal values. How we protect data reflects how much we value privacy, autonomy, and respect for others. Protecting personal data is not just about self-interest; it is about contributing to a safer digital society. When users demand better security and practice good digital habits, standards improve for everyone. Individual choices collectively shape the digital world. This makes cybersecurity a form of civic responsibility.

As this chapter continues to unfold, one message becomes clear: cybersecurity is not optional. It is an essential life skill in the digital age. Just as we learn to lock our doors and protect our possessions, we must learn to secure our digital lives. The tools exist, and the knowledge is accessible. What remains is the willingness to apply them consistently. That willingness is the foundation upon which everything else in this book is built.

At the heart of cybersecurity lies the concept of risk management. Absolute security does not exist, either online or offline, but risks can be reduced to manageable levels. Understanding which behaviors increase exposure allows individuals to make better decisions. Small changes, such as enabling security settings or being cautious with links, can significantly reduce vulnerability.

Cybercriminals often look for easy targets rather than well-protected ones. Awareness alone can be enough to shift you out of that high-risk category.

Personal data protection is also closely tied to control. Knowing where your data lives, who has access to it, and how it is used gives you power. Many people feel powerless online because they do not understand these mechanisms. Gaining control starts with asking questions and reading beyond default settings. Privacy policies may be tedious, but they reveal how your information is handled. Control grows as understanding grows.

Another overlooked aspect of cybersecurity is habit formation. Security is most effective when it becomes routine rather than reactive. Checking permissions, updating software, and reviewing accounts should be as normal as checking your front door before bed. Habits remove reliance on memory and motivation. Over time, these actions become automatic and require little effort. Consistency is more important than complexity when it comes to staying secure.

The digital world also mirrors the physical one in terms of responsibility. Just as society expects individuals to act responsibly in public spaces, digital spaces require the same consideration. Reckless behavior online can harm others just as easily as oneself. Sharing compromised information, forwarding scams, or ignoring security warnings has consequences. Cybersecurity is therefore an act of respect toward others. Responsible digital behavior strengthens the entire online ecosystem.

Technology itself is neutral; it reflects how it is used. Cybersecurity challenges arise not because technology exists, but because it can be misused. This perspective helps remove fear and blame from the conversation. Instead of viewing technology as dangerous, we can view education as the solution. Informed users transform technology into a tool for empowerment rather than exploitation. Knowledge changes the balance of power.

As you move deeper into this book, you will encounter both technical concepts and behavioral strategies. Some ideas may feel familiar, while others may challenge long-held assumptions. Growth often begins with discomfort, especially when habits must change. This discomfort is temporary, but the benefits are lasting. Every step taken toward better security is an investment in your future. Progress matters more than perfection.

Cybersecurity and personal data protection are no longer optional skills reserved for specialists. They are essential life skills in a connected world. The purpose of this chapter has been to build awareness and establish urgency without fear. Awareness leads to action, and action leads to resilience. You are not powerless in the face of cyber threats. With the right knowledge and mindset, you can protect what matters most.

This introduction marks the beginning of a practical journey. Each chapter ahead will focus on specific threats and solutions, building upon what you have learned here. The goal is not just to inform, but to equip you. By the end of this book, cybersecurity will no longer feel abstract or overwhelming. It will feel manageable, logical, and within your control.

Reflection:

Writing this chapter reminded me how easily we underestimate the value of our personal data. We protect our physical belongings instinctively, yet often neglect our digital ones. This imbalance is not due to carelessness, but a lack of understanding. Once people realize how interconnected their digital lives are, priorities begin to shift. My hope is that this chapter sparks that shift for you. Awareness is the quiet beginning of meaningful change.

"The greatest risk in the digital age is not that we use technology, but that we use it without understanding how to protect ourselves."
— Unknown

CHAPTER .2

THE ANATOMY OF CYBER THREATS AND ATTACKS

Exploring the Different Types of Cyber Attacks and How They Impact Individuals and Organizations.

Cyber threats come in many forms, but all share a common goal: unauthorized access to data or systems. These threats exploit weaknesses in technology, processes, or human behavior. Understanding how cyber attacks work is essential to defending against them. Attacks are rarely random and are often carefully planned to maximize impact. Cybercriminals study their targets just as closely as defenders study threats. This chapter begins by breaking down the structure and intent behind modern cyber attacks.

One of the most common cyber threats is malware, a broad term for malicious software designed to harm or exploit systems. Malware includes viruses, worms, trojans, spyware, and ransomware. Each type operates differently, but all are created to infiltrate devices without consent. Some malware steals information quietly, while others disrupt systems openly. Many infections occur through seemingly harmless downloads or links. Once inside, malware can spread rapidly and cause significant damage.

Another major category of cyber threats involves social engineering attacks. These attacks rely on manipulating human psychology rather than exploiting technical flaws. Cybercriminals impersonate trusted entities to trick individuals into revealing sensitive information. Emails, phone calls, and text messages are commonly used in these schemes. The success of social engineering lies in urgency, fear, or curiosity. Understanding this tactic helps individuals pause and think before reacting.

Network-based attacks target the infrastructure that connects devices and systems. These attacks aim to intercept, disrupt, or overload network traffic. Distributed denial-of-service attacks, for example, flood systems with requests until they become unusable. Other attacks involve intercepting data as it travels across unsecured networks. Weak or misconfigured networks provide easy entry points for attackers. Protecting networks is therefore a critical part of cybersecurity defense.

Cyber attacks also vary in scale and intent. Some attackers target individuals for financial gain, while others aim at organizations or governments. Small-scale attacks may involve stealing login credentials, while large-scale operations can disrupt critical infrastructure. Motivations range from profit and espionage to activism and sabotage. Understanding attacker motivation helps predict behavior and improve defenses. Not all threats are equal, but all deserve attention.

Attackers often follow a predictable lifecycle when executing a cyber attack. This process includes reconnaissance, infiltration, exploitation, and persistence. During reconnaissance, attackers gather information about potential targets. Infiltration occurs when they gain initial access through a vulnerability. Exploitation allows them to achieve their objective, such as stealing data. Persistence ensures continued access even if defenses improve.

Technology alone cannot stop cyber threats without informed users. Many attacks succeed because of simple mistakes, such as clicking malicious links or using weak passwords. Cybercriminals depend on these errors to bypass sophisticated defenses. This is why education is as important as technology in cybersecurity. When users understand how attacks work, they become much harder to deceive. Knowledge turns potential victims into active defenders.

As cyber threats continue to evolve, so do the methods used to carry them out. Automation, artificial intelligence, and global connectivity have increased the scale of attacks. What once required significant resources can now be done with minimal effort. This reality makes understanding cyber threats more important than ever. Awareness reduces surprise, and reduced surprise limits damage. The next sections of this chapter will explore specific attack types in greater detail and explain how they affect both individuals and organizations.

Phishing remains one of the most widespread and effective cyber attack methods in use today. These attacks are designed to appear legitimate, often mimicking trusted companies or individuals. Attackers craft messages that create urgency, such as warnings about account closures or suspicious activity. Victims are encouraged to click links or provide sensitive information quickly. Once credentials are stolen, attackers can access accounts and escalate their attacks. Phishing succeeds because it exploits trust rather than technology.

Ransomware attacks have grown rapidly due to their high profitability. In these attacks, malware encrypts a victim's data and demands payment for its release. Individuals may lose access to personal files, while organizations can face operational shutdowns. Even when ransoms are paid, there is no guarantee data will be restored. Ransomware often spreads through email attachments or unpatched software vulnerabilities. Prevention and backups are the most effective defenses against this threat.

Credential-based attacks focus on exploiting weak or reused passwords. Attackers use automated tools to test stolen credentials across multiple platforms. This technique, known as credential stuffing, takes advantage of the fact that many users reuse passwords. Once access is gained, attackers can steal data or impersonate the victim. Strong, unique passwords significantly reduce the success of these attacks. This highlights the importance of basic security hygiene.

Man-in-the-middle attacks occur when attackers intercept communication between two parties. These attacks are common on unsecured public networks. Sensitive data such as login credentials or financial information can be captured in transit. Victims are often unaware that interception has occurred. Encryption and secure connections are essential defenses against this threat. Awareness of network security plays a critical role in prevention.

Supply chain attacks target trusted third-party vendors to reach larger groups of victims. Instead of attacking users directly, attackers compromise software updates or services. This method allows malicious code to spread widely and quietly. Victims trust the source, making detection difficult. Supply chain attacks demonstrate how interconnected digital systems have become. Trust must be paired with verification in modern cybersecurity.

Insider threats represent another complex category of cyber risk. These threats come from individuals with legitimate access to systems. Sometimes the actions are malicious, while other times they are accidental. Human error can be just as damaging as intentional misuse. Proper training, access controls, and monitoring reduce insider risk. Security is strongest when people and processes are aligned.

Cyber attacks are rarely isolated events; they often combine multiple techniques. An attacker may use phishing to gain access, malware to spread, and ransomware to monetize the attack. Understanding this layered approach helps defenders recognize early warning signs. Early detection can prevent minor incidents from becoming major breaches. Awareness allows faster response and reduced damage. Preparation turns chaos into manageable incidents.

The anatomy of cyber threats reveals a critical truth: attackers rely on predictability. They exploit common behaviors, outdated systems, and weak defenses. Breaking these patterns disrupts their success. By understanding how attacks are structured, individuals and organizations gain a strategic advantage. Knowledge transforms cybersecurity from reactive to proactive. This understanding sets the stage for learning how to protect what matters most.

Advanced persistent threats represent some of the most sophisticated cyber attacks in existence. These attacks are typically carried out by well-funded groups with long-term objectives. Instead of causing immediate damage, attackers remain hidden while collecting data over extended periods. Victims may not realize they have been compromised for months or even years. These threats often target governments, corporations, and critical infrastructure. Understanding them highlights how patience and stealth can be more dangerous than speed.

Zero-day attacks exploit vulnerabilities that are unknown to software developers. Because no fix exists at the time of exploitation, defenses are limited. Attackers who discover these flaws gain a significant advantage. Zero-day attacks are often used in targeted operations rather than mass attacks. Their existence underscores the importance of layered security rather than reliance on a single defense. Even fully updated systems can be at risk.

Cyber attacks also differ based on opportunity rather than intent. Opportunistic attackers scan the internet for exposed systems and weak credentials. They are less selective and aim for volume rather than precision. These attacks are common and affect individuals and small organizations frequently. Simple misconfigurations or default passwords are enough to attract attention. Good basic security practices dramatically reduce exposure to these threats.

Targeted attacks, by contrast, are carefully customized for specific victims. Attackers research their targets using publicly available information. Social media profiles, company websites, and public records provide valuable intelligence. Messages and malware are then tailored to increase credibility. These attacks are harder to detect because they appear legitimate. Awareness of personal information exposure reduces their effectiveness.

Automation has transformed the scale of cyber attacks. Tools can now scan thousands of systems in minutes. Attacks that once required technical expertise are now accessible to novices. This has lowered the barrier to entry for cybercrime. Automation increases speed but also increases noise. Well-configured defenses can detect and block many automated attacks.

Financial incentives drive the majority of cyber attacks today. Stolen data can be sold, used for fraud, or leveraged for extortion. Even small amounts of data can be profitable when stolen at scale. This economic motivation ensures that cyber threats will continue to evolve. As long as cybercrime remains lucrative, attackers will adapt. Defense must therefore evolve just as quickly.

Understanding the anatomy of cyber threats allows patterns to emerge. Attacks follow logic, structure, and repeatable methods. This predictability is a weakness that defenders can exploit. Education transforms uncertainty into clarity. When you know how attacks work, they lose much of their power. Awareness is the first real line of defense.

As this chapter draws toward completion, the key takeaway is perspective. Cyber threats are not mysterious forces but engineered processes. They rely on human error, technical gaps, and misplaced trust. Addressing these areas dramatically reduces risk. The next chapters will shift focus from threats to protection. With a clear understanding of how attacks work, you are now ready to learn how to stop them.

Another important dimension of cyber threats is the role of misinformation and disinformation. While not always classified as traditional cyber attacks, these tactics exploit digital platforms to manipulate behavior. False information can be spread rapidly through compromised accounts or coordinated campaigns. The goal is often to influence decisions, damage reputations, or create confusion. These attacks target perception rather than systems, yet their impact can be just as severe. Understanding this threat expands the definition of cybersecurity beyond technical breaches.

Timing also plays a significant role in how cyber attacks succeed. Attackers often strike during holidays, emergencies, or periods of high stress. During these times, people are more distracted and less vigilant. Organizations may operate with reduced staff, delaying detection and response. Cybercriminals exploit these moments strategically. Awareness of timing helps explain why attacks often coincide with major events. Preparedness must account for human behavior under pressure.

The aftermath of a cyber attack is often more damaging than the initial breach. Recovery can involve financial loss, reputational damage, and emotional distress. For organizations, trust once lost is difficult to regain. Individuals may spend months repairing credit or restoring accounts. The ripple effects can extend far beyond the original incident. Understanding consequences reinforces why prevention is critical. Cybersecurity is not just about stopping attacks, but about minimizing long-term harm.

Many cyber attacks succeed because warning signs are ignored. Unusual login alerts, system slowdowns, or unexpected messages are often dismissed. Attackers rely on this delay to deepen their access. Early detection is one of the most effective ways to limit damage. Paying attention to small anomalies can prevent major incidents. Cybersecurity rewards attentiveness and curiosity. Asking questions is a powerful defensive tool.

Training and awareness transform users from vulnerabilities into safeguards. When people understand how attacks unfold, they respond more effectively. This reduces panic and improves decision-making under pressure. Cybersecurity awareness does not eliminate risk, but it dramatically reduces impact. Informed users act faster and make fewer mistakes. Knowledge shortens recovery time and limits exposure.

The anatomy of cyber threats reveals a consistent truth: attacks are designed, not accidental. They follow patterns shaped by incentives, opportunity, and human behavior. This makes them understandable and, therefore, preventable. Complexity should not discourage action. Even simple defensive steps disrupt many attack strategies. Defense does not require perfection, only persistence.

Cyber threats are constantly evolving, and understanding their evolution is key to staying protected. Early attacks were relatively simple, often exploiting basic software flaws or using straightforward scams. Over time, attackers have become more sophisticated, combining multiple techniques to achieve their goals. Advanced attacks now include stealth, automation, and manipulation of human psychology. This evolution means that defenses must also adapt continuously. Recognizing trends in cyber threats allows users and organizations to anticipate risks rather than react to them.

The rise of cloud computing has introduced new attack vectors. Cloud environments centralize data, which can be both convenient and risky. Misconfigured cloud storage or weak access controls can expose sensitive information to attackers. Cloud-based attacks often exploit trust between services and users. Understanding the specific risks of cloud computing is essential for modern cybersecurity. Protecting cloud assets requires both technical knowledge and good operational practices.

Cybercriminals also leverage anonymity to their advantage. The internet allows them to hide behind layers of obfuscation, including VPNs, Tor networks, and stolen accounts. This anonymity complicates attribution, making it difficult to identify perpetrators. It also emboldens attackers, since legal consequences feel distant. Users must assume that attackers are persistent and capable. Recognizing the intent and sophistication of attackers informs defensive strategies.

Attackers often exploit human behavior, knowing that people are the weakest link in cybersecurity. This includes phishing, social engineering, and exploiting predictable habits. Cybercriminals rely on urgency, curiosity, and fear to manipulate victims. Training and awareness help reduce this vulnerability. Users who understand common tactics are less likely to be deceived. Cybersecurity is as much about psychology as it is about technology.

Finally, organizations face additional challenges because attacks are increasingly targeted and multifaceted. Large-scale operations combine ransomware, phishing, and network exploitation. Critical infrastructure, financial systems, and healthcare networks are common targets. Defending against these attacks requires coordinated efforts, continuous monitoring, and rapid response. Individual users also play a role in this ecosystem by practicing good cybersecurity habits. Understanding the broader context emphasizes that cybersecurity is both personal and collective.

Reflection:

Exploring the anatomy of cyber threats has reinforced how strategic and calculated these attacks are. They are not random; they are meticulously planned to exploit vulnerabilities, whether technical or human. As a reader, understanding this can transform fear into proactive vigilance. Cybersecurity is about preparation, education, and responsibility. Every small step taken to secure your data contributes to a safer digital environment for yourself and those around you.

CHAPTER .3

WHY PERSONAL DATA IS A TARGET FOR CYBERCRIMINALS

Recognizing the Value of Your Personal Information and the Risks of Its Exposure

Personal data has become one of the most valuable commodities in the digital age. Every click, purchase, and interaction online generates information that can be collected, analyzed, and monetized. Cybercriminals are acutely aware of this value, and they constantly develop strategies to access it. From social security numbers to email addresses and even shopping habits, each piece of data has potential financial or strategic worth. Unlike physical assets, digital data can be copied and distributed endlessly, increasing its attractiveness to attackers. Understanding the value of your information is the first step toward protecting it effectively.

Identity theft is one of the most common consequences of stolen personal data. When cybercriminals acquire your information, they can impersonate you in order to open accounts, make purchases, or even commit crimes under your name. This type of fraud can have long-lasting effects on your finances, credit score, and reputation. Many people assume identity theft only affects the wealthy, but in reality, anyone with personal information can be targeted. The accessibility of stolen data on the dark web makes it even easier for criminals to commit fraud. Protecting your personal data is therefore not optional; it is a necessity for maintaining control over your identity.

Financial information is particularly valuable to cybercriminals because it can be directly converted into money. Bank account details, credit card numbers, and digital payment credentials are prime targets. Attackers may also use your information to bypass security questions and access other accounts. Small details, such as your date of birth or address, can provide the keys to unlocking accounts. Even temporary access can be profitable for criminals, making all data points potentially dangerous. The more aware you are of what you share and how it can be exploited, the better you can defend against attacks.

Social media accounts are another goldmine for cybercriminals. Platforms like Facebook, Instagram, and LinkedIn hold vast amounts of personal information. Birthdays, location check-ins, friend networks, and personal interests can all be leveraged for malicious purposes. Cybercriminals may use this information for targeted phishing attacks or to create convincing social engineering schemes. Even seemingly harmless posts can reveal patterns and vulnerabilities. The more information shared publicly, the more opportunities exist for exploitation.

Personal data is also valuable to businesses and advertisers, which raises concerns beyond criminal intent. Companies track user behavior to develop marketing strategies, predict trends, and sell products. While this data collection is often legal and legitimate, it also creates a risk if those databases are breached. High-profile data breaches have exposed millions of users' personal information to attackers. The convergence of business data collection and criminal exploitation illustrates why safeguarding personal data is critical. Users must navigate this landscape thoughtfully and intentionally.

The variety of ways cybercriminals can exploit personal data is staggering. Beyond financial gain, stolen data can be used for blackmail, espionage, or even identity resale on underground markets. Some attackers seek to manipulate victims for political or social influence. Others aim to infiltrate organizations using stolen employee credentials. Recognizing these diverse motivations underscores the importance of proactive data protection. The more you understand potential threats, the better prepared you are to mitigate them.

Many people underestimate how much information they generate daily. Emails, app usage, GPS data, and even health information can reveal patterns about behavior, location, and preferences. Attackers use this data to build detailed profiles for targeted attacks. Every piece of seemingly trivial information can be combined with other data to create a complete picture. Awareness of the extent of personal data generation is a crucial step in reducing risk. Limiting unnecessary sharing and monitoring digital footprints becomes essential in protecting oneself.

Data breaches have shown that no one is immune, regardless of wealth or status. Large corporations, healthcare providers, and government agencies have all experienced breaches that exposed sensitive user information. When such breaches occur, individuals often have little recourse beyond monitoring accounts and changing passwords. Proactive measures, such as using strong passwords, encryption, and secure connections, are far more effective than reactive ones. Learning to treat personal data as a valuable asset is key to preventing compromise. Cybersecurity is as much about mindset as it is about technology.

The digital economy has created an environment where personal information drives value for many actors. Cybercriminals, advertisers, and even social networks capitalize on data. Understanding why your personal information is sought after allows you to make conscious choices about sharing it. Protecting your data requires vigilance, informed decisions, and the consistent application of security practices. The next chapters will provide actionable strategies for defending your personal information in a variety of contexts. Awareness, combined with practical steps, empowers you to reclaim control over your digital life.

Cybercriminals often focus on patterns of behavior rather than single pieces of information. By analyzing online activity, attackers can identify vulnerabilities and predict opportunities for exploitation. This can include recognizing weak passwords, frequent use of certain apps, or predictable responses to emails and notifications. Understanding these patterns allows criminals to craft personalized attacks that are far more effective. Awareness of your own digital habits is a critical part of defense. Small adjustments in behavior can significantly reduce risk exposure.

Healthcare data has become a particularly attractive target for cybercriminals. Medical records contain a wealth of personal information, including social security numbers, insurance details, and medical history. This information can be sold on the dark web or used for identity theft and insurance fraud. Healthcare organizations often manage large volumes of data with limited resources, making them vulnerable to breaches. Patients are typically unaware of how exposed their information may be. Protecting personal health data requires vigilance both from institutions and from individuals.

Education and employment records also hold considerable value. Academic transcripts, student IDs, and employment details can be used to steal identities or gain unauthorized access to services. Attackers often target these records because they are rich with personal identifiers and less well-protected than financial data. Even seemingly minor details, such as graduation dates or employee numbers, can be exploited in combination with other data. Awareness of these risks encourages more cautious sharing and handling of personal information. Preventing exposure is much easier than recovering from misuse.

Personal data is not only targeted for theft but also for manipulation. Attackers use information to influence decisions or coerce individuals into specific actions. Phishing schemes, targeted ads, and even social engineering scams leverage personal knowledge to manipulate victims. These tactics are subtle and often exploit trust or authority. Recognizing that your data can be used to influence behavior helps you remain cautious. Guarding your personal information protects both your assets and your autonomy.

Children and minors are increasingly targets for cybercriminals. Their digital identities are often less protected, and they are less likely to recognize scams or phishing attempts. Attackers can exploit this naivety to steal information or gain access to family accounts. Monitoring and educating young users is critical for their safety. Parents and guardians must actively manage privacy settings and online exposure. The digital safety of children relies on proactive, informed guidance.

Attackers also exploit the interconnectedness of personal and professional information. Credentials used in one context, like an email for work, can be leveraged to access personal accounts. Similarly, personal details shared publicly can be combined with professional data to facilitate attacks. Awareness of these links is essential to maintaining security across multiple spheres. Compartmentalizing information reduces risk and limits potential damage. A holistic approach to data protection considers both personal and professional exposures.

The value of personal data increases with volume and accuracy. The more comprehensive and detailed the information, the more profitable it becomes for attackers. This is why social media profiles, online purchases, and digital communications are so frequently targeted. Even small pieces of data, when combined, can reveal much more than anticipated. Recognizing the cumulative value of your information is key to taking data protection seriously. Every bit of information shared online should be treated as valuable.

Ultimately, understanding why cybercriminals target personal data empowers individuals to act proactively. Awareness of motivations, methods, and the types of information most at risk informs defensive strategies. Protecting your personal data requires consistent effort, mindfulness, and adoption of best practices. In the digital era, data is both an asset and a vulnerability. Treating it with care is not optional—it is essential. The following chapters will provide the tools and techniques necessary to safeguard your information effectively.

The ease with which personal data can be stolen makes it a constant target for cybercriminals. Even a single compromised password or unsecured account can provide a gateway to larger systems. Attackers often start with low-risk or easily accessible information and escalate their attacks from there. Public Wi-Fi, poorly secured apps, and reused credentials all create opportunities for exploitation. Cybercriminals capitalize on these small openings to gain greater access. Recognizing these vulnerabilities encourages individuals to implement preventive measures consistently.

Digital footprints also make individuals predictable targets. Every website visited, search query entered, or social post shared contributes to a larger profile. Attackers can piece together seemingly minor details to create comprehensive insights about routines, preferences, and vulnerabilities. Awareness of this reality emphasizes caution in what is shared online. Even information shared with friends can be intercepted or leaked. Understanding digital footprints is critical to reducing exposure. Practicing selective sharing protects both privacy and security.

Data aggregation has increased the profitability of personal information. Companies collect data for analytics, marketing, and product development, creating vast repositories of user information. When these databases are compromised, cybercriminals gain access to thousands or millions of profiles at once. Individual actions, such as monitoring privacy settings and opting out of unnecessary data collection, become crucial. Limiting exposure reduces the attractiveness of your data as a target. Proactive management of personal information is essential in today's data-driven environment.

Cybercriminals also exploit trust in digital ecosystems. Users naturally trust emails from known contacts, websites with familiar designs, and notifications that appear official. This trust is manipulated through phishing, malware-laden links, and fraudulent communications. Attacks often mimic legitimate services to deceive even cautious users. Developing a critical eye toward digital interactions enhances security. Recognizing when trust is being exploited allows you to respond safely and confidently.

The consequences of data compromise are far-reaching. Beyond financial loss, personal data theft can affect professional reputation, relationships, and mental well-being. Victims often face months of recovery, dealing with credit monitoring, password resets, and fraud investigations. Identity theft, in particular, can cause long-lasting challenges that affect daily life. The emotional impact is often underestimated but significant. Understanding these risks reinforces the importance of preventive action and consistent cybersecurity practices.

Even small actions can make a significant difference in protecting personal data. Using strong, unique passwords, enabling multi-factor authentication, and monitoring account activity are foundational steps. Being cautious about what is shared online, especially on social media, reduces vulnerability. Regularly reviewing privacy settings on apps and platforms ensures that sensitive information remains controlled. Awareness combined with action transforms personal data from an easy target into a protected asset. Every precaution matters when cybercriminals are constantly seeking opportunities.

The digital world will continue to expand, and personal data will remain a valuable commodity. As technology advances, new forms of data will emerge, creating fresh targets for attackers. Biometric information, IoT devices, and wearable technology all contribute additional layers of personal data. Staying informed about emerging risks ensures that protective strategies evolve alongside threats. Individuals who understand the value of their data are better positioned to safeguard it. Knowledge and vigilance are the strongest tools in preventing data exploitation.

Recognizing why personal data is targeted is essential for developing effective cybersecurity habits. Attackers are motivated by financial gain, exploitation, or strategic advantage. They rely on human error, trust, and lack of awareness to succeed. Understanding these factors empowers users to make informed decisions. Cybersecurity is therefore both a mindset and a practice. Protecting personal data requires vigilance, education, and consistent application of security principles.

CHAPTER .4

THE ROLE OF ENCRYPTION IN PROTECTING YOUR DATA

How Encryption Works to Safeguard Your Information from Unauthorized Access

Encryption is one of the most powerful tools available for protecting personal data. At its core, encryption converts readable information into an unreadable format using algorithms. Only those with the correct decryption key can access the original data. This process ensures that even if a cybercriminal intercepts your data, it remains useless without authorization. Encryption protects everything from emails to financial transactions and personal files. Understanding how encryption works is the first step toward appreciating its importance in cybersecurity.

Modern encryption relies on complex mathematical algorithms to secure information. Symmetric encryption uses a single key for both encryption and decryption, while asymmetric encryption employs a pair of keys—public and private. Each method has its own advantages and applications depending on the context. Symmetric encryption is fast and efficient, ideal for large datasets, while asymmetric encryption is commonly used for secure communications. The choice of encryption method influences both security and usability. Regardless of the type, the goal remains the same: prevent unauthorized access.

Data in transit and data at rest both benefit from encryption. Data in transit includes information sent over networks, such as emails, messaging apps, and web traffic. Encrypting this data ensures that it cannot be intercepted and read during transmission. Data at rest refers to stored information, like files on a hard drive or data in cloud storage. Encrypting stored data protects it from unauthorized access if devices are lost, stolen, or compromised. Both forms of encryption are essential in modern cybersecurity strategies.

End-to-end encryption provides an additional layer of protection for communications. This method ensures that only the sender and recipient can read messages. Even service providers cannot access the content of end-to-end encrypted communications. Messaging apps, email services, and some cloud storage platforms now offer this feature. By preventing interception, end-to-end encryption drastically reduces the risk of data exposure. Users should prioritize services that implement robust end-to-end encryption to protect sensitive information.

Encryption also plays a critical role in protecting financial transactions. Online banking, digital payments, and e-commerce rely heavily on encryption to secure user data. Payment information, account credentials, and transaction details are encrypted to prevent theft. Without encryption, cybercriminals could easily intercept sensitive financial data. This is why encrypted connections, such as HTTPS, are mandatory for online commerce. Encryption ensures trust in the digital economy.

While encryption is highly effective, it is not foolproof. Weak passwords, mismanaged encryption keys, and outdated algorithms can undermine its protection. Cybercriminals may attempt to exploit these weaknesses to bypass security measures. Regular updates, strong key management, and the use of proven algorithms are critical to maintaining security. Understanding potential weaknesses allows users to take proactive steps to safeguard data. Encryption is most effective when combined with good digital hygiene.

Despite its complexity, encryption can be accessible to everyday users. Many software applications and online services implement encryption automatically, requiring minimal user intervention.

Password managers, secure messaging apps, and cloud storage services often include encryption as a built-in feature. Users can benefit from these protections simply by enabling security settings and practicing strong password hygiene. Awareness of encryption and its use empowers individuals to protect their data effectively. It transforms abstract technical concepts into practical digital defenses.

Encryption is not only a defense against cybercriminals but also a safeguard for privacy and autonomy. Governments, corporations, and hackers may attempt to access personal data without consent. Strong encryption ensures that sensitive information remains private, even when stored or transmitted digitally. By understanding and applying encryption, users maintain control over their digital identities. It reinforces trust in online services and strengthens overall cybersecurity. Knowledge of encryption equips individuals with a critical layer of protection in a data-driven world.

Cybersecurity is most effective when multiple layers of protection are applied. Encryption works best in combination with strong passwords, multi-factor authentication, and secure device practices. Each layer addresses different vulnerabilities, creating a comprehensive defense strategy. Relying on a single protective measure increases risk, whereas layered security enhances resilience. Encryption is a cornerstone of this multi-layered approach, safeguarding data against interception and theft. Awareness and consistent application ensure its maximum effectiveness.

Encryption is a tool that empowers individuals to take control of their digital lives. By converting data into secure formats, it prevents unauthorized access and reduces the impact of breaches. Even when technology evolves and attackers become more sophisticated, encryption remains a fundamental defense. Understanding its role and implementing it thoughtfully strengthens both privacy and security. The following chapters will build on this foundation, providing additional strategies to protect devices, accounts, and personal information. Encryption is not just a technical feature; it is a critical pillar of modern personal cybersecurity.

CHAPTER .5

COMMON CYBERSECURITY MISCONCEPTIONS

Debunking Myths That Lead to Personal Data Compromise and Inadequate Protection

One of the biggest obstacles to effective cybersecurity is misinformation. Many people operate under false assumptions about what keeps them safe online. Believing these misconceptions can leave individuals and organizations vulnerable to attacks. Cybersecurity is not just a concern for tech experts; it affects everyone. Understanding and correcting these myths is a critical first step in protecting personal data. This chapter explores common misunderstandings and provides clarity to empower users.

A frequent misconception is that "I have nothing worth stealing." Many individuals underestimate the value of their personal data. Even seemingly trivial information—email addresses, birthdays, or shopping habits—can be exploited by cybercriminals. Small data points can be combined to launch sophisticated attacks, including identity theft and phishing. Assuming you are not a target can create dangerous complacency. Recognizing the value of your data encourages proactive security measures.

Another widespread belief is that antivirus software alone provides complete protection. While antivirus programs are important, they cannot stop every threat. Malware, ransomware, and phishing attacks continue to evolve faster than signature-based antivirus solutions. Relying solely on antivirus software may create a false sense of security. Layered security, including strong passwords, encryption, and regular updates, is essential. Awareness of the limitations of technology prevents overconfidence.

Many users also believe that strong passwords are sufficient to protect accounts. While they are a foundational component, passwords alone cannot defend against phishing or credential theft. Multi-factor authentication provides an additional layer of security, making unauthorized access more difficult. Failing to implement multi-factor authentication leaves accounts unnecessarily exposed. Combining passwords with other protective measures significantly enhances security. Understanding the limits of passwords is crucial for a holistic approach.

Some assume that mobile devices are inherently secure because they are newer or smaller. However, smartphones and tablets are increasingly targeted by cybercriminals. Mobile malware, malicious apps, and unsecured Wi-Fi networks put sensitive information at risk. Overconfidence in mobile security can lead to negligence, such as skipping updates or installing unverified apps. Protecting mobile devices is just as important as securing computers and networks. Education about mobile threats is key to maintaining comprehensive protection.

Another misconception is that public Wi-Fi is safe if it requires a password. Password-protected networks can still be intercepted, allowing attackers to monitor traffic or inject malware. Using VPNs and avoiding sensitive transactions on public Wi-Fi are necessary precautions. Believing that a locked network is automatically secure can expose users to serious risks. Understanding the nuances of network security helps prevent unintended data exposure. Public Wi-Fi should always be approached with caution.

Some individuals think that cyber threats are only external. Insider threats, human error, and social engineering attacks demonstrate that risk can come from within. Even trusted employees or acquaintances can inadvertently compromise sensitive information. Training, monitoring, and clear policies are essential to mitigate internal risks. Awareness of this reality ensures that individuals and organizations adopt comprehensive security practices. No environment is completely safe without active vigilance.

Cybersecurity myths also extend to assumptions about cloud security. Some believe that cloud providers automatically guarantee complete protection. While providers implement strong security measures, users remain responsible for configuring permissions, managing access, and monitoring activity. Blind trust in cloud security can lead to exposed data. Understanding shared responsibility is critical to protecting cloud-based information. Awareness of these responsibilities empowers users to secure their digital assets.

Believing that cyberattacks are always detectable is another dangerous misconception. Many attacks, particularly sophisticated ones, occur silently over extended periods. Early signs can be subtle, and breaches may go unnoticed for months. Assuming that detection is automatic reduces vigilance and delays response. Proactive monitoring, regular audits, and awareness of unusual activity are essential. Recognizing the stealthy nature of attacks improves readiness and response time.

Debunking these misconceptions is essential to building a strong foundation in personal cybersecurity. Awareness and education empower individuals to take meaningful steps to protect their data. Accepting that threats are real, evolving, and sometimes invisible encourages proactive measures. Cybersecurity is not about fear—it's about informed, consistent action. Understanding the truth about common myths transforms users from vulnerable targets into active defenders.

Chapter .6

Securing Your Devices: From Smartphones to Laptops

Essential Steps to Protecting Your Devices from Malware and Unauthorized Access

Every device you use—from smartphones to laptops—represents a potential entry point for cybercriminals. These devices store personal information, financial data, and private communications that must be protected. Securing devices is a critical aspect of personal cybersecurity. Without proper measures, even the strongest passwords and encryption may not prevent unauthorized access. Cybercriminals actively exploit unprotected devices to steal information or deploy malware. Understanding device vulnerabilities is the first step toward comprehensive security.

Physical security is as important as digital safeguards. Devices that are lost or stolen can provide attackers with direct access to sensitive information. Simple measures like screen locks, strong passwords, and device tracking features greatly reduce this risk. For laptops and desktops, consider locking your computer when away from your desk. Smartphones should be secured with biometric authentication or strong PINs. Physical vigilance complements software-based security measures, creating a layered defense.

Regular software updates are essential for device security. Operating systems, applications, and firmware frequently receive updates to patch vulnerabilities. Cybercriminals often exploit outdated software to gain access to devices. Ignoring updates increases exposure to malware, ransomware, and unauthorized access. Enabling automatic updates ensures your device remains protected with minimal effort. Staying current is one of the simplest and most effective security measures.

Installing reputable security software adds another layer of protection. Antivirus and anti-malware programs detect and remove harmful software before it can cause damage. These programs often include features such as real-time scanning, firewall integration, and web protection. While not infallible, security software significantly reduces risk. Choosing well-reviewed and regularly updated solutions is crucial. Relying solely on default security features may leave gaps in protection.

Device permissions are often overlooked yet critical to security. Apps frequently request access to contacts, location, camera, and storage. Granting unnecessary permissions increases the risk of data exposure. Regularly review app permissions and disable access that is not essential. Limiting permissions minimizes the potential damage if an app is compromised. Vigilance in managing permissions strengthens device security.

Secure connections are vital when using any device online. Avoid unprotected public Wi-Fi for sensitive transactions. When necessary, use a trusted VPN to encrypt your internet connection. Secure networks prevent attackers from intercepting data transmitted from your devices. Wi-Fi routers should also be configured with strong passwords and up-to-date firmware. Network security extends the protection of individual devices across digital communication channels.

Device backups are a critical part of security strategy. Regularly backing up data ensures that information can be restored in the event of a malware attack, hardware failure, or accidental deletion. Backups should be stored in encrypted, secure locations, ideally both locally and in the cloud. Testing backups periodically confirms that recovery processes work correctly. Data loss can be devastating, but proper backup practices mitigate the impact.

Two-factor authentication (2FA) adds another crucial layer to device security. Linking accounts and devices to multi-factor authentication reduces the risk of unauthorized access, even if passwords are compromised. Many operating systems and apps now offer 2FA as a standard feature. Activating 2FA provides additional assurance that your devices and accounts remain protected. This simple step greatly enhances the security of all connected devices.

Understanding the unique risks of each device is also important. Smartphones are often lost or stolen, making remote wipe and tracking essential. Laptops may be more vulnerable to malware due to their broader use and access to networks. Tablets often bridge personal and work activities, requiring careful management of apps and permissions. Tailoring security measures to each device type ensures comprehensive protection. Awareness of device-specific vulnerabilities informs better defensive strategies.

Securing your devices requires ongoing attention, awareness, and layered defenses. No single measure provides complete protection, but combining physical safeguards, updates, security software, permissions management, secure connections, backups, and multi-factor authentication significantly reduces risk. Devices are the gateways to your digital life; protecting them safeguards both your data and your privacy. By taking proactive steps, you transform vulnerable devices into secure tools that support safe and confident digital engagement.

CHAPTER .7

PASSWORD SECURITY: THE FIRST LINE OF DEFENSE

Why Strong, Unique Passwords Are Critical and How to Manage Them Effectively

Passwords are the first line of defense in protecting your digital identity. They guard access to email, banking, social media, and countless other accounts. Weak or reused passwords are one of the most common causes of cyber breaches. Cybercriminals use automated tools to guess passwords, often exploiting predictable patterns. A single compromised password can provide access to multiple accounts, magnifying the damage. Understanding the importance of password security is essential for protecting personal data.

Strong passwords combine complexity with memorability. They should include a mix of upper- and lowercase letters, numbers, and special characters. Avoid using easily guessed information, such as birthdays, names, or common words. Longer passwords are generally more secure, as they increase the time and effort required for brute-force attacks. Password managers can help generate and store strong passwords safely. By using these tools, you can maintain complex, unique credentials for every account.

Reusing passwords across multiple accounts is a significant security risk. If one account is compromised, attackers can gain access to others using the same credentials. Many breaches occur because users rely on a single password for convenience. Creating unique passwords for each account prevents a domino effect during an attack. It may require additional effort, but password managers simplify this process. This practice is a cornerstone of personal cybersecurity.

Two-factor authentication (2FA) enhances password security by adding an additional verification step. Even if a password is stolen, attackers cannot access an account without the second factor, which may be a code sent via SMS, an authentication app, or a hardware token. Enabling 2FA dramatically reduces the likelihood of unauthorized access. Many services now offer 2FA as an optional or default security measure. Using it consistently strengthens your defense against credential-based attacks.

Passwords should be updated periodically, particularly for critical accounts. Regular changes reduce the window of opportunity for attackers to exploit compromised credentials. Updates are especially important if a breach has been reported or if you suspect suspicious activity. While frequent password changes may seem inconvenient, they are a small effort compared to the potential damage from unauthorized access. Staying proactive is essential for long-term security.

Avoid storing passwords in insecure locations, such as sticky notes or unencrypted files. Physical notes are vulnerable to theft, and unprotected digital files can be accessed if a device is compromised. Password managers provide encrypted storage and auto-fill capabilities, combining security with convenience. Using these tools reduces reliance on memory while maintaining strong security practices. Proper storage is an often-overlooked component of effective password management.

Phishing attacks often target passwords directly. Cybercriminals create convincing fake login pages or send fraudulent emails to trick users into revealing their credentials. Awareness of these tactics and verifying URLs and sources before entering passwords is crucial. Never share passwords via email or messaging apps.

Being vigilant against phishing reinforces password protection. Education complements technical measures in keeping accounts secure.

Biometric authentication, such as fingerprint or facial recognition, is increasingly used to supplement passwords. While convenient, biometric systems are not infallible and should be combined with traditional passwords or PINs. Biometric data itself must be securely stored to prevent misuse. This layered approach adds security without sacrificing usability. Combining passwords with biometric authentication enhances protection while simplifying access.

Password security is the foundation for all other cybersecurity measures. Strong, unique passwords combined with 2FA and careful storage drastically reduce the risk of unauthorized access. Awareness of common attacks and proper habits enhances resilience. Taking responsibility for your own credentials is empowering and practical. Passwords protect not only your data but also your digital reputation and identity. Mastering this first line of defense is essential for safe digital engagement.

Cybercriminals often exploit predictable human behavior when targeting passwords. Many users create passwords that are easy to remember but also easy to guess, such as "123456" or "password." Others incorporate keyboard patterns like "qwerty" or sequential numbers, which are also common targets. Automated attack tools can attempt thousands of combinations in seconds, taking advantage of these predictable patterns. Awareness of these tendencies is crucial to strengthening password security. By consciously avoiding predictable choices, users significantly increase the difficulty for attackers.

Password managers not only store credentials but also help generate strong, random passwords. These tools create complex passwords that are extremely difficult to crack. Some password managers also alert users if their stored credentials have appeared in data breaches. This combination of secure generation, storage, and monitoring provides a comprehensive approach. Users no longer need to rely on memory alone, which often leads to weaker or reused passwords. Integrating password managers into daily routines is a practical step toward robust cybersecurity.

Two-factor authentication (2FA) should be enabled wherever available, particularly for sensitive accounts. Even if a password is compromised, the attacker cannot bypass the second layer without the physical device or authentication token. Common forms of 2FA include SMS codes, authentication apps, and hardware keys. Authentication apps and hardware keys are generally more secure than SMS, which can be intercepted through SIM swapping attacks. Understanding the differences in 2FA methods allows users to select the most secure options. Layering security reduces vulnerabilities significantly.

Security questions are another often-overlooked risk. Many services require answers to questions such as "What is your mother's maiden name?" or "What is your first pet's name?" While intended as an additional layer of protection, these answers can sometimes be discovered through social media or public records. Using fictitious answers or incorporating them into password manager entries can mitigate this risk. Security questions should never be treated as trivial or secondary. Thoughtful management of these answers strengthens overall account security.

Regular monitoring of account activity is critical for early detection of compromise. Many services provide alerts for unusual login locations, failed login attempts, or device access. Promptly responding to these alerts can prevent further unauthorized access. Users should review account settings periodically, including devices linked, app access, and password recovery options. Active engagement with account security is a proactive defense strategy. Being vigilant and responsive enhances the effectiveness of strong passwords.

Training and habit formation are crucial for maintaining password security. Users should develop the habit of creating strong, unique passwords for every account and updating them when breaches occur. Education about phishing, social engineering, and other password-targeting attacks complements technical measures. Strong habits reduce the likelihood of human error, which is often the weakest link in cybersecurity. Cybersecurity is a continuous process, not a one-time effort. Consistency and awareness transform password management from a chore into a protective routine.

Compromised accounts can have far-reaching consequences. Beyond financial loss, attackers can access personal communications, sensitive documents, and even social connections. Cybercriminals may impersonate victims for scams or identity theft. The interconnected nature of digital accounts means a single weak password can cascade into multiple compromised services. Awareness of potential consequences reinforces the need for diligence. Password security is not just about protecting individual accounts but safeguarding overall digital identity.

The use of unique passwords for every account cannot be overstated. Even if a less critical account is breached, using distinct passwords ensures other accounts remain secure. This principle also applies to secondary accounts and subscriptions. Treating each account independently prevents domino-effect compromises. Coupled with 2FA and monitoring, this strategy provides a robust defense. Users who implement these practices reduce risk dramatically and gain peace of mind.

Cybersecurity awareness is key to sustaining password hygiene. Staying informed about new types of attacks, common breaches, and emerging best practices empowers users to act proactively. Knowledge combined with consistent action creates a resilient digital presence. Strong password practices form the foundation upon which additional security layers, like encryption and multi-factor authentication, are built. Prioritizing this foundational step ensures that all other cybersecurity measures are more effective. Password security is not optional—it is essential.

Even with strong passwords and 2FA, users must remain vigilant against social engineering attacks. Cybercriminals may attempt to trick individuals into revealing credentials through phone calls, emails, or instant messages. These attacks exploit trust, urgency, or fear to prompt hasty decisions. Awareness and skepticism are your best defenses against these tactics. Verifying requests before sharing sensitive information prevents unnecessary compromises. Combining technical security with informed behavior creates a more resilient defense.

Password expiration policies, often enforced by organizations, are another important consideration. Changing passwords periodically limits the window of opportunity for attackers who may have gained unauthorized access. However, overly frequent changes can lead to weaker passwords or reliance on predictable patterns. Striking a balance between security and usability is key. Using a password manager helps maintain strong, unique passwords even with scheduled updates. Strategic password rotation enhances security without adding unnecessary complexity.

Monitoring dark web activity is an emerging practice for maintaining password security. Some services alert users if their credentials appear in data breaches or are available for sale online. This early warning allows individuals to change passwords before attackers exploit them. Staying proactive rather than reactive is critical in cybersecurity. While no system is foolproof, early detection minimizes potential damage. Being informed about compromised credentials reinforces a proactive security mindset.

Public and shared computers pose significant password risks. Logging in from a public terminal, such as at a library or café, exposes credentials to potential interception. Key-loggers, malware, and unsecured networks all increase vulnerability. Whenever possible, avoid logging into sensitive accounts on shared devices. If necessary, use virtual keyboards or temporary passwords, and ensure all sessions are logged out afterward. Treating public devices with caution preserves the integrity of your accounts.

Password security is also tied to email protection. Since email accounts often serve as recovery points for other accounts, compromising an email password can grant access to multiple services. Ensuring email accounts are secured with strong, unique passwords and 2FA is paramount. Monitoring for suspicious activity and promptly addressing potential compromises prevents cascading breaches. Protecting your email protects all other connected accounts. This single step significantly strengthens overall cybersecurity.

Security culture extends to families and organizations. Encouraging everyone to adopt strong password practices creates a safer digital environment for all. Shared accounts should have carefully managed credentials and restricted access. Discussions about phishing, password hygiene, and multi-factor authentication raise awareness and build consistent habits. Cybersecurity is a collective responsibility, and shared knowledge enhances individual security. Strong password habits are most effective when reinforced across all users.

Backups complement password security by mitigating the impact of account compromise. Even if credentials are stolen, regular backups allow users to recover important data without paying ransom or losing information. Encrypted backups ensure that sensitive data remains safe even if stored remotely. Combining password protection with backup strategies creates a multi-layered defense. This approach reduces the consequences of both unauthorized access and malware attacks. Redundancy reinforces resilience.

The evolution of attack methods necessitates continuous adaptation of password strategies. As attackers develop new tools and techniques, users must remain vigilant and flexible. Staying informed about trends in cybercrime helps anticipate potential threats. Regularly reviewing accounts, updating credentials, and monitoring activity are critical practices. Cybersecurity is not static; it requires ongoing effort and awareness. Maintaining strong password habits ensures long-term protection in a dynamic digital landscape.

Ultimately, password security is both a technical and behavioral practice. Strong, unique passwords, combined with 2FA, monitoring, and careful handling of credentials, form a foundational defense. Awareness of attack methods, habits that minimize exposure, and proactive management of accounts ensures that users remain in control of their digital identities. Passwords are not just lines of text—they are the key to protecting your digital life. Mastering password security is the first step in building a comprehensive cybersecurity strategy.

In addition to traditional passwords, pass-phrases offer a more secure and memorable alternative. A passphrase is a sequence of words or a sentence that is longer and harder to guess than typical passwords. For example, a phrase like "SunsetsBringCalm&CoffeeEveryMorning" combines length, complexity, and memorability. This approach increases resistance to brute-force attacks while remaining manageable for human recall. Pass-phrases also encourage the use of symbols, numbers, and varied capitalization naturally. Adopting pass-phrases is a practical way to enhance password security without adding undue burden.

Users must also understand the risks of password sharing. Sharing credentials, even with trusted friends or family, introduces vulnerabilities. Shared passwords can be accidentally exposed, stored insecurely, or misused. In professional environments, sharing passwords undermines accountability and increases the potential for internal breaches. Passwords should remain personal and confidential at all times. Establishing this principle as a habit reinforces overall cybersecurity hygiene.

Securing backup authentication methods is equally important. Recovery codes, secondary emails, and security questions should be protected with the same rigor as primary passwords. If attackers gain access to recovery methods, they can bypass primary security measures. Using strong, unique information for recovery options prevents easy circumvention. Password security extends beyond the visible credentials to all systems supporting account access. Every access point matters when defending against compromise.

Periodic security audits help maintain strong password hygiene. Reviewing accounts for weak passwords, unused services, and unusual login activity identifies potential vulnerabilities. This audit process includes verifying that all important accounts have 2FA enabled and that credentials have not been exposed in known breaches. Regular audits encourage consistent security practices and reduce the risk of unnoticed compromises. Staying proactive in this way ensures that security measures remain effective. Monitoring and review are essential components of password management.

Finally, cultivating a mindset of vigilance strengthens password security over time. Recognizing the evolving tactics of cybercriminals helps maintain alertness. Being cautious with credentials, avoiding shortcuts, and continually reviewing security practices instills habits that protect both personal and professional accounts. Cybersecurity is a continuous journey rather than a one-time action. Strong password habits form the foundation for more advanced protective measures. By prioritizing vigilance and discipline, users safeguard their digital lives against threats.

The consequences of weak or compromised passwords extend far beyond minor inconvenience. Attackers can access financial accounts, personal communications, and even professional networks. Identity theft, fraud, and reputational damage are common outcomes of insufficient password security. Recovering from these incidents can take months or even years, highlighting the importance of prevention. Strong password habits reduce the likelihood of such breaches and provide peace of mind. Understanding these stakes motivates consistent attention to password management.

Password management is not static; it evolves as technology and threats advance. New tools, such as password managers and biometric authentication, make it easier to maintain secure accounts. Awareness of emerging threats, such as credential stuffing and phishing attacks, allows users to adapt their practices. Combining multiple layers of protection—strong passwords, 2FA, secure storage, and vigilant monitoring—ensures the greatest resilience. Users who embrace evolving strategies are best positioned to protect their digital identities. Adaptation is the key to long-term security.

Education is central to cultivating strong password habits. Sharing knowledge about best practices with family, friends, and colleagues strengthens collective security. Teaching others about the risks of reused or weak passwords helps prevent inadvertent compromises. Cybersecurity is a shared responsibility, and informed users act as both defenders and educators. A culture of awareness reduces vulnerabilities across networks and communities. Knowledge, when applied consistently, is a powerful tool for protection.

Password security also reinforces confidence in digital interactions. Users who rely on strong passwords and multi-factor authentication can engage with online services more securely. Whether managing finances, communicating with friends, or conducting professional tasks, secure credentials provide peace of mind. Confidence in one's digital defenses encourages responsible behavior and reduces susceptibility to attacks. Security empowers users to navigate the digital world without fear. Passwords are the foundation of this empowerment.

REFLECTION:

Reflecting on password security, it's clear that this seemingly simple element underpins much of our digital safety. A strong, unique password protects not only accounts but also personal identity, financial assets, and privacy. The combination of awareness, disciplined habits, and technology transforms a single line of defense into a robust shield. Investing effort into password management is investing in your own security and peace of mind. Every strong password is a step toward reclaiming control over your digital life.

"Passwords are the keys to your digital kingdom; guard them wisely, change them regularly, and never underestimate their power."
— Unknown

CHAPTER .8

MULTI-FACTOR AUTHENTICATION: ADDING LAYERS OF SECURITY

How Multi-Factor Authentication Enhances Your Digital Security and Reduces Vulnerabilities

Multi-factor authentication (MFA) is a critical enhancement to traditional password security. While passwords alone provide a first line of defense, MFA adds additional layers that significantly reduce the risk of unauthorized access. This method requires users to provide two or more forms of verification before gaining entry to an account. These factors can include something you know (a password), something you have (a smartphone or hardware token), or something you are (biometric verification). By combining multiple factors, MFA makes it much harder for cybercriminals to compromise accounts. Understanding and implementing MFA is essential for modern cybersecurity.

The most common forms of MFA include SMS codes, authentication apps, and hardware tokens. SMS codes send a one-time password to a registered phone number, providing an extra verification step. Authentication apps, such as Google Authenticator or Authy, generate time-sensitive codes that are more secure than SMS, as they cannot be intercepted easily. Hardware tokens are physical devices that produce one-time codes or connect to computers via USB for authentication. Each method offers varying levels of convenience and security. Users should select the option that balances usability with maximum protection.

MFA dramatically reduces the risk of credential-based attacks. Even if a password is compromised, attackers cannot bypass the additional verification factor. This protects accounts from phishing, key-logging, and brute-force attacks. Studies have shown that enabling MFA can block up to 99% of automated attacks. It is particularly critical for high-value accounts, such as email, banking, and cloud storage services. The added security ensures that even in the event of a breach, access remains limited and controlled.

Biometric authentication, such as fingerprint or facial recognition, adds a convenient and secure layer to MFA. Unlike passwords, biometrics cannot be easily guessed or stolen. Many devices and applications now integrate biometrics for login and verification. However, biometric data must be stored securely, as it is sensitive and immutable. Using biometrics in combination with other authentication factors provides both ease of use and strong security. MFA with biometrics offers a modern solution for protecting personal and professional accounts.

Implementing MFA requires careful consideration of account recovery processes. Losing access to an authentication device or app can lock users out of their accounts. Backup codes, secondary email addresses, or alternative authentication methods should be set up in advance. Planning for contingencies ensures that MFA enhances security without creating unnecessary access barriers. Proper setup and management are critical for maintaining both security and usability. Thoughtful implementation is key to maximizing the benefits of MFA.

Education and awareness are vital for successful MFA adoption. Users must understand why MFA is important, how to enable it, and the best practices for maintaining it. Many individuals fail to implement MFA simply because they underestimate its value or perceive it as inconvenient. Highlighting the protective benefits, including prevention of identity theft and account compromise, encourages adoption. The more users understand MFA, the more effective it becomes. Education transforms MFA from an optional feature into an essential security practice.

MFA also supports compliance with organizational and regulatory requirements. Many industries, such as finance and healthcare, require multi-factor authentication to protect sensitive data. Implementing MFA reduces liability and ensures adherence to security standards. Organizations that encourage MFA adoption help create a culture of security awareness. Employees and individuals alike benefit from the extra layer of protection. Compliance and security work hand-in-hand through effective MFA deployment.

While MFA significantly strengthens security, it is not a replacement for other cybersecurity measures. Strong passwords, encryption, device security, and awareness of phishing attacks remain essential. MFA complements these measures by adding a critical verification layer that reduces the impact of compromised credentials. A comprehensive cybersecurity strategy integrates MFA into a broader set of protective practices. Each layer works together to safeguard personal and professional information. MFA is a cornerstone of modern defense but must be used as part of a multi-layered approach.

Understanding MFA empowers users to take control of their accounts and personal data. By implementing multiple verification factors, users can significantly reduce vulnerability to cyberattacks. The combination of passwords, MFA, and good digital hygiene creates a formidable defense. Awareness and proper application of these tools transform security from reactive to proactive. MFA is both a practical and powerful step toward securing your digital life. Adopting it is a key milestone in building a resilient cybersecurity posture.

CHAPTER .9

PHISHING ATTACKS: HOW TO RECOGNIZE AND AVOID THEM

Understanding the Tactics Cybercriminals Use in Phishing and How to Defend Against Them

Phishing attacks are one of the most common and effective methods cybercriminals use to steal personal information. These attacks typically involve fraudulent emails, messages, or websites designed to appear legitimate. The goal is to trick users into revealing sensitive information, such as passwords, credit card numbers, or social security numbers. Phishing can target individuals or organizations, and the consequences can range from minor inconveniences to severe financial and reputational damage. Recognizing the tactics used in phishing is essential for protecting personal data. Awareness is the first defense against these deceptive attacks.

Phishing attacks often exploit urgency or fear to provoke immediate action. Messages may claim that an account has been compromised, that a payment is overdue, or that immediate verification is required. By creating a sense of panic, attackers reduce the likelihood that users will carefully inspect the message. Understanding this psychological manipulation helps users pause and evaluate the authenticity of communications. Vigilance and critical thinking are powerful tools against these tactics. Users who slow down and question unusual requests reduce their risk of compromise.

Spear phishing represents a more targeted form of attack. Unlike generic phishing emails, spear phishing targets specific individuals or organizations with personalized content. Attackers often research their victims to include accurate names, positions, or recent activities. This personalization increases the likelihood that the victim will trust the message and take action. Recognizing spear phishing requires careful attention to details, including sender addresses, URLs, and the context of the request. Awareness of targeted attacks enhances preparedness and response.

Phishing attempts are not limited to email; they also occur via text messages, social media, and even phone calls. SMS-based phishing, known as smishing, uses fraudulent messages to lure users into revealing sensitive information. Voice phishing, or vishing, involves phone calls where attackers impersonate trusted entities. Social media platforms are increasingly exploited for phishing by sending malicious links through direct messages. Being aware of these diverse channels helps users apply caution across all digital communications. Comprehensive vigilance is necessary to defend against multi-channel phishing threats.

Technical measures can also help defend against phishing. Email services often include spam filters and phishing detection algorithms that flag suspicious messages. Browser security features warn users when visiting potentially malicious websites. Anti-malware and endpoint protection software provide additional layers of defense. However, these tools are not foolproof, and user judgment remains critical. Combining technology with awareness maximizes protection. Security is strongest when tools and informed behavior work together.

Recognizing common phishing indicators is crucial for prevention. Suspicious URLs, misspellings, grammatical errors, and unexpected attachments are often red flags. Requests for personal or financial information that legitimate organizations would not ask for via email are particularly concerning. Hovering over links to verify their destination before clicking can prevent accidental exposure. Training and practice improve the ability to spot subtle signs of phishing. Developing a habit of scrutiny reduces the likelihood of falling victim to attacks.

Reporting phishing attempts strengthens overall security. Many organizations and email providers allow users to report suspected phishing messages. Reporting helps security teams block malicious senders and warn other users. In addition, sharing awareness within personal or professional networks increases vigilance and reduces the success rate of attacks. Collective action amplifies individual defense. Contributing to a safer digital environment benefits everyone.

Even with strong precautions, phishing attempts continue to evolve. Attackers adapt tactics to bypass filters and exploit new technologies. Staying informed about emerging phishing trends is necessary for ongoing protection. Awareness, skepticism, and continuous learning are key components of an effective defense strategy. Understanding that phishing is a persistent threat motivates vigilance. Prevention requires both technical safeguards and proactive user behavior.

Educating others about phishing is also an essential part of cybersecurity culture. Family members, friends, and colleagues benefit from guidance on recognizing suspicious communications. Promoting awareness and sharing best practices help create safer digital communities. Empowered and informed users reduce the likelihood of successful phishing attacks. Education, vigilance, and technology together form a strong defense against one of the most pervasive cyber threats.

Phishing attacks often rely on manipulating trust in familiar brands or institutions. Attackers frequently impersonate banks, government agencies, or popular online services. The emails or messages may include logos, formatting, and language that appear authentic. Victims are more likely to click links or download attachments when they believe the communication is from a trusted source. Verifying the sender's email address or contact information can reveal subtle inconsistencies. Developing a habit of questioning unexpected requests reduces the effectiveness of these attacks.

Another common tactic is the use of malicious links or attachments. Links may redirect users to fake websites that look identical to legitimate platforms, prompting them to enter sensitive information. Attachments can contain malware designed to steal data or compromise devices. Hovering over links to inspect their destination before clicking is an essential preventive measure. Users should also avoid downloading attachments from unknown or unsolicited sources. Awareness of these techniques is crucial for maintaining device and data security.

Phishing attacks can also exploit current events or crises. Cybercriminals often craft messages that reference urgent news, natural disasters, or major events. These messages appeal to emotions such as fear, empathy, or curiosity, prompting immediate action. Users must be cautious about clicking links or providing information in response to urgent or emotionally charged communications. Independent verification from official sources is essential before taking any action. Emotional awareness is as important as technical knowledge in defending against phishing.

Corporate and organizational email systems are frequent phishing targets. Employees may receive messages appearing to come from management, IT, or trusted partners. These messages often request credentials, sensitive documents, or financial transfers. Organizations implement security awareness training to educate staff about recognizing and reporting phishing attempts. Simulated phishing exercises can reinforce good habits and improve detection rates. A culture of vigilance within organizations reduces the likelihood of successful attacks.

Phishing attacks are increasingly sophisticated, blending social engineering with technical exploits. For example, some messages include malware-laden links that exploit vulnerabilities in software. Others may use “man-in-the-middle” tactics to intercept communication between users and legitimate services. Even careful users can be targeted by these advanced strategies. Regular software updates, endpoint protection, and network monitoring provide essential defenses. However, user awareness remains the most critical component of phishing prevention.

Attackers often use repetition to increase their chances of success. Receiving multiple similar messages can create a sense of legitimacy or pressure to act. Being aware that repeated communications can be a tactic helps users avoid falling for persistent attacks. Patience, skepticism, and verification are effective tools to counter this strategy. Users should never feel compelled to respond hastily to repeated requests. Understanding attacker psychology strengthens overall cybersecurity posture.

Training individuals to recognize and report phishing is an ongoing process. Awareness programs emphasize identifying suspicious links, verifying sources, and avoiding information disclosure. Encouraging reporting of suspicious messages helps organizations and communities block malicious actors. These practices also cultivate responsible digital citizenship. The combination of training, vigilance, and technical safeguards reduces phishing-related risks. Collective awareness is a force multiplier in cybersecurity.

Phishing is not a static threat; it constantly adapts to bypass defenses. Cybercriminals refine tactics based on emerging trends, technological changes, and user behavior. Staying informed about the latest phishing methods is crucial to remaining protected. Engaging in continuous learning and maintaining a skeptical mindset strengthens defenses. Users must recognize that vigilance is an ongoing responsibility. Awareness and adaptation are key to mitigating phishing threats.

Even the most careful individuals can be targeted by sophisticated phishing campaigns. The key is not perfection but preparedness. Developing routines for verifying communications, using technical safeguards, and reporting suspicious activity creates resilience. Phishing attacks are preventable with consistent awareness and proactive measures. Understanding these dynamics empowers users to protect both their personal and professional information. Preparedness transforms fear into effective defense.

Phishing attacks often exploit human curiosity and the desire for rewards. Messages may claim that you have won a prize, are eligible for a refund, or have exclusive access to an offer. The excitement of potential gain can override caution, leading users to click links or provide personal information. Recognizing the emotional manipulation inherent in such tactics is essential. Always verify offers independently through official channels. Developing a habit of pausing before reacting protects against these opportunistic attacks.

Cybercriminals frequently use email spoofing to create a false sense of legitimacy. Spoofed emails mimic real addresses, making it appear as if the message comes from a trusted sender. Careful inspection of the sender's address and email headers can reveal inconsistencies. Users should also be cautious of generic greetings, such as "Dear Customer," which are common in mass phishing attempts. Learning to spot subtle anomalies increases the likelihood of detecting fraudulent messages. A critical eye is a key defense against email spoofing.

Clone phishing is another advanced tactic used by attackers. In this method, a legitimate email previously sent to a user is copied and modified to include malicious links or attachments. Recipients may be more likely to trust the cloned email because it appears familiar. Users should verify any unexpected changes or requests, even in previously trusted communications. Confirming authenticity with the sender or organization prevents exploitation. Understanding evolving phishing techniques strengthens overall digital security.

Phishing is not limited to external threats; insider attacks can also occur. Employees or acquaintances with access to internal systems may exploit trust to gain sensitive information. Training and strict access controls are essential in reducing the likelihood of successful internal phishing attempts. Awareness campaigns should emphasize the importance of reporting suspicious behavior promptly. A combination of technical safeguards and human vigilance is necessary to mitigate insider threats. Security is a shared responsibility across all levels.

Multi-layered defenses are essential to combat phishing effectively. Technical solutions, such as spam filters, email authentication protocols, and web filtering, block many attacks before reaching the user. Human awareness, skepticism, and verification complement these tools. Security policies, such as limiting email attachments or requiring 2FA, further reduce risk. Combining these strategies creates a robust framework for preventing successful phishing attacks. Layered security enhances resilience against constantly evolving threats.

Regularly educating users about new phishing trends is crucial for long-term defense. Attackers continuously refine their strategies, using current events, sophisticated impersonation, and emerging technologies to exploit vulnerabilities. Awareness programs and ongoing training ensure that individuals stay informed and vigilant. Knowledge about tactics such as vishing, smishing, and spear phishing equips users to recognize and respond appropriately. Cybersecurity education transforms potential victims into proactive defenders. Continuous learning is essential in an ever-changing threat landscape.

Psychological tactics in phishing exploit trust, authority, and urgency. Attackers often create scenarios that pressure users into acting without due consideration. Recognizing the manipulation of human behavior allows users to respond rationally rather than emotionally. Pausing, verifying, and questioning unusual requests are simple yet effective strategies. Understanding that attackers target psychology as much as technology empowers users. Awareness of these tactics is critical for successful defense.

Phishing attacks often evolve alongside technological trends. Social media, mobile apps, and cloud services are increasingly targeted by attackers. Users must adapt their awareness strategies to these platforms as effectively as they would for email. Verifying links, monitoring permissions, and exercising caution across all digital channels is essential. Being vigilant on multiple platforms ensures comprehensive protection. Adaptability is a cornerstone of modern cybersecurity.

Phishing attacks often target the most frequently used accounts, such as email and banking platforms. Cybercriminals know that gaining access to these accounts can provide gateways to other services. A single compromised email can allow attackers to reset passwords on social media, shopping, or work-related accounts. Users should prioritize securing high-value accounts with strong passwords and multi-factor authentication. Monitoring account activity regularly helps detect suspicious access early. Protecting key accounts creates a strong foundation for overall digital security.

Mobile devices have become a prime target for phishing attacks. SMS messages, messaging apps, and social media platforms are commonly exploited to distribute malicious links. Mobile users may be more vulnerable due to smaller screens, which make it harder to inspect URLs or verify sender details. Awareness of mobile-specific threats is essential to prevent accidental exposure. Using authentication apps, secure connections, and cautious link-clicking practices strengthens mobile security. Vigilance across all devices is necessary to maintain comprehensive protection.

Corporate environments face unique phishing risks. Employees may receive messages that appear to be internal communications or requests from management. These messages often aim to capture login credentials, financial information, or confidential files. Implementing security awareness training helps employees recognize and report suspicious emails. Organizations can also employ email authentication protocols, such as SPF, DKIM, and DMARC, to reduce spoofing. Combining employee education with technical safeguards significantly lowers the risk of successful attacks.

Awareness campaigns can include simulated phishing exercises. These controlled tests send fake phishing emails to employees or users to gauge their responses. The goal is to identify vulnerabilities and reinforce training without compromising actual data. Regular testing increases recognition of phishing tactics and encourages safe behavior. Continuous reinforcement ensures that users remain alert over time. Proactive engagement strengthens the overall security posture and reduces the effectiveness of real phishing attempts.

Phishing attacks are constantly evolving, requiring users to stay informed and vigilant. Cybercriminals refine their methods, incorporating new technologies and exploiting current events to increase success rates. The sophistication of attacks makes reliance on technical safeguards alone insufficient. Human awareness, skepticism, and cautious behavior remain the most effective defenses. Users must adopt a proactive mindset, treating every unexpected request with careful consideration. Continuous learning and adaptation are essential to staying one step ahead of attackers.

Developing a habit of verifying requests before responding is crucial. Simple actions such as checking sender addresses, hovering over links, and contacting the purported source directly can prevent exposure. Multi-factor authentication further protects accounts even if credentials are inadvertently shared. By combining careful verification with layered security, users minimize the risk of compromise. Routine diligence transforms vigilance into a sustainable practice. Small, consistent actions create significant protection against phishing threats.

Phishing attacks also highlight the importance of education and community awareness. Sharing knowledge about suspicious communications, common tactics, and best practices strengthens collective security. Families, colleagues, and friends benefit when individuals communicate lessons learned from potential threats. Community awareness amplifies the impact of personal vigilance and reduces the success of phishing campaigns. Cybersecurity is a shared responsibility that extends beyond individual accounts. Teaching and reinforcing good practices fosters a culture of safety.

Organizations play a crucial role in mitigating phishing threats. Policies, training programs, and technological safeguards must work together to create a secure environment. Employees should be encouraged to report suspicious activity without fear of reprisal. Simulated phishing exercises and regular updates on emerging threats reinforce positive behaviors. A proactive security culture ensures that phishing risks are managed consistently and effectively. Coordination between technology and human awareness is key to organizational resilience.

CHAPTER .10

THE DANGERS OF PUBLIC WI-FI AND HOW TO PROTECT YOUR DATA

Why Using Public Wi-Fi Poses Risks and How You Can Secure Your Internet Connections

Public Wi-Fi networks are convenient but often insecure, making them prime targets for cybercriminals. Cafes, airports, hotels, and other public spaces offer open networks that lack robust security measures. Users connecting to these networks may unknowingly expose sensitive information, such as login credentials, personal messages, and financial data. Attackers can intercept communications, monitor traffic, or inject malicious content. Understanding the risks associated with public Wi-Fi is the first step in protecting your data. Awareness and precautionary measures are essential when accessing networks outside your trusted environment.

One of the most common threats on public Wi-Fi is the "man-in-the-middle" attack. In this scenario, a cybercriminal intercepts the communication between your device and the destination server. This allows the attacker to capture passwords, credit card numbers, and other sensitive information in transit. Even encrypted websites are not entirely immune if the attacker can redirect traffic or exploit vulnerabilities. Being aware of this threat underscores the importance of using secure connections and protective measures. Understanding the mechanics of these attacks empowers users to make safer choices online.

Using a Virtual Private Network (VPN) is one of the most effective ways to secure your connection on public Wi-Fi. A VPN encrypts all data transmitted between your device and the internet, preventing attackers from intercepting sensitive information. VPNs also mask your IP address, adding another layer of privacy and anonymity. Reliable VPN services are essential, as some free options may compromise security or log user activity. By consistently using a VPN, you can safely access public networks without exposing critical data. Encryption is a key element in maintaining digital safety.

Avoiding automatic connections to open networks is another important precaution. Many devices automatically join previously used or available networks, sometimes without user consent. Attackers can create fake hotspots that mimic legitimate public Wi-Fi, tricking devices into connecting. Disabling automatic connections and manually verifying networks reduces the likelihood of connecting to malicious access points. Users should also confirm network names with staff or signage when in public spaces. Vigilance in connecting to networks helps prevent inadvertent exposure.

Sensitive activities should be limited on public Wi-Fi whenever possible. Online banking, shopping, or accessing confidential documents should ideally be done on secure, trusted networks. If necessary, additional security measures such as VPNs and multi-factor authentication can mitigate risks. Users should also ensure that websites employ HTTPS, indicating encrypted communications. Combining behavioral caution with technical safeguards strengthens overall protection. Being mindful of what you do online in public spaces reduces vulnerability significantly.

Device security settings play a crucial role in protecting data on public networks. Ensuring that firewalls are enabled, sharing settings are restricted, and security updates are current helps prevent unauthorized access. Disabling file and printer sharing and using strong passwords for device accounts are essential precautions. These settings create barriers that make it more difficult for attackers to exploit vulnerabilities. Maintaining up-to-date security software complements these precautions. Layered protection reinforces resilience against public network threats.

Phishing and malware distribution are also risks on public Wi-Fi. Attackers can use fake login portals or malicious advertisements to trick users into downloading malware. Being skeptical of unsolicited prompts, avoiding unknown links, and verifying sources reduces the likelihood of infection. Security tools such as antivirus software and browser filters provide additional safeguards. Awareness of the tactics used by attackers strengthens the overall defense strategy. Public networks demand heightened vigilance at all times.

Public Wi-Fi often lacks accountability and monitoring, making it easier for attackers to operate undetected. Unlike private networks, public networks do not track activity or enforce strict security policies. Users are responsible for their own protection and must assume that any activity could be observed. Practicing cautious behavior, using encrypted connections, and minimizing sensitive transactions is essential. Taking personal responsibility for security reduces exposure to cyber threats. Awareness and precaution create a safer digital experience.

Even familiar public locations are not immune to Wi-Fi threats. Cafes, libraries, and transportation hubs are frequented by many people, including potential attackers. Physical proximity to a network user can allow interception of unencrypted data. Treating all public networks as potentially compromised encourages consistent protective behavior. Regularly reviewing network security practices and updating knowledge about public Wi-Fi risks enhances preparedness. Vigilance and consistent habits are the best defenses against these common threats.

Securing your connection on public Wi-Fi is a combination of technology and behavior. VPNs, updated devices, strong security settings, and cautious browsing practices work together to mitigate risk. Understanding the threats and adopting protective habits empowers users to take control of their digital safety. Being proactive transforms a potentially dangerous environment into a manageable one. Public Wi-Fi does not have to compromise your data if approached with awareness, preparation, and layered protection.

Many users underestimate the dangers of connecting to free public Wi-Fi, assuming that "everyone else is using it safely." This false sense of security can lead to careless behavior, such as logging into multiple accounts without precautions. Cybercriminals rely on this assumption, knowing that convenience often outweighs caution. Even simple browsing activity can reveal personal information, such as device type, operating system, and browsing habits. Awareness of these subtle vulnerabilities helps users make more informed decisions. Treating public Wi-Fi as inherently risky encourages safer online behavior.

Fake Wi-Fi hotspots, often called "evil twins," are a common tactic used by attackers. These malicious networks mimic legitimate public Wi-Fi names, luring users into connecting. Once connected, all data transmitted can be intercepted, monitored, or manipulated. Users should confirm network names with staff, signage, or official sources before connecting. Checking for the presence of secure HTTPS connections is also essential. Remaining skeptical of unknown or unfamiliar networks reduces the likelihood of falling victim to this type of attack.

Public Wi-Fi often lacks encryption, leaving traffic exposed to interception. Websites without HTTPS transmit data in plain text, making it easy for attackers to capture login credentials, messages, or financial information. Even HTTPS websites can be compromised if users are connected to malicious networks that employ SSL stripping techniques. Utilizing VPNs encrypts all data, preventing attackers from reading or altering communications. Combining VPN usage with HTTPS websites provides a strong layer of protection. Encryption is a vital tool for safe browsing on public networks.

Device settings can significantly improve security when using public networks. Firewalls block unauthorized access attempts, while disabling file sharing and network discovery prevents accidental exposure. Users should ensure that devices are set to "public network" mode rather than "private," which can leave them more vulnerable. Keeping operating systems and applications up to date addresses known vulnerabilities that attackers might exploit. Layering these technical safeguards creates a more secure environment. Proper configuration reduces the chance of compromise, even on risky networks.

Limiting sensitive activities while on public Wi-Fi is a practical precaution. Avoid logging into banking accounts, accessing work-related systems, or transmitting personal documents unless absolutely necessary. If such activities must occur, using a secure VPN or mobile hotspot provides safer alternatives. Logging out from accounts and clearing browser caches afterward further reduces risk. These behavioral measures, combined with technical protections, create a comprehensive defense. Awareness and discipline are critical in protecting personal data in public spaces.

Monitoring for suspicious activity is another essential practice. Users should regularly check bank statements, email account activity, and connected device logs for unauthorized access. Alerts from security software or multi-factor authentication notifications can provide early warning of potential compromises. Prompt action can prevent attackers from escalating access to additional accounts or services. Maintaining vigilance even after disconnecting from public Wi-Fi is essential. Security does not end when the session ends; follow-up and monitoring are key components.

Educating users about the risks of public Wi-Fi strengthens overall cybersecurity. Awareness campaigns can inform individuals about the dangers of unencrypted networks, fake hotspots, and phishing attempts. Sharing best practices, such as VPN usage and careful network selection, reduces vulnerability. Collective education encourages responsible behavior across communities, workplaces, and families. Knowledge empowers users to navigate public networks safely. Information is a critical line of defense in environments outside one's control.

Even seemingly secure networks in hotels, airports, or cafes may have hidden vulnerabilities. Network administrators may fail to implement robust security measures, leaving data susceptible to interception. Users should assume that any public Wi-Fi could be compromised and take protective measures accordingly. This cautious approach reduces risk and promotes safe online habits. Vigilance combined with technological safeguards ensures maximum protection. Treating all public networks with respect and caution is essential.

Public Wi-Fi networks are often exploited by attackers to deploy malware. Malicious software can be injected into devices through unsecured connections, leading to compromised data, identity theft, or ransomware infections. Users may unknowingly download malware by clicking links, opening attachments, or visiting compromised websites. Ensuring antivirus and anti-malware software is up-to-date helps prevent these infections. Additionally, avoiding downloads or suspicious prompts while on public Wi-Fi reduces exposure. Combining preventative software with cautious browsing habits creates a stronger defense.

Wi-Fi eavesdropping, or sniffing, is another serious threat on public networks. Attackers can capture data transmitted over open networks using packet-sniffing tools. Personal information, passwords, and messages sent in plain text are especially vulnerable. Encryption, such as HTTPS and VPNs, protects data from interception and tampering. Users should always check for secure website connections and enable VPNs when accessing sensitive information. Being aware of eavesdropping risks encourages safer online behavior in public spaces.

Attackers sometimes create malicious captive portals, the login pages that appear when connecting to public Wi-Fi. These portals may appear legitimate but are designed to capture credentials or install malware. Users should verify portal authenticity by confirming with network staff or using trusted sources before entering information. Avoid automatically logging in or providing personal details unless the network is verified. Recognizing the signs of suspicious portals protects against credential theft and device compromise. Vigilance and verification are critical for safe access.

Mobile hotspot alternatives offer a safer option than public Wi-Fi. Using cellular data through a personal hotspot provides an encrypted connection that is less susceptible to interception. This method may consume mobile data but significantly reduces exposure to public network threats. Combining hotspot usage with secure applications, VPNs, and strong authentication ensures maximum safety. Users who frequently handle sensitive information while traveling benefit from this approach. Prioritizing security over convenience is essential in high-risk environments.

Even seemingly routine activities, such as checking email or social media, can be risky on public Wi-Fi. Attackers can exploit cookies, cached data, or insecure sessions to gain access to accounts. Logging out of accounts after use and clearing browser caches helps mitigate these risks. Secure browsing practices, combined with encryption and VPNs, protect data from unauthorized access. Small, consistent habits contribute to long-term security. Awareness of subtle risks is just as important as guarding against obvious threats.

Cybersecurity education plays a key role in safe public Wi-Fi usage. Users must understand how attackers exploit unsecured networks and what steps to take to prevent compromise. Training programs, online resources, and community awareness campaigns can help individuals make informed choices. Teaching users about VPNs, network verification, and device security reinforces good habits. Knowledgeable users are more likely to act cautiously and avoid mistakes that lead to breaches. Education empowers proactive, safe online behavior.

Organizations and businesses also bear responsibility for securing public Wi-Fi. Hotels, cafes, and airports should implement encryption, authentication, and monitoring protocols to protect users. Providing clear instructions for safe connection, including recommended VPN use, enhances user safety. When organizations prioritize network security, the risk of exploitation decreases significantly. Users benefit from environments where security measures are thoughtfully implemented. Safe infrastructure complements individual precautions.

Despite all precautions, users should always assume some level of risk on public networks. Treating public Wi-Fi as potentially compromised encourages consistent protective behavior. Relying solely on trust in network providers or apparent security can lead to complacency. Layering safeguards, maintaining awareness, and practicing caution ensures the best possible protection. Vigilance and proactive measures transform public Wi-Fi from a threat into a manageable risk. Responsible usage is the key to digital safety in public spaces.

Phishing attacks are often combined with public Wi-Fi risks. Cybercriminals may send emails or display fake login prompts specifically targeting users connected to unsecured networks. The combination of open access and social engineering makes public Wi-Fi a particularly dangerous environment. Users should be cautious of any unexpected login requests or prompts for personal information while connected. Verifying the source and avoiding unsolicited inputs helps prevent credential theft. Awareness of combined threats reinforces safer online behavior.

Public Wi-Fi networks also make it easier for attackers to perform session hijacking. If a user logs into an account without secure encryption, attackers can intercept session cookies and impersonate the user. This can lead to unauthorized account access, identity theft, or fraudulent transactions. Utilizing VPNs and ensuring websites use HTTPS protects against session hijacking. Regularly logging out of accounts and clearing cached data further mitigates risk. Consistent attention to security practices reduces exposure to these attacks.

Device operating systems and applications must be up-to-date to maintain security on public networks. Vulnerabilities in outdated software are commonly exploited by attackers on open Wi-Fi. Regularly installing updates patches security gaps and improves overall resilience. Users should also review app permissions and disable unnecessary network access. Combining software maintenance with careful network behavior minimizes the likelihood of compromise. Staying current is a simple yet effective preventive measure.

Public Wi-Fi often exposes users to network spoofing. Attackers can create fake access points with names similar to legitimate networks, tricking users into connecting. Once connected, attackers can monitor or manipulate traffic without detection. Always verify network names, avoid automatically connecting, and use VPNs to reduce exposure. Awareness of spoofing tactics ensures safer connections in public spaces. Treating unfamiliar networks with caution significantly lowers risk.

Public Wi-Fi presents an ongoing challenge for digital safety, but adopting layered protection strategies can mitigate risks. Users must combine technical tools like VPNs, updated devices, and encryption with careful browsing habits. Avoiding sensitive transactions, logging out after sessions, and verifying network authenticity are crucial behavioral practices. Awareness and education about phishing, spoofing, and malware on public networks reinforce these strategies. Maintaining consistent vigilance ensures that personal and professional data remain secure. The combination of preparation, caution, and technology transforms public Wi-Fi from a potential threat into a safe utility.

Travelers and remote workers face additional challenges on public networks. Using hotel, airport, or café Wi-Fi for work requires heightened caution, as attackers may target these users for corporate data. Business-sensitive communications should be conducted over secured connections or private networks whenever possible. Multi-factor authentication further protects accounts and reduces the impact of potential compromises. Users should also be mindful of device visibility settings and disable unnecessary sharing features. Proactive attention ensures secure work and travel environments.

Cybersecurity education is essential for public Wi-Fi users. Training, online resources, and awareness campaigns help individuals understand the risks and adopt safe practices. Encouraging friends, family, and colleagues to follow safe connection habits creates a wider network of protection. Sharing experiences and best practices increases vigilance across communities. Knowledge empowers users to make informed decisions and avoid common pitfalls. Education turns potential vulnerabilities into manageable challenges.

Monitoring and responding to suspicious activity is a critical component of safe public Wi-Fi usage. Users should track account activity, enable alerts for unusual logins, and promptly address any anomalies. Proactive monitoring allows for quick response to potential compromises before they escalate. Combined with preventative measures, vigilant observation ensures comprehensive security. Users who regularly check their digital environment are better equipped to prevent or minimize damage. Awareness, preparation, and action together create a strong defense.

REFLECTION:

Reflecting on public Wi-Fi security, it is clear that convenience must never come at the cost of safety. By understanding the risks, implementing technical safeguards, and practicing vigilant behavior, users can enjoy connectivity without compromising their data. Public networks challenge our digital responsibility, requiring awareness, preparation, and discipline. The small steps of cautious use, encryption, and monitoring collectively form a resilient approach to online safety. Protecting your information in public spaces is not optional—it is essential for maintaining control of your digital life.

"Safety in public Wi-Fi is not about avoiding it, but about connecting wisely, protecting your data, and staying vigilant at every step."
— Unknown

CHAPTER .11

SECURING YOUR SOCIAL MEDIA PROFILES

Steps to Safeguard Your Online Presence and Limit Exposure to Identity Theft

Social media platforms have become integral to modern life, but they also present significant privacy and security risks. Sharing personal information, photos, or location details can make users targets for cybercriminals. Attackers may exploit overshared data for identity theft, phishing, or social engineering attacks. Understanding the vulnerabilities of social media accounts is essential for protecting personal information. Awareness and proactive security measures help users maintain a safe online presence. Securing profiles is not just about privacy—it is a critical step in safeguarding identity.

Strong, unique passwords are the foundation of social media security. Many users reuse passwords across multiple accounts, creating an easy path for attackers. Implementing unique credentials for each platform minimizes the impact of any single breach. Password managers simplify this process by securely storing complex passwords. Multi-factor authentication (MFA) adds an additional layer of protection, preventing unauthorized access even if credentials are compromised. Combining strong passwords with MFA significantly strengthens social media defenses.

Privacy settings are another crucial aspect of securing social media accounts. Most platforms allow users to control who can see posts, contact them, or access personal information. Regularly reviewing and adjusting these settings ensures that sensitive information is only shared with intended audiences. Limiting public visibility of personal details, such as birthdates, contact information, or address, reduces the risk of identity theft. Awareness of platform-specific privacy features empowers users to control their digital footprint. Proper configuration of these settings is a proactive security measure.

Being cautious about third-party apps and integrations is essential. Many social media users connect their accounts to external apps for games, quizzes, or services. These apps often request access to personal data, which can be exploited if the app is malicious or compromised. Regularly reviewing app permissions and revoking access to unnecessary or unknown apps reduces exposure. Awareness of the data being shared with third parties strengthens overall account security. Limiting access is a simple but effective way to reduce risk.

Phishing attacks on social media are increasingly common. Attackers may send malicious links via direct messages, friend requests, or comments. These links often lead to fake login pages or malware downloads. Users should verify sender identities, avoid clicking on suspicious links, and report potentially malicious activity to platform administrators. Education about social engineering tactics on social media helps prevent unauthorized access. Vigilance combined with technical safeguards ensures a safer online environment.

Regular monitoring of account activity is vital. Many platforms provide logs of recent logins, devices used, and suspicious activity alerts. Reviewing these reports helps detect unauthorized access early, allowing users to take corrective action. Promptly changing passwords, revoking device access, and updating security settings are essential steps if suspicious activity is detected. Monitoring reinforces overall account security and enhances user awareness. Being proactive can prevent minor issues from escalating into full-scale breaches.

Avoiding oversharing personal information is a key behavioral practice. Posts about vacations, routines, or personal achievements can be used by attackers for social engineering. Sharing location in real-time or posting photos with identifiable landmarks increases exposure. Users should consider the long-term impact of what they post and limit public availability of sensitive information. Privacy-conscious behavior reduces the likelihood of identity theft or targeted attacks. Thoughtful posting habits complement technical security measures.

Educating friends and family about safe social media practices extends protection beyond personal accounts. Cybercriminals often exploit weaker accounts in a user's network to gain access or spread malicious content. Encouraging safe password habits, privacy settings, and vigilance in connected accounts strengthens collective security. Community awareness helps reduce the success of social engineering and phishing attacks. Promoting a culture of digital responsibility benefits everyone within a social network. Shared knowledge is a powerful tool for online safety.

Using official apps and avoiding third-party clones can prevent exposure to malicious software. Fake or altered versions of social media apps can harvest credentials or inject malware. Downloading apps only from trusted sources, such as official app stores, reduces the risk. Keeping applications updated ensures that security patches address known vulnerabilities. Awareness of app authenticity protects users from preventable attacks. Combining safe usage habits with technical precautions creates a secure social media environment.

Social engineering remains one of the most dangerous threats on social media. Attackers often impersonate friends, family, or trusted organizations to gain trust and solicit sensitive information. Messages requesting login details, financial help, or personal data should be approached with skepticism. Verifying the identity of the sender before responding is crucial. Users must learn to recognize red flags such as urgent requests, unusual language, or suspicious links. Developing a habit of cautious interaction reduces vulnerability to these manipulative tactics.

Privacy settings should be reviewed regularly, as social media platforms frequently update policies and features. New defaults or changes may expose information previously kept private. Users should periodically audit friend lists, posts, and shared media to ensure appropriate visibility. Limiting profile information to essential details minimizes exposure to attackers. Awareness of platform updates and proactive adjustments maintain consistent security. Staying informed about changes is key to long-term account protection.

Two-factor authentication (2FA) is an essential security measure for social media accounts. By requiring a secondary verification method, such as a text message or authentication app, 2FA blocks unauthorized access even if passwords are compromised. Users should enable 2FA on all critical accounts, especially those linked to email or financial information. This additional layer creates a formidable barrier against hackers. Coupled with strong, unique passwords, 2FA significantly enhances account security. Multi-layered authentication ensures resilience against common attack methods.

Cautious interaction with third-party applications prevents unnecessary data exposure. Many apps request extensive access to personal profiles, friends lists, or private messages. Reviewing permissions and removing unnecessary connections reduces the potential for data harvesting. Users should be wary of apps promising rewards or entertainment that require extensive access. Minimizing external access protects against identity theft and account compromise. Regular audits of connected applications reinforce a safer social media presence.

Monitoring account activity allows early detection of potential security breaches. Notifications about unfamiliar logins, new devices, or unusual messages are warning signs of unauthorized access. Prompt action, including changing passwords, revoking device access, and reviewing connected apps, helps contain risks. Users should treat these alerts seriously and investigate suspicious activity immediately. Early intervention prevents attackers from escalating access to other accounts or platforms. Vigilant monitoring is a key habit for maintaining long-term account safety.

Being mindful of the information shared in posts and comments helps prevent social engineering attacks. Details about travel plans, daily routines, or family events can be exploited by malicious actors. Users should consider the audience and potential consequences of sharing personal information publicly. Limiting visibility to trusted contacts reduces the chance of exposure. Thoughtful posting habits complement technical safeguards, creating a balanced approach to social media security. Awareness of what is shared online is as important as account protection.

Phishing attacks on social media often use enticing content to lure victims. Messages or posts may include fake offers, quizzes, or links that appear legitimate. Users should hover over links, verify URLs, and avoid clicking on suspicious content. Reporting malicious content to the platform helps prevent further spread and protects other users. Awareness of the tactics used by attackers strengthens individual and collective defenses. Careful scrutiny of interactions ensures safer engagement with online communities.

Educating friends and family about safe social media practices amplifies protection. Attackers often target weaker accounts in a user's network to gain access or spread malicious content. Sharing tips on password security, privacy settings, and phishing recognition helps reduce risks for everyone connected. Collective awareness reinforces strong cybersecurity habits. Encouraging vigilance within your network creates a more secure digital environment. Empowering others enhances your own security indirectly.

Location sharing on social media can inadvertently reveal sensitive information. Features that automatically tag locations in posts or check-ins can allow attackers to track patterns, plan targeted scams, or even locate a user physically. Users should disable automatic location tagging and be selective about sharing current locations. Avoid posting real-time updates of travel or daily routines to reduce exposure. Thoughtful management of location information helps prevent stalking, burglary, and identity theft. Awareness of digital footprints enhances overall security on social platforms.

Photo and video sharing can also present risks beyond immediate visibility. Metadata embedded in images, such as geolocation or device information, can reveal private details. Users should remove metadata before posting or use platform tools to strip identifying information. Sharing images publicly without considering potential implications may provide attackers with material for social engineering. Reviewing privacy settings for shared media ensures that only intended audiences can access content. Thoughtful media management is a critical component of social media safety.

Social media account recovery options must be secured carefully. Many platforms allow password resets via email or phone number, which can be exploited if these channels are compromised. Users should ensure recovery email accounts and phone numbers are protected with strong passwords and multi-factor authentication. Limiting the number of recovery options and regularly reviewing them reduces the risk of account takeover. Awareness of recovery vulnerabilities strengthens the overall security posture. Properly managed recovery mechanisms serve as a safeguard in case of breach.

Regularly auditing connected devices adds another layer of protection. Many social media accounts allow access from multiple devices, including phones, tablets, and computers. Removing unused or unrecognized devices prevents unauthorized access and ensures that only trusted devices remain connected. Users should also log out from shared or public devices to avoid lingering session risks. Maintaining control over device access reinforces overall account security. Device management is a proactive habit that complements other protective measures.

Awareness of platform-specific scams is crucial. Each social media site may have unique vulnerabilities and attack methods, such as fake giveaways, impersonation accounts, or malicious apps. Users should stay informed about these risks through official security updates, forums, or trusted news sources. Understanding the context of each platform helps users adopt tailored security practices. Educated users are more likely to identify threats and respond appropriately. Knowledge of platform-specific tactics strengthens digital resilience.

Engaging in responsible friend and follower management supports account security. Accepting requests only from known individuals and reviewing connections periodically reduces exposure to malicious actors. Fake accounts, bots, and impersonators are common tools used by attackers to gain trust and access personal information. Vigilant management of your network prevents unwanted access and protects personal data. Encouraging security awareness among friends and contacts amplifies overall protection. Careful curation of social connections is an important preventative measure.

Two-factor authentication should be complemented with backup codes and secure storage. If a primary device for 2FA is lost, backup codes ensure access while maintaining security. These codes should be stored safely, offline, or in secure password managers. Planning for contingencies prevents being locked out while still protecting against unauthorized access. Preparedness strengthens the reliability and effectiveness of multi-factor authentication. Secure account recovery is as critical as initial access protection.

Social media users should also be wary of oversharing professional information. Details such as workplace, position, or colleagues' information can be exploited by attackers for targeted scams or corporate espionage. Limiting exposure of work-related details to trusted connections reduces organizational and personal risk. Combining privacy settings with cautious sharing habits ensures safer engagement. Awareness of professional boundaries on social media is essential for maintaining both personal and organizational security. Thoughtful disclosure prevents potential exploitation.

Phishing attempts on social media are increasingly sophisticated, often leveraging trusted relationships to trick users. Attackers may send direct messages pretending to be friends or organizations, asking for login credentials, money, or personal information. Users should verify unusual requests through separate channels before responding. Recognizing the signs of social engineering—urgency, unfamiliar links, or unexpected attachments—helps prevent compromise. Being cautious even with messages from known contacts reduces the risk of falling victim. Awareness and skepticism are powerful defenses in online interactions.

Suspicious links embedded in posts or ads can also compromise security. Clicking on these links may lead to fake login pages, malware downloads, or credential theft. Users should hover over links to inspect URLs and avoid clicking on anything that appears unfamiliar or suspicious. Browser extensions or security software can help detect malicious content and warn users before they proceed. Combining vigilance with technical tools enhances protection against online threats. Careful navigation and link verification are essential habits for safe social media use.

Regularly updating apps and devices strengthens account security. Many social media platforms release updates that patch vulnerabilities and improve safety features. Users who neglect updates may leave themselves exposed to exploits. Enabling automatic updates or checking for updates frequently ensures that devices and apps are fortified against known threats. Updating also includes reviewing permissions and security settings to maintain optimal protection. Staying current with technology is a proactive approach to reducing risks.

Educating peers and family members on secure social media practices extends protection beyond individual accounts. Attackers often exploit weaker accounts in a network to gain access to other users. Sharing guidance on password security, privacy settings, and phishing awareness reduces vulnerabilities for everyone connected. Promoting safe online behavior in your circles creates a more secure digital environment. Collective vigilance strengthens the overall resilience of communities against cyber threats. Teaching others reinforces your own security habits as well.

Monitoring account notifications and unusual activity alerts allows for early intervention. Most platforms provide reports of new logins, unrecognized devices, or changes to account settings. Users should respond promptly by changing passwords, revoking device access, and reviewing connected apps. Acting quickly can prevent minor security breaches from escalating. Continuous observation ensures that accounts remain under the user's control. Regular monitoring complements other preventive measures and is key to long-term social media safety.

Being mindful of public posts and interactions helps reduce risk. Sharing personal opinions, photos, or updates in public view can inadvertently expose information to attackers. Limiting the audience for sensitive content and thinking critically about what is shared minimizes opportunities for social engineering. Awareness of digital footprints ensures that online behavior does not compromise security. Responsible posting habits are as important as technical protections. Thoughtful content management enhances overall account security.

Securing your social media accounts also requires safe password management. Using unique, complex passwords for each platform prevents a single breach from compromising multiple accounts. Password managers can help maintain strong, secure credentials without the need for memorization. Regularly updating passwords adds an additional layer of protection against potential threats. Combined with two-factor authentication, this approach creates a robust barrier against unauthorized access. Strong password hygiene is a fundamental step in safeguarding social media profiles.

Avoiding the use of public or shared devices for logging into social media accounts is another important precaution. Public computers or unsecured devices can store login credentials or be infected with malware. Users should log out completely after any session and avoid saving passwords on unfamiliar devices. Using personal devices with updated security software reduces the risk of compromise. Consistent attention to device security ensures that accounts remain protected across all access points. Safe device usage habits reinforce broader account security practices.

Maintaining security across multiple social media platforms requires consistent practices. Each account should have strong, unique passwords, two-factor authentication enabled, and privacy settings reviewed regularly. Users should avoid linking sensitive accounts, such as email or banking, directly to social media, as compromise of one platform can cascade into others. Periodic audits of connected apps, devices, and account activity help identify potential vulnerabilities. Being proactive across all platforms reduces the likelihood of a successful attack. Consistency and vigilance are the cornerstones of long-term social media safety.

Engaging responsibly with content and contacts further reduces exposure. Users should verify friend requests, avoid accepting connections from unknown individuals, and be cautious about sharing personal information in comments or messages. Attackers often exploit weak or careless behavior to gain access. Educating yourself and your network about safe interactions strengthens collective security. Thoughtful engagement ensures that social media remains a safe environment for communication. A mindful approach to interactions complements technical safeguards and reinforces account safety.

Awareness of current threats is crucial for social media security. Attackers continually evolve their tactics, employing sophisticated phishing, impersonation, and malware distribution techniques. Staying informed about emerging risks, platform updates, and new security tools empowers users to respond effectively. Knowledgeable users are better equipped to recognize and mitigate threats before damage occurs. Ongoing education and vigilance are key components of resilient account protection. Staying current allows users to adapt to the dynamic landscape of online security.

Regular monitoring of notifications and unusual activities helps detect early signs of compromise. Platforms typically offer alerts for new logins, password changes, or suspicious device activity.

Responding quickly to these alerts—by changing passwords, revoking device access, and reviewing connected applications—prevents minor incidents from escalating. Active monitoring reinforces other protective measures and ensures users maintain control over their accounts. Vigilance and responsiveness are crucial habits for long-term safety. Timely action often determines whether an account remains secure or falls victim to attack.

CHAPTER .12

CYBERSECURITY FOR FAMILIES: PROTECTING CHILDREN ONLINE

How to Implement Digital Safety Measures for Children and Minimize Their Online Risks

The internet offers children immense opportunities for learning, entertainment, and social interaction, but it also presents numerous risks. Cyberbullying, inappropriate content, online predators, and identity theft are just a few of the dangers children may encounter. Parents and guardians must actively participate in guiding and monitoring online activity to ensure a safe digital experience. Awareness of the risks and implementation of protective strategies is essential in today's connected world. Fostering open communication, education, and responsible habits helps children navigate the online space securely. Proactive involvement is the first line of defense in protecting young users.

Establishing clear rules for internet use sets expectations and boundaries. Children should understand which websites, applications, and platforms are acceptable, as well as time limits for online activity. Guidelines should include rules for sharing personal information, interacting with strangers, and using social media safely. Regular discussions about online experiences create opportunities for learning and problem-solving. Consistency and clarity in rules reinforce healthy digital behavior. Structured guidance fosters responsible and secure internet use.

Parental control tools and software provide an additional layer of protection. These tools allow monitoring of browsing activity, limiting access to inappropriate content, and setting usage schedules. Features may include filtering, website blocking, and alerts for potentially risky behavior. Selecting tools appropriate for a child's age and maturity ensures effective protection without stifling independence. Combining software safeguards with ongoing guidance strengthens overall security. Technology should support, not replace, parental involvement.

Education is a critical component of cybersecurity for children. Teaching kids about online privacy, password security, and safe communication helps them make informed decisions. Lessons should include recognizing phishing attempts, avoiding suspicious links, and understanding the consequences of oversharing. Interactive discussions and real-life examples make learning engaging and memorable. Encouraging curiosity while promoting caution empowers children to navigate the internet safely. Knowledge is one of the most effective defenses against online threats.

Monitoring and supervision should be balanced with respect for privacy. Parents can maintain awareness of online activity while fostering trust and independence. Open communication about internet experiences encourages children to report uncomfortable interactions or suspicious content. Rather than enforcing strict surveillance, guiding children through responsible online behavior is more effective in the long term. Encouraging self-awareness and problem-solving skills reinforces safe digital habits. Building trust strengthens both security and family relationships.

Setting up strong account protections is essential for children using online services. Unique passwords, two-factor authentication, and parental verification measures protect accounts from unauthorized access. Children should understand the importance of not sharing credentials and the potential consequences of weak security. Parents can model good security practices to reinforce these lessons. Account security is a foundational aspect of safe online engagement. Instilling these habits early promotes lifelong cybersecurity awareness.

Social media and gaming platforms require special attention. Many children interact with peers on these platforms, which can expose them to cyberbullying, harassment, or inappropriate content. Parents should guide safe usage, privacy settings, and responsible interactions. Discussions about identifying and reporting inappropriate behavior help children respond effectively. Encouraging moderation and healthy boundaries supports positive digital experiences. Awareness of platform-specific risks protects children from potential harm.

Educating children about digital footprints is equally important. Everything shared online can leave a lasting trace, influencing privacy and reputation. Teaching kids to consider the long-term impact of their posts and interactions fosters responsible behavior. Awareness of digital permanence encourages thoughtful decision-making. Digital literacy includes understanding how personal data can be tracked and misused. Preparing children to manage their online presence builds resilience against future risks.

Cybersecurity for families also involves modeling responsible behavior. Children learn from observing how adults handle online safety, privacy, and communication. Demonstrating strong password habits, cautious sharing, and critical thinking online reinforces lessons. Family discussions about news stories, cyber threats, and safe practices provide context and engagement. Leading by example strengthens children's understanding and motivation to follow safe practices. Role modeling is a powerful tool in teaching cybersecurity responsibility.

Children are often curious and eager to explore new online platforms, which can expose them to unforeseen risks. They may unknowingly share personal information, click on malicious links, or interact with strangers posing as peers. Parents and guardians must educate children about these dangers while encouraging safe exploration. Explaining the "why" behind rules fosters understanding and compliance. Children who grasp the consequences of unsafe behavior are more likely to make responsible choices. Awareness combined with guidance reduces exposure to online threats.

Age-appropriate guidance ensures that children learn cybersecurity skills gradually and effectively. Younger children may require strict supervision and filtered access, while older children can be taught to evaluate risks independently. Tailoring education to developmental levels promotes comprehension without overwhelming them. Age-appropriate tools and conversations empower children to practice good habits safely. Parents should adjust guidance as children mature and as technology evolves. Progressive education builds competence and confidence over time.

Monitoring online interactions helps prevent exposure to cyberbullying and inappropriate content. Children should feel comfortable reporting any harassment, threatening behavior, or uncomfortable interactions. Parents can assist by teaching children to recognize warning signs, block harmful users, and report incidents to platform administrators. Active engagement strengthens resilience and encourages safe social interaction online. Communication and supervision work hand-in-hand to protect children from harm. Awareness of potential threats creates a proactive defense system.

Online gaming can present unique cybersecurity risks. Many games include chat features that allow strangers to communicate directly with children. While gaming can be social and educational, it can also expose children to inappropriate language, harassment, or predatory behavior. Parents should review game ratings, supervise interactions, and configure privacy settings to limit exposure. Teaching children safe gaming habits, such as not sharing personal information or locations, reinforces security. Proper guidance ensures gaming remains a positive and safe experience.

Social media literacy is an essential component of family cybersecurity. Children should learn to critically evaluate friend requests, posts, and messages. They should understand that not everyone online has good intentions, and appearances can be deceiving. Discussing examples of scams, phishing attempts, and manipulation helps children recognize warning signs. Practical lessons and simulations improve their ability to respond appropriately to threats. Knowledge and practice empower children to make safe, informed decisions online.

Parents should implement secure password practices for all family accounts. Each child should have unique passwords, ideally managed with a family password manager. Teaching children about the importance of not sharing passwords fosters a sense of responsibility. Multi-factor authentication should be enabled on accounts where possible to add an extra layer of protection. Strong account security reduces the likelihood of unauthorized access and misuse. Password habits developed early promote lifelong cybersecurity awareness.

Creating a family internet agreement can formalize expectations. This agreement can outline acceptable websites, apps, time limits, and behavior online. It should also include steps for reporting suspicious or harmful activity. Engaging children in developing the agreement increases buy-in and accountability. Reviewing and updating the agreement regularly ensures that it remains relevant as technology and maturity evolve. Agreements provide a framework for discussion, enforcement, and ongoing education.

Teaching children about the permanence of online activity is critical. Even posts, messages, or images shared privately can be copied, saved, or spread beyond intended audiences. Educating children on the concept of digital footprints encourages caution and reflection. Children who understand that their online actions have lasting consequences are more likely to make thoughtful choices. Awareness of the potential impact of their behavior strengthens their ability to protect privacy. Digital literacy is an essential part of modern childhood education.

Children often use multiple devices, including smartphones, tablets, and computers, which increases their exposure to potential threats. Each device should be secured individually with strong passwords, updated operating systems, and antivirus protection. Configuring parental controls on all devices ensures consistent oversight. Educating children on the safe use of each device reinforces secure habits. Device security combined with supervision provides a layered defense against cyber threats. Consistency across devices reduces gaps in protection.

Communication about online risks should be ongoing rather than one-time discussions. Children benefit from regular conversations about the types of threats they may encounter, such as phishing, scams, or inappropriate content. These discussions help children understand why rules exist and how to respond when faced with suspicious situations. Encouraging children to ask questions and share experiences promotes active learning. Open dialogue reinforces trust and strengthens family cybersecurity practices. Knowledge paired with communication empowers children to act responsibly.

Implementing content filtering and monitoring tools can protect children from inappropriate or harmful material. Filters can block access to adult content, violence, or other unsuitable media. Monitoring tools allow parents to review browsing history and app usage without being overly intrusive. Balancing supervision with trust ensures that children feel guided rather than controlled. These tools act as safety nets while children learn to navigate the digital world responsibly. Layered protective measures create a safer online environment.

Social interactions online must be guided with caution. Children should be taught not to share personal information with strangers and to recognize signs of grooming or manipulation. Online friendships should be discussed openly, emphasizing the importance of verifying identities and maintaining privacy. Encouraging responsible social engagement teaches children to interact safely while still enjoying social benefits. Education about digital etiquette and potential risks fosters both safety and confidence. Awareness and guidance help children navigate social platforms responsibly.

Gaming platforms with multiplayer capabilities pose unique risks. Many games allow direct messaging and interaction with unknown players, which can expose children to harmful content or solicitations. Parents should review game ratings, enable privacy settings, and supervise communication channels. Discussing potential dangers and appropriate responses prepares children to handle uncomfortable situations. Teaching them to report or block inappropriate behavior enhances both safety and digital literacy. Safe gaming practices protect children while allowing them to enjoy interactive experiences.

Children should understand the concept of digital responsibility. Teaching them that their online behavior can have long-lasting consequences instills accountability. This includes thinking before posting, respecting others online, and safeguarding personal information. Reinforcing these lessons through conversation and examples helps children internalize responsible habits. Digital responsibility promotes safe participation in online communities. Early guidance builds a foundation for lifelong cybersecurity awareness.

Regular review of family cybersecurity practices ensures continued protection. As children grow and technology evolves, guidelines, monitoring, and security tools should be updated. Involving children in these reviews fosters engagement and shared responsibility. This proactive approach allows adjustments to changing circumstances while maintaining safety. Families that adapt and evolve their strategies are better equipped to handle new threats. Continuous evaluation reinforces resilience and preparedness.

Encouraging children to use secure communication methods enhances online safety. Using encrypted messaging apps and avoiding sharing sensitive information over public platforms reduces risk. Teaching them to recognize and report suspicious contacts ensures timely intervention. Safe communication habits protect both the child and the wider family network. Empowering children with knowledge and tools creates confident, informed digital citizens. Security is strengthened when children are active participants in their own protection.

Children's curiosity often leads them to explore new websites, apps, and social media platforms, sometimes without understanding the associated risks. Parents should guide exploration by providing safe options and teaching children to evaluate new online environments critically. Demonstrating how to verify website authenticity and recognize suspicious content helps children develop critical thinking skills. Encouraging questions and discussions about their online experiences fosters awareness and confidence. Gradual exposure under supervision allows children to learn safely while maintaining curiosity. Balancing exploration with guidance ensures both learning and protection.

Parental involvement should evolve as children mature. Younger children require stricter monitoring and control, while older children can gradually take more responsibility for their online activity. Regular discussions about safe online practices, emerging threats, and responsible behavior help children internalize cybersecurity principles. Establishing trust and communication ensures that children seek guidance when they encounter risky situations. Age-appropriate autonomy promotes confidence while maintaining safety. Adaptable guidance prepares children for responsible independent internet use.

Online safety education should include discussions about the permanence of digital content. Children must understand that posts, messages, and images shared online can have lasting consequences. Encouraging thoughtful sharing and privacy-conscious habits helps minimize future risks, such as cyberbullying or reputational damage. Parents should model responsible online behavior to reinforce these lessons. Awareness of digital footprints fosters lifelong habits of cautious and informed sharing. Teaching digital responsibility early empowers children to navigate technology safely.

Creating a family cybersecurity plan formalizes safety practices. This plan can include rules for device usage, time limits, approved apps, and guidelines for online interactions. Involving children in the creation of the plan encourages accountability and ownership of their behavior. Periodic reviews of the plan ensure it remains relevant as technology, platforms, and children's maturity evolve. A well-defined strategy provides clarity and consistency for the whole family. Proactive planning strengthens security and reduces ambiguity about expectations.

Children should be guided on how to respond to online threats, including cyberbullying, scams, and harassment. Teaching them to report incidents, block malicious users, and communicate concerns promptly is essential. Practicing response scenarios can build confidence and preparedness. Parents should reinforce that reporting is not a sign of weakness but a proactive step toward safety. Empowering children with response strategies reduces anxiety and increases resilience. Preparedness ensures that children can act quickly and safely when confronted with online risks.

Regular monitoring of children's online activity must be balanced with respect for their privacy. Open conversations about internet usage foster trust while allowing parents to identify potential risks. Tools such as activity logs, content filters, and device usage reports can provide insights without being overly intrusive. Combining monitoring with education encourages children to take responsibility for their own cybersecurity. Respecting privacy while maintaining oversight builds a culture of shared responsibility. Balanced supervision strengthens both security and trust.

Children should learn to protect personal information actively. This includes avoiding oversharing names, addresses, phone numbers, and other sensitive data. Teaching them to use pseudonyms or generic usernames when possible adds an extra layer of privacy. Understanding the consequences of data exposure helps children make thoughtful decisions about what to share online. Awareness of data privacy and protection reinforces responsible online behavior. Protecting personal information is a critical skill for navigating the digital world safely.

Safe communication practices should extend beyond social media and gaming. Children must understand that emails, messaging apps, and video chat platforms also carry risks. Teaching them to verify contacts, avoid sharing sensitive information, and recognize red flags builds comprehensive online safety awareness. Practicing safe habits across all digital communication channels strengthens overall cybersecurity. Consistency in teaching and modeling behavior enhances protection. Holistic education ensures children are prepared for all aspects of online interaction.

Ensuring children's online safety is a continuous effort that combines technology, education, and communication. Parents and guardians play a critical role in establishing rules, monitoring activity, and teaching responsible behavior. Regular discussions about online experiences help children feel supported and informed. Providing age-appropriate guidance while fostering independence encourages both confidence and safety. Combining proactive measures with open dialogue creates a resilient and secure digital environment. Families that work together can empower children to explore the internet safely and responsibly.

Parental tools and monitoring software are invaluable for mitigating risks. Filters, alerts, and usage tracking help parents identify potential issues before they escalate. These tools also provide opportunities for teaching moments, where children can learn from mistakes under guidance. Technology should complement—not replace—conversations about safety, privacy, and responsible behavior. By integrating these measures thoughtfully, families create a layered approach to cybersecurity. Combining technical tools with education strengthens protection and builds lifelong habits.

Education remains the cornerstone of cybersecurity for children. Teaching children about phishing, malware, identity theft, and social engineering equips them with practical skills to recognize threats. Real-world examples, role-playing, and interactive lessons can make learning engaging and memorable. Encouraging critical thinking about online interactions fosters resilience against manipulation or deception. Knowledge empowers children to make safe choices and avoid risky behavior. Cybersecurity education is most effective when it is ongoing, age-appropriate, and interactive.

Open communication fosters trust and encourages children to seek help when needed. Children should feel comfortable reporting cyberbullying, suspicious contacts, or accidental exposure of personal information. Establishing a supportive environment reinforces the importance of safety and helps children develop confidence in their decision-making. Parents should respond to concerns calmly and constructively, turning potential incidents into learning opportunities. Trust strengthens both security and family relationships. A culture of openness ensures children are proactive participants in their own protection.

Chapter .13

The Importance of Software Updates and Patch Management

How Regular Updates Keep Your Devices Secure and Guard Against Known Vulnerabilities

Software updates are essential for maintaining the security and performance of digital devices. Developers release updates to fix bugs, patch vulnerabilities, and improve functionality. Neglecting updates leaves systems exposed to known threats that attackers can exploit easily. Cybercriminals often target outdated software because vulnerabilities are widely documented and easier to exploit. Regular updates ensure that security flaws are addressed promptly. Keeping devices current is a fundamental step in protecting personal and professional data.

Patch management is a critical aspect of cybersecurity strategy. Patches are specific updates designed to correct security weaknesses or functional issues in software. Organizations and individuals must implement a structured approach to applying patches in a timely manner. Delaying updates increases the window of opportunity for attackers. Automation tools can simplify patch deployment and ensure consistency across devices. Effective patch management reduces risk and strengthens overall digital resilience.

Operating systems are particularly vulnerable when not updated regularly. Outdated OS versions may contain security holes that allow malware, ransomware, or unauthorized access. Updating the operating system ensures the latest security features are active and known vulnerabilities are addressed. Users should also enable automatic updates where possible to reduce human error and oversight. Staying current protects not only the device but also the data stored within it. A secure operating system is the foundation for overall device safety.

Applications, including web browsers, office software, and messaging platforms, also require constant attention. Vulnerabilities in these programs can serve as entry points for attacks, especially if they interact with the internet. Regularly updating applications ensures that security fixes are applied and compatibility issues are resolved. Users should be proactive in checking for updates and configuring automatic notifications when available. Maintaining software hygiene prevents exploitation by cybercriminals. Comprehensive update practices protect both personal information and device integrity.

Firmware updates for hardware devices are equally important. Routers, IoT devices, and peripherals often include embedded software that can have security weaknesses. Manufacturers release firmware updates to patch vulnerabilities and enhance performance. Ignoring these updates can expose the entire network to potential compromise. Users should follow manufacturer guidance and apply firmware updates consistently. Secure hardware supports the overall cybersecurity framework and reduces exposure to attacks.

Cybersecurity threats are constantly evolving, and attackers actively search for unpatched systems. Exploit kits and automated malware tools specifically target outdated software. Applying updates promptly reduces the attack surface and limits opportunities for cybercriminals. Awareness of emerging threats emphasizes the urgency of regular maintenance. Neglecting updates is akin to leaving doors unlocked in a high-risk environment. Consistent patching and updating practices are critical for defense.

Organizations often implement formal patch management policies to maintain security. These policies prioritize critical updates, schedule regular maintenance, and track compliance across all systems. Individuals can adopt similar approaches by setting reminders, using update management tools, and staying informed about critical patches. Structured processes prevent overlooked updates and ensure timely application. Proactive planning improves overall security posture. Treating updates as essential rather than optional is key to digital safety.

Education about the importance of updates is vital for all users. Many people delay or ignore updates due to inconvenience or lack of understanding. Communicating the risks associated with outdated software encourages timely adoption of patches. Awareness campaigns and user-friendly guidance can shift perceptions and promote responsible behavior. Informed users are more likely to prioritize updates and maintain secure systems. Education complements technical measures by fostering proactive habits.

Ignoring software updates is one of the most common mistakes that users make, often due to inconvenience or lack of awareness. Many cyberattacks exploit vulnerabilities that have already been patched in newer versions of software. Failing to update leaves systems defenseless against threats that could otherwise be easily mitigated. Users should prioritize critical updates, especially those addressing security vulnerabilities. Developing a routine for checking and applying updates reduces the likelihood of exploitation. Awareness of the risks associated with outdated software emphasizes the necessity of timely maintenance.

Automatic updates simplify the patching process and reduce human error. Most modern operating systems and applications offer options to install updates automatically. Enabling this feature ensures that essential patches are applied promptly without requiring constant attention. Users should verify that automatic updates are functioning correctly and not disabled accidentally. While automatic updates are convenient, it is still important to periodically check for updates manually. A combination of automation and oversight ensures comprehensive coverage.

Updates often include performance enhancements in addition to security fixes. Outdated software can suffer from glitches, slowdowns, or compatibility issues that affect user experience. Installing updates maintains optimal device performance while simultaneously enhancing security. Ignoring updates may result in both reduced efficiency and increased vulnerability. Recognizing the dual benefits of updates encourages users to maintain consistent practices. Keeping software current supports productivity and protection simultaneously.

Many cybercriminals use exploit kits that specifically target unpatched software. These kits scan for vulnerable systems and deliver malware, ransomware, or spyware to unprotected devices. Systems with the latest updates are significantly less likely to be compromised by automated attacks. Understanding this threat underscores the urgency of maintaining up-to-date software. Timely updates act as a defensive shield against a range of attacks. Knowledge of how attackers exploit outdated software reinforces proactive behavior.

Organizations often segment updates based on priority and criticality. Critical security patches should be applied immediately, while minor updates may be scheduled for later deployment. Individuals can adopt a similar strategy by identifying high-risk applications and prioritizing their updates. This approach ensures that the most vulnerable areas are protected first. Structured prioritization prevents delays and reduces overall risk. Applying updates strategically enhances security efficiency without overwhelming users.

Patch management also involves verifying the authenticity of updates. Users should download patches only from official sources or trusted platforms. Installing updates from unverified sources may inadvertently introduce malware or compromise system integrity. Careful attention to source authenticity ensures that updates enhance rather than jeopardize security. Verification is a simple but essential step in maintaining digital safety. Ensuring trustworthiness complements the act of updating itself.

Updates may occasionally introduce new features that require user adaptation. While these changes are usually beneficial, users should familiarize themselves with updates to prevent misuse or misconfiguration. Taking the time to understand updates ensures that new security features are properly utilized. Awareness of update content enhances both functionality and protection. Users who embrace updates as a learning opportunity strengthen their overall cybersecurity posture. Knowledgeable engagement maximizes the benefits of patching.

Scheduling regular update checks is a proactive habit that ensures consistent protection. Users can set reminders or incorporate update checks into routine device maintenance. Regular checks prevent the accumulation of unpatched software, which can increase exposure to attacks. Consistency in updating reduces gaps in security and enhances overall digital hygiene. Integrating update habits into daily or weekly routines makes protection habitual rather than reactive. Persistent attention to updates is a hallmark of responsible digital behavior.

Vulnerabilities in outdated software are often widely documented, making them prime targets for attackers. Cybercriminals actively search for systems that have not applied the latest patches, exploiting known weaknesses. Even minor delays in updating can provide an opportunity for attacks such as ransomware infections or data theft. Understanding that updates are proactive defenses highlights their critical role in cybersecurity. Regular maintenance ensures that systems remain resilient against evolving threats. Neglecting updates is akin to leaving the front door unlocked in a dangerous neighborhood.

Enterprise environments face unique challenges with patch management, but lessons apply to individuals as well. Large networks may require careful testing before updates are deployed to prevent compatibility issues. Individuals can adopt a simpler but structured approach by prioritizing critical updates first, then applying optional or feature updates later. This systematic approach ensures that the most serious vulnerabilities are addressed promptly. Structured patching minimizes disruption while maximizing security. Organization and planning are key elements of effective patch management.

User education plays a crucial role in successful update practices. Many users ignore update prompts due to inconvenience, assumptions that updates are unnecessary, or lack of understanding of their importance. Explaining the security risks associated with outdated software encourages timely action. Awareness campaigns, tutorials, and reminders help shift behavior toward proactive updating. Informed users are more likely to prioritize security alongside convenience. Knowledge transforms updates from an optional task into a critical habit.

Mobile devices are particularly susceptible to vulnerabilities if updates are neglected. Smartphones, tablets, and IoT devices frequently receive security patches to address emerging threats. Mobile operating systems and apps should be updated promptly to prevent compromise. Users should enable automatic updates whenever possible and periodically review device settings. Mobile security is an integral part of personal cybersecurity, as these devices often hold sensitive personal and financial information. Maintaining mobile updates ensures protection across all points of access.

Legacy software and unsupported applications pose ongoing risks. Older programs may no longer receive patches, leaving them exposed to newly discovered vulnerabilities. Users should identify outdated software and consider alternatives or upgrades that are actively maintained. Continuing to use unsupported software increases the likelihood of successful attacks. Awareness of software lifecycle and support policies is essential for long-term digital safety. Transitioning to updated platforms reduces risk and ensures compatibility with modern security standards.

Cybersecurity best practices recommend combining updates with other protective measures. Strong passwords, firewalls, antivirus software, and safe browsing habits complement the protective effects of updates. Updates alone cannot provide total security, but they form a critical layer of defense. Integrating updates into a broader security strategy strengthens overall resilience. Multi-layered protection is the most effective approach in defending against cyber threats. Software maintenance and behavioral practices work hand-in-hand for comprehensive protection.

Monitoring update notifications regularly prevents missed patches. Users should ensure that alerts from operating systems, applications, and security tools are active and visible. Ignoring notifications can result in critical vulnerabilities remaining unpatched for extended periods. Developing a habit of responding promptly to notifications reinforces consistent protection. Timely attention to alerts prevents small gaps from becoming major security risks. Vigilance in monitoring supports ongoing cybersecurity diligence.

Backup strategies complement software updates by providing a safety net. In the event an update causes unexpected issues or conflicts, having recent backups ensures data integrity. Regular backups allow users to restore systems to a known good state, minimizing downtime and potential loss. Combining backup practices with timely updates enhances overall digital security and stability. Preparedness strengthens both confidence and resilience in managing devices. Redundancy and updates together form a robust defense against cyber threats.

Regularly reviewing update histories can help identify gaps or missed patches. Most operating systems and applications provide logs or notifications indicating when updates were installed. Checking these records ensures that critical patches have been applied and helps track patterns of compliance. Users should address any skipped updates immediately to maintain security integrity. Awareness of historical update activity supports proactive management and reduces vulnerabilities. Routine review fosters accountability and discipline in maintaining digital safety.

Understanding the difference between security updates and feature updates is important. Security updates address vulnerabilities that could be exploited by attackers, while feature updates often add new functionality or performance improvements. Both are valuable, but security patches should always take priority. Users who delay security updates in favor of optional features may inadvertently expose themselves to risks. Recognizing the criticality of different updates ensures informed decision-making. Prioritizing security over convenience is a cornerstone of effective cybersecurity.

Patch management strategies should include testing when possible. While this is particularly relevant in organizational environments, individuals can also benefit by verifying that updates do not conflict with essential applications or system configurations. This precaution prevents disruptions and ensures compatibility. Even minor conflicts can cause software instability or data access issues. Thoughtful application of updates enhances both security and usability. A deliberate approach reduces frustration and strengthens confidence in maintaining updated systems.

Update notifications may sometimes be ignored due to perceived frequency or inconvenience. Users should develop routines that incorporate updates into regular device maintenance schedules. Setting aside time weekly or monthly to check for and apply updates can ensure consistent protection. Combining scheduled checks with automatic updates creates redundancy, reducing the chance of vulnerabilities persisting. Discipline in maintaining a schedule reflects a proactive approach to cybersecurity. Consistency is key to minimizing exposure to preventable risks.

Cybercriminals actively exploit known vulnerabilities in software for both targeted and opportunistic attacks. Outdated software is often an easy entry point for malware, ransomware, and unauthorized access. Keeping software updated significantly reduces the attack surface and strengthens overall security posture. Awareness of the threat landscape reinforces the necessity of timely updates. Cybersecurity is a dynamic challenge, and regular patching is a fundamental defense. Vigilant maintenance of software ensures that known weaknesses are addressed before attackers can exploit them.

Education about the importance of updates should extend to all family members or users of shared devices. Children, teens, and other household members should understand why updating devices protects both their information and the broader network. Simple explanations about security risks and practical demonstrations can encourage compliance. Shared understanding promotes a culture of cybersecurity awareness within the household. Knowledgeable users are more likely to participate actively in maintaining device safety. Family-wide engagement enhances collective protection.

Firmware and driver updates for hardware devices should not be overlooked. Routers, printers, smart home devices, and other peripherals often have security vulnerabilities that require patching. Applying these updates maintains compatibility, improves performance, and mitigates risks. Devices that are left unpatched may serve as entry points for attacks targeting the entire network. Users should consult manufacturer instructions and schedule firmware updates consistently. Hardware maintenance is as important as software updates in ensuring comprehensive digital security.

Software updates and patch management are not just technical tasks—they are essential habits for anyone serious about cybersecurity. Treating updates as optional exposes devices and data to unnecessary risk, whereas consistent maintenance provides a strong foundation for protection. Updates safeguard against known vulnerabilities, improve functionality, and often include performance enhancements. Users who integrate updates into their routine develop a proactive mindset toward digital safety. Embracing the habit of timely patching transforms a reactive defense into a proactive one. Regular attention to updates strengthens overall digital resilience.

Family and household devices require coordinated update strategies. When multiple users share devices, it is important to ensure that everyone understands the importance of updates. Shared responsibility helps prevent overlooked patches and reinforces a culture of cybersecurity awareness. Teaching children, teens, and other users to respect update protocols fosters collective protection. Coordinated efforts reduce vulnerabilities across all connected devices. A household that prioritizes updates as a team maintains a safer digital environment for everyone.

Automation and tools play an important role in sustaining update discipline. Automatic updates, notifications, and centralized management tools reduce the likelihood of missing critical patches. Users should leverage these technologies to simplify the update process while retaining oversight. Technology should serve as an aid, not a replacement for understanding the importance of updates. Combining automation with education ensures both efficiency and informed engagement. Effective use of tools reinforces proactive security practices.

Understanding the consequences of neglecting updates reinforces motivation to maintain them. Outdated software can lead to malware infections, identity theft, data loss, and compromised privacy. Cybercriminals often target unpatched systems because they are predictable and easily exploited. Recognizing the tangible risks associated with outdated software encourages users to prioritize updates consistently. Awareness of potential consequences fosters responsible habits. Preventive measures, such as patching, reduce the likelihood of expensive or harmful incidents.

Finally, software updates should be viewed as a cornerstone of a broader cybersecurity strategy. Alongside strong passwords, antivirus protection, cautious online behavior, and backups, timely updates form a multi-layered defense. Users who consistently maintain updates protect themselves, their families, and their networks from avoidable threats. Updates are simple yet powerful tools that enhance security, performance, and confidence in digital life. Treating them as essential rather than optional transforms device maintenance into a proactive, protective practice.

REFLECTION:

Reflecting on the importance of software updates, I have realized that vigilance and consistency are more powerful than advanced tools alone. Keeping devices updated is a straightforward, low-effort step that prevents a vast array of potential attacks. Personally, I have observed that users who integrate updates into their routine experience fewer issues, enjoy better device performance, and feel more secure online. This chapter has reinforced that cybersecurity is not only about defense but also about disciplined habits and informed engagement. Updates are small actions with outsized benefits, and embracing them reflects a commitment to personal and digital safety.

"An updated system is a defended system; every patch applied is a step toward a safer digital life."
— Unknown

CHAPTER .14

USING ANTIVIRUS SOFTWARE: WHAT YOU NEED TO KNOW

Choosing and Using Antivirus Programs to Detect and Remove Malicious Software

Antivirus software is one of the foundational tools for protecting devices against malware, spyware, ransomware, and other malicious programs. These programs actively scan, detect, and remove threats before they can compromise systems or steal personal information. While antivirus software alone cannot guarantee complete security, it significantly reduces the risk of infection. Modern antivirus solutions often include real-time protection, automatic updates, and threat alerts to help users stay ahead of emerging threats. Selecting the right antivirus software requires understanding features, performance, and compatibility with your devices. A well-chosen antivirus program forms a crucial layer of defense in a comprehensive cybersecurity strategy.

Understanding the types of malware that antivirus software protects against is essential. Viruses can corrupt or delete files, worms can spread across networks, and trojans disguise themselves as legitimate programs. Spyware secretly monitors activity, while ransomware locks files and demands payment for release. Antivirus programs identify these threats using signature databases, behavioral analysis, and heuristic scanning. Being familiar with these malware types helps users understand the importance of active protection. Awareness of potential threats ensures that users value and maintain their antivirus solutions.

Installing antivirus software correctly is critical for effective protection. Users should download programs only from reputable sources, such as official vendor websites or trusted app stores. Installation should include enabling real-time protection and automatic updates to ensure continuous coverage. Some programs offer additional features, like firewalls or phishing protection, which can further enhance security. Proper configuration ensures that the antivirus software can perform its intended functions without gaps. Correct installation is the first step toward reliable defense.

Regular scanning of devices complements real-time protection. Full system scans detect hidden threats that may have bypassed initial defenses, while quick scans focus on commonly targeted areas. Scheduling regular scans ensures consistent monitoring without relying solely on manual action. Scanning can detect malware that may have been inadvertently downloaded, accessed through email attachments, or transferred via external drives. Combining real-time protection with scheduled scans creates a more robust security posture. Vigilance in scanning increases confidence that devices remain safe and secure.

Keeping antivirus software up to date is essential. Threats evolve constantly, and new malware variants are created daily. Antivirus vendors release frequent updates to signature databases, algorithms, and detection methods to combat these threats. Failing to update software leaves devices vulnerable to newly emerging attacks. Users should enable automatic updates whenever possible and periodically check that the software is current. Timely updates ensure that the antivirus program remains effective against the latest threats.

Choosing antivirus software requires consideration of compatibility, system performance, and security features. Lightweight programs minimize impact on device speed, while comprehensive suites may include additional tools like VPNs, firewalls, or parental controls. Users should balance protection with usability to avoid frustration and maintain consistent use. Reading reviews, consulting experts, and testing trial versions can guide informed decisions. Selecting the right program ensures long-term adoption and effective defense. A thoughtful choice maximizes security benefits without compromising device functionality.

Antivirus software is not a replacement for safe online behavior. Even the best programs cannot prevent phishing attacks, social engineering, or poor password practices. Users must combine antivirus protection with cautious browsing, strong passwords, and awareness of suspicious emails or links. This layered approach reduces risk and ensures that multiple defenses are in place. Relying solely on antivirus software creates a false sense of security. Comprehensive protection requires both technology and responsible behavior.

Antivirus solutions often include real-time alerts and threat notifications. Users should understand these alerts and respond promptly, such as quarantining suspicious files or blocking malicious websites. Ignoring warnings can lead to infections and data compromise. Familiarity with alert protocols ensures that users act appropriately when a threat is detected. Quick, informed responses minimize the potential impact of malware. Awareness and action are crucial components of effective antivirus usage.

Antivirus software relies on multiple detection methods to identify and block threats effectively. Signature-based detection compares files against known malware signatures, while heuristic analysis identifies suspicious behavior even in previously unknown threats. Some advanced solutions incorporate machine learning and artificial intelligence to detect subtle or evolving malware patterns. Understanding how your antivirus works helps users appreciate its importance and limitations. Combining multiple detection approaches enhances overall protection. Awareness of detection methods ensures informed usage and realistic expectations.

Real-time protection is a critical feature in modern antivirus software. It continuously monitors files, downloads, emails, and web traffic for suspicious activity. This proactive approach prevents malware from executing and spreading before damage occurs. Users should ensure that real-time protection is always enabled, as disabling it even temporarily increases vulnerability. Real-time alerts allow users to respond immediately to potential threats. Maintaining continuous monitoring is essential for minimizing exposure to cyber risks.

Regularly reviewing quarantined files is an important maintenance step. Antivirus programs often isolate suspicious files to prevent harm while allowing users to examine them. Reviewing these files helps determine whether they are false positives or genuine threats. Users should follow program guidance to safely delete or restore files as appropriate. Ignoring quarantined files can lead to overlooked infections or wasted storage space. Proper management of quarantined files maintains both security and system performance.

Antivirus software may sometimes conflict with other applications or system settings. Users should be aware of potential compatibility issues, especially when using multiple security programs simultaneously. Conflicts can reduce effectiveness or slow down devices. Consulting vendor documentation and adjusting settings can resolve conflicts while maintaining protection. Awareness of potential interference ensures that antivirus software functions optimally. Proper configuration preserves both security and usability.

Education about safe computing complements antivirus protection. Users must understand that no software can defend against all threats if poor habits persist. Avoiding suspicious downloads, phishing emails, and unsafe websites reduces the likelihood of infections. Antivirus programs act as a safety net, but proactive behavior is the first line of defense. Combining technical tools with responsible behavior maximizes digital security. Informed users are less likely to fall victim to malware or cybercrime.

Choosing antivirus software with automatic updates ensures ongoing protection. Threats evolve daily, and signature databases must be current to detect the latest malware. Automatic updates remove the burden of manual intervention and reduce the chance of missing critical patches. Users should verify that update functionality is active and functioning correctly. Staying current with the latest security definitions strengthens overall defense. Timely updates are essential for effective malware protection.

Mobile antivirus solutions are increasingly important as smartphones and tablets become primary computing devices. Mobile malware, malicious apps, and phishing attacks target personal and financial information. Installing antivirus software on mobile devices protects sensitive data and prevents unauthorized access. Users should select solutions that are lightweight, efficient, and compatible with mobile operating systems. Mobile protection is an integral part of comprehensive digital security. Ensuring consistent protection across all devices minimizes vulnerabilities.

Antivirus software may also include additional tools like firewalls, anti-phishing modules, and VPN integration. These features enhance overall security by addressing multiple attack vectors. Users should explore available options and enable features that align with their specific needs. Leveraging integrated tools simplifies security management and strengthens protection. Combining antivirus functionality with additional layers creates a more robust defense. Multi-faceted security solutions offer broader and more effective protection.

Antivirus software is only effective if it is actively maintained and properly configured. Users should routinely verify that the program is running, that real-time protection is enabled, and that updates are current. Neglecting maintenance can leave devices exposed despite having software installed. Periodic checks ensure that the antivirus functions as intended and provides full protection. Awareness and proactive management are essential for maintaining a secure environment. Regular maintenance habits maximize the effectiveness of the software and prevent lapses in defense.

Many antivirus programs include scheduled scanning features, which allow users to automate checks for malware. Full system scans should be run regularly to catch hidden threats, while quick scans can target high-risk areas more frequently. Scheduling scans at times when the device is idle ensures minimal disruption while maintaining consistent monitoring. Users should review scan results carefully and take recommended actions to resolve detected issues. Combining scheduled scans with real-time monitoring enhances security and provides peace of mind. Routine scanning strengthens the overall cybersecurity posture.

Understanding false positives is important when using antivirus software. Occasionally, legitimate files may be flagged as malicious due to heuristics or behavioral detection. Users should review these files carefully and, when in doubt, consult the antivirus vendor or perform additional verification. Mismanaging false positives can lead to unnecessary deletion of important files or unwarranted concern. Awareness of this phenomenon ensures measured, informed responses to alerts. Proper handling of false positives maintains both security and system functionality.

Antivirus software is most effective when integrated into a broader cybersecurity strategy. Safe browsing habits, strong passwords, and updated software complement antivirus protection. Users must avoid assuming that antivirus alone is sufficient. A holistic approach addresses multiple potential vulnerabilities and strengthens overall digital safety. Combining behavioral practices with technological safeguards creates layered defenses that significantly reduce risk. Integration of multiple strategies ensures comprehensive protection against cyber threats.

Mobile and IoT devices require attention beyond traditional computers. Smartphones, tablets, smart home devices, and connected gadgets are increasingly targeted by malware. Antivirus solutions for mobile devices help protect sensitive personal information, including banking credentials and private communications. Users should ensure that all connected devices have adequate protection and that updates are applied consistently. A comprehensive approach to antivirus protection includes all endpoints, not just computers. Extending coverage across devices strengthens overall network security.

Education and awareness are as important as technology. Users must understand how malware spreads, the risks of phishing, and the importance of avoiding unsafe downloads. Teaching family members or colleagues to recognize suspicious behavior enhances collective protection. Antivirus software works best when combined with informed, vigilant behavior. Empowering users with knowledge complements technical measures and reduces exposure. Awareness ensures that technology and human behavior work together for effective cybersecurity.

Choosing the right antivirus solution requires evaluating features, cost, performance, and support. Users should select software that fits their device capabilities, user experience preferences, and security needs. Free solutions may offer basic protection, while paid versions often include additional features like VPNs, advanced scanning, or parental controls. Research, reviews, and trial versions can help determine the best option. A well-chosen solution ensures both protection and usability. Thoughtful selection maximizes the benefits of antivirus investment.

Antivirus software plays a crucial role in defending against evolving cyber threats, but it is most effective when users remain actively engaged. Users should not treat installation as a one-time task but rather as the beginning of ongoing management. Regularly reviewing settings, monitoring alerts, and performing scans ensures that protection is consistently effective. Neglecting these practices can allow malware to bypass defenses or remain undetected. Active involvement enhances the reliability of the antivirus solution. Vigilance transforms antivirus software from a passive tool into an active guardian.

Integration with other security measures strengthens overall protection. Firewalls, password managers, VPNs, and safe browsing habits create a layered defense system that complements antivirus capabilities. Each component addresses a different vulnerability, reducing the likelihood that a single breach could compromise sensitive information. Users should view antivirus software as part of this comprehensive approach rather than a standalone solution. Understanding the interplay between these security layers ensures maximum protection. Layered security provides resilience against both known and emerging threats.

Monitoring system performance alongside antivirus activity is also important. Some antivirus programs can be resource-intensive, affecting device speed or causing conflicts with other applications. Users should optimize settings to balance security with performance, ensuring that protection does not interfere with daily tasks. Performance monitoring also helps identify issues that may signal malware infections or misconfigurations. Adjusting configurations as needed ensures effective and efficient protection. Awareness of system behavior complements technical safeguards.

Antivirus solutions often include additional features, such as email scanning, phishing protection, and web filtering. These tools prevent malicious links, spam, and infected attachments from reaching users. Enabling and properly configuring these features enhances security beyond traditional malware scanning. Users should familiarize themselves with available options and ensure that all relevant protections are active. Leveraging these features reduces exposure to common attack vectors. Comprehensive configuration maximizes the benefits of the antivirus software.

Education and training are essential for maximizing antivirus effectiveness. Users must understand the types of threats they are likely to encounter and how the software responds. Training should include recognizing suspicious files, responding to alerts, and practicing safe computing habits. Well-informed users are less likely to engage in behaviors that undermine antivirus protection. Knowledge empowers users to act as active participants in their own cybersecurity. Education complements technology by turning awareness into actionable safety practices.

Incorporating antivirus software into your daily digital routine is a simple yet powerful step toward protecting your devices and personal data. Regular updates, real-time monitoring, and scheduled scans ensure that the system remains resilient against evolving threats. Users should view antivirus management as an ongoing responsibility rather than a one-time installation.

Consistent engagement maximizes the program's effectiveness and reduces the risk of malware infections. A proactive approach transforms antivirus software into a reliable, ever-present defense. Maintaining vigilance is key to sustaining strong cybersecurity.

For households and families, antivirus practices should be standardized across all devices. Children, teens, and adults alike must understand the importance of running scans, updating software, and responding to alerts. Shared knowledge and responsibility foster a culture of safety and collective cybersecurity awareness. Parents and guardians can lead by example, demonstrating safe computing practices and the importance of routine antivirus maintenance. Engaging all household members creates a united approach to digital protection. Consistent habits across users strengthen overall network security.

Selecting the right antivirus solution requires balancing security features, performance, and usability. Lightweight programs prevent slowdowns, while comprehensive suites offer additional tools such as firewalls, VPNs, and anti-phishing modules. Evaluating reviews, testing trial versions, and consulting expert recommendations helps users choose the best solution for their needs. Choosing thoughtfully ensures long-term adoption and effective protection. A well-suited antivirus program empowers users to navigate the digital world safely. Strategic selection is a critical step in personal cybersecurity planning.

Antivirus software is most effective when complemented by safe computing habits. Avoiding suspicious downloads, phishing links, and untrusted websites reduces reliance on reactive defense measures. Users should treat antivirus as one layer in a multi-faceted security strategy, supported by backups, password hygiene, and cautious online behavior. The combination of proactive habits and technological safeguards significantly decreases the risk of compromise. Human awareness and responsible behavior amplify the protective power of antivirus tools. Technology and education together form a resilient cybersecurity posture.

Reflection:

Reflecting on antivirus software, I realize it is a powerful shield only when paired with awareness, vigilance, and proper management. Installing a program is not enough; consistent updates, scans, and user education determine its true effectiveness. In my own experience, proactive antivirus practices have prevented countless potential incidents and provided peace of mind. Cybersecurity is not just about technology—it's about habits, discipline, and informed action. Antivirus software exemplifies how small, consistent practices can have a significant impact on digital safety.

"Antivirus software protects your devices, but knowledge and vigilance protect your life online."
— Unknown

CHAPTER .15

FIREWALLS AND VPNs: PROTECTING YOUR DIGITAL BORDERS

How Firewalls and Virtual Private Networks (VPNs) Keep Your Data Safe from External Threats

Firewalls and VPNs are essential tools for maintaining a secure digital environment. Firewalls act as gatekeepers, controlling incoming and outgoing network traffic to prevent unauthorized access. VPNs, on the other hand, create encrypted tunnels that safeguard data transmitted over the internet, ensuring privacy and protection from eavesdroppers. Both tools work together to shield devices and networks from cyber threats. Understanding how these technologies function is critical for anyone seeking to protect personal and professional information. Effective use of firewalls and VPNs enhances cybersecurity and provides peace of mind.

Firewalls monitor network traffic and enforce security rules to block malicious activity. They can be hardware-based, software-based, or a combination of both, depending on user needs. Firewalls filter traffic based on IP addresses, ports, and protocols, preventing unauthorized access while allowing legitimate communication. Configuring firewalls correctly is essential to prevent vulnerabilities and avoid accidental blocking of necessary services. They also help protect against malware, ransomware, and intrusion attempts. A properly configured firewall is the first line of defense against external cyber threats.

VPNs encrypt internet traffic, making it unreadable to hackers, ISPs, and other potential interceptors. This is especially important when using public Wi-Fi networks, which are often unsecured and prone to attacks. By masking the user's IP address, VPNs also protect online identity and location. VPNs are essential for maintaining privacy when accessing sensitive accounts, conducting financial transactions, or working remotely. Selecting a reliable VPN with strong encryption protocols ensures optimal protection. VPNs create a secure bridge between devices and the internet, safeguarding communications from prying eyes.

Understanding the difference between personal and organizational firewalls is important. Personal firewalls are typically built into operating systems and protect individual devices, while organizational firewalls manage traffic for entire networks. Both types play critical roles in controlling access and preventing unauthorized connections. For individuals, enabling and properly configuring the personal firewall provides a significant layer of security. Organizations often deploy more advanced solutions with intrusion detection and prevention systems. Awareness of the type and configuration of firewalls ensures that users and networks are adequately protected.

VPNs offer additional benefits beyond encryption, including bypassing geographic restrictions and enhancing anonymity. However, users must be cautious in selecting VPN providers. Free VPNs may compromise security or sell user data, while reputable providers invest in strong encryption and privacy policies. Evaluating providers based on reliability, speed, and logging policies is critical. Using a VPN in combination with other security measures maximizes protection. Safe, well-chosen VPNs are a powerful tool for preserving privacy and preventing data interception.

Firewalls can be configured to allow only specific applications or services to communicate with the internet. This minimizes exposure and reduces the risk of malware or unauthorized access. Users should regularly review firewall rules and update them as needed to reflect changing usage patterns. Misconfigured firewalls can create security gaps, making devices vulnerable. Periodic evaluation ensures that the firewall continues to provide effective protection. Firewalls and proper configuration act as barriers, keeping cyber threats at bay.

VPNs are particularly important for remote work and mobile users. Data transmitted over unsecured networks is vulnerable to interception and manipulation. VPNs encrypt these communications, protecting sensitive information such as passwords, emails, and corporate data. Organizations often mandate VPN usage to maintain secure connections between remote employees and corporate systems. Individuals can also benefit by maintaining secure communications for personal banking, shopping, and private communications. VPNs safeguard information wherever users access the internet.

Combining firewalls with VPNs creates layered security. Firewalls block unauthorized access, while VPNs encrypt legitimate traffic to prevent eavesdropping. This combination is particularly effective against hackers, malware, and man-in-the-middle attacks. Layered protection ensures that even if one security measure is bypassed, others remain to safeguard data. Users should implement both technologies for comprehensive defense. Integrated solutions strengthen overall digital security.

Education and awareness are critical for effective firewall and VPN use. Users should understand what is allowed through the firewall, recognize the risks of unprotected connections, and know when to enable VPNs. Safe habits, combined with these technologies, reduce vulnerability and improve privacy. Knowledge empowers users to make informed choices about security configurations. Technology alone is not enough; educated users are an essential part of the defense. Combining awareness with tools ensures optimal protection.

Firewalls operate by analyzing network packets and determining whether to allow or block them based on predefined security rules. This process helps prevent unauthorized access while permitting legitimate traffic to flow. Users should familiarize themselves with firewall settings and ensure essential services are not inadvertently blocked. Periodic reviews of firewall logs can help detect attempted intrusions or suspicious activity. Understanding how traffic is managed enhances awareness of potential vulnerabilities. Effective monitoring and configuration maximize the protective benefits of a firewall.

VPNs rely on encryption protocols to secure data transmitted over public and private networks. Common protocols include OpenVPN, IKEv2/IPSec, and WireGuard, each offering different balances of speed, compatibility, and security. Choosing the right protocol is essential for maintaining privacy without sacrificing performance. Users should also verify that the VPN service does not log sensitive information, ensuring true anonymity. Strong encryption safeguards communications from hackers, cybercriminals, and even internet service providers. Understanding protocol options ensures users make informed decisions for optimal protection.

Many organizations implement firewalls with advanced features such as intrusion detection systems (IDS) and intrusion prevention systems (IPS). IDS monitors network traffic for suspicious behavior and alerts administrators, while IPS can actively block malicious activity. Individuals using home networks can benefit from firewalls with similar functionalities, offering added layers of defense. These features detect patterns of attacks and prevent unauthorized access before damage occurs. Users should ensure these systems are enabled and updated regularly. Advanced firewall features provide proactive threat mitigation.

VPNs are especially valuable when using unsecured Wi-Fi networks, such as those found in cafes, airports, and hotels. Public Wi-Fi is prone to eavesdropping, man-in-the-middle attacks, and other forms of interception. Using a VPN creates an encrypted tunnel, preventing attackers from reading transmitted data. This is particularly important for sensitive communications like banking transactions or confidential emails. Even if the network itself is compromised, a VPN ensures that information remains private. Consistent VPN use reduces exposure to these high-risk environments.

Proper configuration of firewalls is critical to ensure that protection does not interfere with normal operations. Overly strict rules may block necessary applications, while overly lenient rules may leave vulnerabilities exposed. Users should balance security with functionality, allowing legitimate traffic while filtering potential threats. Regular updates to firewall rules ensure that protection remains current as usage patterns evolve. Reviewing logs and alerts helps identify unusual activity and strengthens overall security. Thoughtful configuration maximizes effectiveness without compromising usability.

VPN services may also include features such as kill switches, which disconnect internet access if the VPN connection drops unexpectedly. This prevents data from being transmitted unencrypted and exposed to potential attackers. Users should enable kill switches whenever available to maintain continuous security. Additionally, split tunneling options allow selective routing of traffic through the VPN, balancing security and speed for specific applications. Understanding and utilizing these features enhances both safety and performance. Proper use of VPN features ensures comprehensive protection.

Firewalls and VPNs work best when combined with other cybersecurity measures. Antivirus software, strong passwords, regular updates, and cautious online behavior complement network defenses. No single tool provides complete security, but a layered approach significantly reduces risk. Users should view firewalls and VPNs as integral components within a holistic cybersecurity strategy. Integration of multiple measures creates redundancy and resilience against diverse threats. Layered defenses strengthen both personal and organizational security.

Regular monitoring and maintenance are essential for both firewalls and VPNs to remain effective over time. Firewall logs should be reviewed to detect patterns of suspicious activity or repeated access attempts from unknown sources. Users can adjust rules based on observed traffic to enhance protection while maintaining necessary functionality. Similarly, VPN clients should be kept up to date to ensure encryption protocols are current and vulnerabilities are patched. Neglecting updates or monitoring can leave users exposed to preventable threats. Consistent attention ensures that these tools continue to provide robust security.

Firewalls also play a critical role in protecting connected devices within a home or office network. IoT devices, printers, and smart appliances often lack robust security features, making them potential entry points for attackers. A firewall can limit communication to only trusted devices and services, reducing the network's attack surface. Users should segment their networks when possible, keeping critical devices isolated from less secure ones. Network segmentation combined with firewall rules strengthens overall security. Thoughtful network management prevents a single compromised device from jeopardizing the entire network.

VPN usage should be consistent and intentional to maximize privacy benefits. Many users only enable VPNs sporadically, which leaves intermittent gaps in protection. Ensuring VPN is active whenever transmitting sensitive information, especially over public or untrusted networks, provides continuous security. Additionally, some VPNs offer server selection options that allow users to optimize speed, location, and privacy. Strategic selection of servers enhances security while maintaining performance. Consistent VPN use ensures reliable encryption and data protection.

Firewalls and VPNs are also valuable in defending against remote attacks. Cybercriminals frequently attempt to exploit vulnerabilities in open ports or unsecured connections. Firewalls can block suspicious access attempts, while VPNs ensure that any transmitted data remains encrypted and private. Together, these technologies protect both inbound and outbound communications, reducing the likelihood of breaches. Understanding the protective scope of each tool helps users maximize their effectiveness. Awareness of remote attack vectors reinforces the need for layered defenses.

VPNs also provide an added layer of anonymity online. By masking a user's IP address and routing traffic through secure servers, VPNs make it more difficult for third parties to track location or online activity. This feature is particularly important for journalists, activists, or individuals concerned about privacy. Combined with firewalls and antivirus protection, VPNs help maintain confidentiality and prevent unauthorized monitoring. Users who value privacy should integrate VPN usage into their routine digital activities. Privacy protection becomes a habit rather than an occasional measure.

Educating users about potential pitfalls is equally important. Some VPN services may log user data or sell information to third parties, compromising the very privacy they promise. Users should research providers, review privacy policies, and select reputable services. Similarly, firewall misconfigurations or disabled settings can inadvertently create vulnerabilities. Awareness and proper configuration are as critical as the tools themselves. Knowledgeable users are empowered to make decisions that maximize security and privacy.

Advanced firewall features can significantly enhance network security when properly configured. Stateful inspection, for example, monitors the state of active connections and ensures that only legitimate traffic passes through. Application-layer firewalls examine the data being transmitted, providing additional protection against complex attacks. Users should take the time to understand these features and apply them appropriately to strengthen defense. Regular updates and reviews of firewall settings maintain effectiveness against evolving threats. Advanced configuration ensures that firewalls remain a robust barrier against unauthorized access.

VPNs also offer features that optimize both security and usability. Kill switches, split tunneling, and multi-server options allow users to maintain encryption while balancing speed and accessibility. Enabling a kill switch ensures that data is never transmitted unprotected if the VPN connection drops unexpectedly. Split tunneling allows selected traffic to bypass the VPN, optimizing bandwidth without compromising critical data. Understanding these features helps users fully leverage their VPN for both security and convenience. Proper utilization enhances protection while maintaining a seamless online experience.

Combining firewall and VPN strategies is particularly effective for remote work scenarios. Remote employees often access corporate networks over potentially insecure home or public internet connections. Firewalls control access to internal systems, while VPNs encrypt data transmitted between remote devices and the corporate network. This combination prevents unauthorized access, protects sensitive information, and maintains compliance with security policies. Educating employees on proper use is essential for maximizing the effectiveness of these tools. Organizations that integrate both technologies strengthen their digital perimeter and reduce risks associated with remote work.

Home networks can also benefit from layered protection using firewalls and VPNs. Many households now have multiple connected devices, including smartphones, tablets, smart TVs, and IoT devices. Each device represents a potential entry point for attackers. Configuring the home router with a firewall and using a VPN for sensitive communications reduces exposure. Users should segment networks where possible, isolating devices that may be less secure. This layered approach ensures that a single compromised device does not jeopardize the entire network. Awareness and proactive management are key to comprehensive home cybersecurity.

Education remains critical to the effectiveness of firewalls and VPNs. Users must understand how these tools work, when to activate them, and the types of threats they protect against. Misunderstanding or neglect can reduce their effectiveness and leave devices vulnerable. By fostering awareness, users become active participants in their cybersecurity rather than relying solely on technology. Knowledge empowers individuals to use these tools effectively, maximizing both security and privacy. Combining education with proper configuration creates a robust digital defense.

Firewalls and VPNs are more than just technical tools—they are essential habits for maintaining secure digital boundaries. Consistent configuration, monitoring, and updates ensure that these technologies continue to protect against unauthorized access and data breaches. Users should approach these tools proactively, understanding their functions and using them in combination with other cybersecurity measures. Integrating firewalls and VPNs into daily digital routines creates a strong defense against both targeted and opportunistic cyberattacks. Awareness, discipline, and proper usage transform these tools from passive technologies into active shields. Maintaining vigilance ensures that digital borders remain strong and reliable.

For families and individuals, coordinated use of firewalls and VPNs enhances protection across all devices. Teaching household members how to enable VPNs, respect firewall alerts, and avoid bypassing security protocols fosters collective cybersecurity awareness. A united approach ensures that all connected devices are protected and reduces the risk of compromise from weak links. Parents and guardians can lead by example, demonstrating proper practices and emphasizing the importance of secure connections. Shared responsibility strengthens overall digital safety. Collective engagement builds a culture of cybersecurity within the home.

Choosing the right firewall and VPN solution requires careful consideration. Users should evaluate features, compatibility, performance, and reliability before committing to a service or device. Free or poorly designed solutions may provide limited protection or introduce vulnerabilities. Investing in reputable, well-reviewed technologies ensures optimal security and consistent performance. Thoughtful selection maximizes both usability and defense. A carefully chosen combination of firewall and VPN safeguards devices and data effectively.

Education and ongoing awareness are critical for maximizing the benefits of these technologies. Users must understand what threats they are protecting against, when to activate VPNs, and how to configure firewalls for optimal performance. Awareness reduces the likelihood of mistakes that could compromise security.

Combining technical tools with informed behavior creates a comprehensive defense system. Knowledgeable use ensures that firewalls and VPNs function as intended, providing real-world protection. Continuous learning is a key part of effective cybersecurity.

CHAPTER .16

SAFE ONLINE SHOPPING: PROTECTING YOUR FINANCIAL DATA

Precautions to Take While Shopping Online to Ensure Your Payment Information Remains Secure

Online shopping offers convenience, speed, and access to products from around the world, but it also introduces risks to your financial data. Cybercriminals target shoppers by attempting to steal credit card numbers, personal information, and login credentials. Understanding potential threats and taking proactive precautions is essential to enjoy safe online transactions. Users must combine technological safeguards with vigilant habits to minimize the risk of fraud or identity theft. Being informed about secure shopping practices empowers individuals to protect themselves. Safe online shopping begins with knowledge, awareness, and cautious behavior.

One of the most important steps is ensuring that the websites you use are secure. Look for the padlock icon in the browser's address bar and URLs that start with "https://," indicating that the site uses encryption to protect your data. Avoid entering payment information on sites that lack these security indicators. Reputable retailers usually have well-known domain names and secure connections. Double-check URLs to prevent falling victim to phishing or counterfeit sites. Verifying site authenticity reduces the likelihood of financial data exposure.

Using strong and unique passwords for shopping accounts is essential. Many users reuse passwords across multiple sites, which increases vulnerability if one site is compromised. A breach on one platform can lead to unauthorized access on others. Consider using a password manager to generate and store complex, unique passwords securely. Strong password practices enhance the security of online accounts, protecting personal and financial information. Combined with other security measures, this step creates a critical layer of defense for online transactions.

Credit cards and secure payment methods offer additional protection compared to direct bank transfers or debit cards. Many credit cards provide fraud protection and the ability to dispute unauthorized charges. Consider using digital wallets, virtual credit card numbers, or payment platforms like PayPal that act as intermediaries. These methods reduce the risk of exposing your actual financial information to retailers or potential hackers. Choosing secure payment options adds a buffer against cyber threats. Safe payment practices are an integral part of responsible online shopping.

Keep devices and browsers updated to maintain security. Updates often patch vulnerabilities that cybercriminals could exploit to steal data during online transactions. Antivirus software, firewalls, and secure network connections, such as VPNs, further protect your information. Avoid making purchases over public Wi-Fi networks unless a VPN is used. Securing your devices and connections minimizes opportunities for attackers. A layered approach to device and network security complements safe shopping practices.

Beware of phishing emails, fake promotions, and online scams. Cybercriminals often send emails mimicking legitimate retailers to trick users into revealing payment information. Always verify emails by checking sender addresses and avoiding links in suspicious messages. Navigate directly to the retailer's website instead of clicking embedded links. Awareness and caution prevent falling victim to fraudulent offers or deceptive communications. Vigilance against scams protects both money and personal data.

Monitor financial statements regularly for unauthorized transactions. Early detection of suspicious activity allows you to act quickly to prevent larger losses. Set up alerts for credit card or bank activity to receive notifications of unusual charges. If a transaction appears unauthorized, contact your bank or credit card provider immediately. Monitoring financial accounts complements proactive security measures. Consistent oversight is an essential habit for safe online shopping.

Shopping on reputable websites reduces exposure to risk. Research vendors, read reviews, and ensure that the retailer has a history of secure transactions. Avoid unfamiliar or unverified sellers, especially when purchasing high-value items. Reliable retailers are more likely to implement robust security measures to protect customer data. Combining research with security best practices minimizes the likelihood of financial compromise. Safe shopping begins with informed vendor selection.

Using two-factor authentication (2FA) on shopping accounts adds an important layer of security. Even if a password is compromised, 2FA requires a second form of verification, such as a text message code or authentication app. This additional step significantly reduces the likelihood of unauthorized access. Users should enable 2FA on all accounts that support it, especially those linked to financial information. Combining strong passwords with 2FA provides a robust defense against account breaches. Layered authentication enhances the overall security of online shopping experiences.

Regularly reviewing saved payment methods and billing information is also critical. Avoid storing credit card numbers or bank details on multiple websites unless absolutely necessary. If a site is breached, stored information can be stolen and misused. Remove outdated or unused payment methods promptly to minimize potential exposure. Keeping sensitive data limited to essential accounts reduces the attack surface. Smart management of payment information is a key preventive measure in online shopping security.

Public Wi-Fi networks pose significant risks for online transactions. Hackers can intercept data transmitted over unsecured networks, capturing login credentials, credit card numbers, and personal information. Using a trusted VPN encrypts communications and makes interception extremely difficult. Avoid conducting financial transactions on open or unsecured networks whenever possible. If public Wi-Fi is the only option, always ensure a VPN is active before entering sensitive information. Protecting your connection is just as important as securing your accounts.

Browser security settings can also help safeguard financial data. Enable pop-up blockers, disable autofill for sensitive information, and ensure that browsers are updated with the latest security patches. Avoid clicking on suspicious advertisements or links, which may redirect users to phishing or malicious websites. Security-conscious browsing reduces exposure to threats while shopping online. Combining browser safety with other measures like antivirus software and firewalls strengthens overall protection. A secure browser environment is a foundational component of safe online shopping.

Be cautious with emails offering deals or urgent promotions. Scammers often create fake offers designed to trick users into providing payment details or downloading malware. Never respond to unsolicited requests for personal or financial information. Verify any promotions by visiting the official website directly instead of clicking embedded links. Educating yourself about common scam tactics reduces the risk of falling victim. Awareness and careful verification are vital practices for maintaining security during online shopping.

Monitoring shipping and account activity further enhances protection. Track orders and ensure that delivery addresses are correct to prevent interception or fraud. Enable account notifications to receive alerts of login attempts or suspicious activity. Immediate response to unusual activity can prevent financial loss or identity theft. Users who remain vigilant about transactions and deliveries maintain control over both their purchases and personal data. Regular monitoring reinforces safe online shopping practices.

Consider using disposable or virtual cards for online purchases. Many banks and payment platforms now offer virtual cards that can be used once or have limited validity. This prevents exposure of your primary financial information and reduces risk in case of a breach. Virtual cards are particularly useful for subscriptions, trial services, or unfamiliar vendors. Incorporating this practice into your shopping routine adds an extra layer of security. Limiting financial exposure is a practical strategy for risk reduction.

Using reputable payment platforms adds an additional safeguard for online transactions. Services like PayPal, Apple Pay, and Google Pay act as intermediaries between your bank account and the retailer, reducing exposure of your financial information. These platforms often include fraud protection and monitoring, adding extra layers of security. When shopping with new or unfamiliar vendors, using an intermediary service is especially wise. This practice minimizes the risk of credit card theft or misuse. Choosing trusted payment platforms increases confidence and safety in every purchase.

Shopping on mobile devices requires particular caution. Mobile apps and browsers can be targeted by malicious software designed to steal credentials or intercept payments. Ensure that the apps are downloaded only from official stores and that they are regularly updated. Avoid conducting financial transactions on devices that are unprotected by antivirus software or lacking encryption. Mobile device security is equally important as securing desktop computers. Vigilance across all platforms ensures comprehensive protection for personal and financial data.

Beware of social engineering tactics that may accompany online shopping. Scammers can contact you through emails, text messages, or even phone calls, pretending to be retailers or delivery companies. They often create a sense of urgency, pressuring users into providing sensitive information. Recognizing these tactics and verifying all communications with the official company helps prevent falling victim. Never share passwords, card numbers, or personal information through unsecured channels.

Awareness of social engineering threats complements technical measures like firewalls, antivirus software, and VPNs.

Regularly updating all digital devices ensures that vulnerabilities are minimized. Operating systems, browsers, and apps receive updates that often patch security flaws that could be exploited during online shopping. Skipping updates leaves your device exposed to attacks that could compromise personal or financial data. Automation tools, such as enabling automatic updates, can reduce the risk of neglecting this important step. Updated devices create a secure foundation for safe online transactions. Proactive maintenance strengthens every layer of cybersecurity protection.

Keep detailed records of your online purchases. Retain receipts, confirmation emails, and transaction details for future reference. In case of disputes, fraud, or delivery issues, having accurate records allows you to resolve problems quickly. Reviewing transaction histories also helps detect any unauthorized activity early. Organized documentation enhances both security and accountability in online shopping. Awareness of your purchases reinforces responsible digital practices.

Using alerts and notifications from your bank or payment provider enhances online shopping security. Many financial institutions allow users to receive SMS or email alerts for transactions, withdrawals, or account changes. These alerts help detect suspicious activity quickly, allowing immediate action if unauthorized charges occur. Users should enable all available notification options for accounts used in online shopping. Real-time monitoring complements other protective measures, adding an extra layer of defense. Prompt detection and response reduce the potential damage from fraudulent activity.

Secure Wi-Fi connections are vital when shopping online. Public networks often lack encryption, making it easier for cybercriminals to intercept sensitive data. Whenever possible, use private, password-protected networks for financial transactions. If public Wi-Fi must be used, a VPN should always be active to encrypt communications. This simple precaution dramatically reduces exposure to attackers. Protecting the network connection ensures that online shopping remains safe, even outside the home.

Be cautious with browser autofill and password storage features. While convenient, storing credit card numbers, billing addresses, and passwords in a browser can pose risks if the device is compromised. Consider using a secure password manager instead, which encrypts sensitive data and keeps it protected. Avoid saving financial details on shared or public devices. Responsible management of stored information prevents unintended data exposure. Proper handling of digital credentials strengthens overall security.

Regularly reviewing account statements is essential for maintaining awareness of online activity. Users should reconcile purchases with bank and credit card statements to detect any discrepancies or unauthorized transactions. Early detection of unusual charges allows for prompt reporting to banks or payment providers, minimizing potential financial loss. Consistent monitoring is a simple yet effective preventive measure. Being proactive about reviewing financial activity reinforces safe online shopping practices. Vigilance in tracking transactions protects both money and personal data.

Safe online shopping requires more than just technical tools—it demands consistent habits and informed decision-making. Users must integrate best practices into their routines, combining secure websites, strong passwords, two-factor authentication, and trusted payment methods. Devices should remain updated, protected with antivirus software, and connected through secure networks. Awareness of phishing scams, suspicious promotions, and public Wi-Fi risks adds another critical layer of protection. By maintaining vigilance across all aspects of online shopping, users can significantly reduce their exposure to cyber threats. Consistency and informed behavior transform convenience into security.

Families and households benefit from shared knowledge and collective responsibility. Teaching children, teenagers, and other household members about secure shopping practices fosters a culture of cybersecurity awareness. Parents can demonstrate safe behavior, such as checking for HTTPS, avoiding suspicious links, and using secure payment methods. Shared responsibility ensures that every member of the household is protected and reduces the likelihood of accidental exposure to threats. Collaboration enhances both digital safety and confidence when making online transactions. Collective vigilance strengthens overall security for everyone.

Choosing the right tools is essential for effective protection. Secure payment platforms, reputable VPNs, password managers, and well-reviewed antivirus software provide the technological foundation for safe shopping. Users should research and select services that prioritize privacy, offer strong encryption, and maintain transparent policies. Properly chosen tools reduce the risk of exposure and simplify secure online transactions. Technology works best when combined with careful habits and informed decision-making. Thoughtful selection of tools supports safe, convenient, and worry-free online shopping.

Monitoring and review are equally important for ongoing protection. Regularly checking bank statements, transaction histories, and account notifications allows users to detect suspicious activity early. Timely action prevents financial loss and identity theft. Users should treat monitoring as a proactive habit rather than a reactionary step. Awareness and timely response complement technological safeguards. Consistent vigilance ensures a safe and secure online shopping experience over time.

CHAPTER .17

UNDERSTANDING THE ROLE OF DATA PRIVACY LAWS

How Legislation, Such as GDPR and CCPA, Helps Protect Your Personal Information

Data privacy laws play a critical role in protecting personal information in today's digital landscape. Regulations like the General Data Protection Regulation (GDPR) in Europe and the California Consumer Privacy Act (CCPA) in the United States establish legal frameworks for how organizations collect, store, and use personal data. These laws empower individuals to control their information, requiring transparency, consent, and accountability from companies. Understanding the principles behind these laws helps individuals navigate online services more safely. Awareness of privacy rights allows users to demand better protection and to make informed decisions about sharing data. Data privacy legislation creates both a legal and ethical baseline for safeguarding personal information.

GDPR, enacted in 2018, is one of the most comprehensive data protection laws worldwide. It applies to organizations that handle the personal data of European Union residents, regardless of the company's location. Key provisions include the right to access data, the right to be forgotten, data portability, and explicit consent requirements. Companies are required to implement robust data protection measures and report breaches promptly. GDPR imposes significant penalties for non-compliance, incentivizing organizations to prioritize security and privacy. Understanding

GDPR helps users recognize their rights and the obligations of companies handling their data.

The CCPA, enacted in 2020, focuses on protecting California residents' personal information. It grants rights such as knowing what data is collected, opting out of data sales, and requesting deletion of personal information. Companies must provide clear disclosures about data collection practices and implement mechanisms to respect consumer requests. While CCPA is geographically limited, many companies extend similar privacy practices to users outside California to simplify compliance. Awareness of CCPA empowers individuals to exercise control over how their information is used. Knowledge of privacy rights under such laws enhances digital safety and informed decision-making.

Data privacy laws also encourage companies to adopt stronger cybersecurity measures. Legal obligations for data protection push organizations to implement encryption, secure storage, access controls, and incident response protocols. Compliance requirements reduce the risk of breaches and misuse of personal information. Users benefit from stronger safeguards even if they are unaware of the specific legal requirements. Legislation drives systemic improvements in how organizations handle data, creating safer environments for consumers. Understanding this connection emphasizes the importance of legal frameworks in cybersecurity.

Individuals can take advantage of privacy laws to exercise their rights effectively. Many websites and services now provide options to request data access, delete personal information, or opt out of tracking. Users should familiarize themselves with privacy policies and understand how to submit requests. Exercising these rights helps reduce unnecessary data exposure and increases accountability for organizations. Proactive engagement with data privacy rights reinforces personal protection. Awareness of legal mechanisms strengthens control over personal information.

Legislation also promotes transparency in data collection practices. Companies must clearly inform users about what data is being collected, how it is used, and with whom it is shared. Transparency enables users to make informed choices about sharing information or using services. Clear communication reduces confusion and builds trust between consumers and organizations. Users should read and understand privacy notices and consent forms. Transparency, mandated by law, empowers individuals to maintain control over their personal information. Being informed is the first step in responsible data sharing.

Privacy laws impact both online and offline activities. While much of the focus is on digital data, personal information collected in physical stores, healthcare settings, and other offline interactions is also regulated. Businesses must handle all forms of data responsibly and implement policies that comply with applicable laws. Users should recognize that privacy rights extend beyond the internet. Awareness of offline data protection measures complements digital privacy practices. Comprehensive understanding of privacy laws enhances security in all areas of life.

Understanding data privacy laws helps individuals make more informed decisions about the services they use. When signing up for online platforms, users can review privacy policies to determine how personal data will be collected, stored, and shared. Recognizing the rights granted by laws like GDPR and CCPA allows users to request access, corrections, or deletion of their information. Being proactive in exercising these rights ensures that data is handled responsibly. Awareness of legal protections also encourages safer digital behaviors. Informed decision-making reduces unnecessary exposure of personal information.

Organizations are required to implement technical and organizational measures to comply with data privacy laws. Encryption, access controls, and secure storage practices are among the measures designed to protect user data. Regular audits and assessments are often mandated to ensure ongoing compliance. These requirements not only prevent data breaches but also foster trust between organizations and users. Understanding these obligations gives users confidence that their information is being handled responsibly. Legal enforcement incentivizes businesses to maintain higher security standards.

Consent is a core principle in modern data privacy legislation. Users must provide explicit permission before organizations collect or process personal information, especially sensitive data. Consent should be informed, freely given, and easily revocable. Companies that fail to obtain proper consent may face significant fines and reputational damage. Individuals should be aware of the consent options provided and exercise them to limit unnecessary data collection. Properly managed consent ensures transparency and control over personal information. This principle reinforces the user's role as an active participant in their own data protection.

Data minimization is another key requirement under GDPR and similar laws. Organizations are expected to collect only the data necessary for specific purposes and to retain it only as long as needed. By limiting data collection and storage, the risk of breaches or misuse is reduced. Users benefit from this principle because it limits the amount of personal information exposed to potential threats. Awareness of data minimization encourages individuals to question requests for unnecessary information. Reducing data exposure is a proactive step in maintaining privacy.

Accountability is central to privacy legislation. Organizations must demonstrate compliance with regulations and be able to justify their data handling practices. This includes maintaining records of processing activities, conducting privacy impact assessments, and reporting breaches promptly. Users can leverage this accountability by requesting evidence of compliance or reporting concerns. Legal accountability reinforces best practices across industries and improves overall cybersecurity. Understanding this principle empowers individuals to demand responsible data management.

Cross-border data transfer regulations are an important aspect of privacy laws. Personal data transferred across national boundaries is subject to specific rules to ensure equivalent protection. GDPR, for example, requires that transfers to countries without adequate protection include safeguards such as standard contractual clauses. Awareness of these rules helps users understand the potential risks of using international services. Companies are legally obliged to protect data even when it moves globally. Knowledge of cross-border regulations strengthens informed decisions about using international platforms.

Privacy laws also shape corporate behavior in terms of transparency and communication. Organizations must provide clear information about data processing activities, potential risks, and user rights. This transparency empowers users to make choices aligned with their comfort levels regarding data sharing. Users should actively engage with privacy notices and understand their options for controlling information. Clear communication reduces confusion and builds trust between users and service providers. Legal transparency enhances both individual protection and accountability.

Privacy laws have a significant impact on digital marketing and advertising practices. Organizations must obtain consent before using personal data for targeted advertising, and users have the right to opt out of such practices. This reduces the amount of personal information shared without explicit permission and limits exposure to potential data misuse. Understanding these rights helps users navigate online advertisements more safely. Companies must also provide mechanisms to respect user choices, such as "Do Not Sell My Data" links or preference settings. Awareness of these protections allows individuals to maintain greater control over their digital footprint.

Enforcement mechanisms are a critical component of data privacy legislation. Regulatory bodies have the authority to investigate complaints, conduct audits, and impose fines for non-compliance. High-profile cases, such as large fines issued under GDPR for mishandling user data, serve as warnings to organizations worldwide. Knowledge of enforcement capabilities empowers individuals to take action if their rights are violated. Legal oversight ensures that organizations prioritize the protection of personal information. Users benefit from a system that holds companies accountable for their data practices.

Data portability is another important feature of modern privacy laws. Users have the right to request and receive their personal data in a structured, commonly used, and machine-readable format. This allows individuals to transfer information between service providers seamlessly and without unnecessary barriers. Data portability increases control over personal information and encourages competition among service providers. Understanding this right empowers users to make informed choices about their digital services. Portability reinforces the principle that personal data belongs to the individual, not the company.

Privacy laws also encourage organizations to implement "privacy by design" principles. This approach requires that data protection measures are integrated into the development of systems, applications, and processes from the outset. Security and privacy are considered at every stage, reducing the risk of vulnerabilities and breaches. Users benefit from products and services designed with their safety in mind. Awareness of privacy by design encourages individuals to select services that prioritize protection. Thoughtful design creates a safer environment for digital interactions.

Individuals should also understand the concept of the "right to be forgotten." This right allows users to request the deletion of personal data that is no longer necessary, inaccurate, or collected without proper consent. Organizations must comply unless there are overriding legal or contractual reasons to retain the information. Exercising this right helps reduce unnecessary exposure of personal data and strengthens control over online presence. Awareness of the right to be forgotten allows users to take action to maintain privacy and limit potential misuse. Deletion of unnecessary information is a proactive step in digital self-protection.

Privacy laws also extend to children's data, recognizing their heightened vulnerability. Regulations like GDPR and the Children's Online Privacy Protection Act (COPPA) impose stricter requirements for collecting information from minors. Parents and guardians must be aware of these protections and ensure that children's online activities comply with applicable regulations. Understanding these safeguards helps families create safer digital experiences for younger users. Legal protections for children emphasize the importance of responsible data handling by organizations. Awareness of children's privacy rights supports both protection and education.

Data privacy laws influence how companies handle consent management and user notifications. Organizations must provide clear, accessible mechanisms for users to give, withdraw, or modify consent for data processing activities. These requirements ensure that users remain in control of their personal information at all times. Understanding these mechanisms helps individuals exercise their rights effectively and prevent unwanted data collection. Companies that comply with these rules demonstrate accountability and build trust with their customers. Knowledge of consent management empowers users to make informed decisions about sharing data.

Data breach notification requirements are another critical component of privacy laws. Organizations are often required to inform affected individuals and regulatory authorities promptly when a breach occurs. Timely notification allows users to take protective actions, such as changing passwords or monitoring financial accounts. Awareness of these notification rights helps users respond quickly and mitigate potential damage. Organizations that prioritize breach transparency demonstrate a commitment to accountability and user protection. Understanding breach response procedures strengthens overall cybersecurity preparedness.

Privacy laws also impact third-party data sharing practices. Companies that share user data with vendors, advertisers, or partners must ensure that these third parties comply with applicable privacy regulations. Users should be aware of who may have access to their information and under what circumstances. Reviewing privacy policies and data-sharing disclosures allows individuals to make informed choices about service usage. Understanding third-party obligations enhances control over personal data and reduces the risk of unauthorized exposure. Legal oversight ensures that personal information is protected beyond the primary organization.

International regulations create additional layers of protection. Laws like GDPR set standards for global data protection, influencing practices even for companies operating outside the European Union. Compliance often extends to multinational services to maintain consistency and avoid penalties. Users who understand international regulations can assess the safety of using global platforms and demand stronger protections. Awareness of cross-border privacy requirements increases confidence when interacting with international services. Legal frameworks create a safer, more accountable digital ecosystem for users worldwide.

Individuals can actively exercise their privacy rights through tools provided by organizations. Many websites now offer dashboards where users can review collected data, request deletion, or export information. Familiarity with these tools allows individuals to maintain control over their digital footprint. Proactive use of these resources reinforces safe online behavior and personal cybersecurity practices. Knowledge of actionable rights ensures that privacy laws translate into practical protection. Taking advantage of these tools empowers users to assert their data privacy in tangible ways.

Data privacy laws are more than just regulations—they are a framework that empowers individuals to take control of their personal information. By understanding rights such as access, deletion, portability, and consent, users can actively manage how their data is collected and used. Organizations are legally obligated to respect these rights, implement safeguards, and report breaches, which creates accountability and encourages responsible data practices. Knowledge of these laws allows individuals to make informed decisions about which services to use and how to protect their digital identities. Awareness of legal protections also fosters confidence in interacting with digital platforms. Ultimately, understanding privacy legislation is a key element of comprehensive personal cybersecurity.

Exercising privacy rights requires a proactive approach. Users should regularly review privacy settings on accounts, check for data-sharing disclosures, and submit requests for information access or deletion when necessary. Being attentive to how companies handle personal data reduces unnecessary exposure and ensures that organizations comply with their obligations. Individuals who take action demonstrate digital responsibility and contribute to a culture of accountability. Engaging with privacy laws transforms passive online participation into active, informed decision-making. Knowledge and action together create a robust defense for personal data.

Education is essential for maximizing the benefits of privacy laws. Users must understand not only their rights but also how to implement them in practical scenarios. This includes reading privacy policies, monitoring data use, and using available tools to exercise rights effectively. Awareness empowers individuals to protect themselves from misuse of personal information and cyber threats. Organizations that provide clear guidance and easy-to-use privacy tools enhance this process, making compliance accessible to all users. Continuous learning ensures that privacy protections evolve with changing technologies and practices.

Privacy laws also serve as a guide for developing safe online habits. Understanding the principles behind consent, data minimization, transparency, and accountability encourages users to think critically about sharing information. It reinforces the importance of strong passwords, cautious interactions, and selective engagement with online platforms. By integrating legal knowledge with practical cybersecurity practices, individuals achieve a higher level of protection. Awareness of the law informs everyday digital behavior, making privacy a conscious choice rather than a passive expectation. Legal knowledge and practical habits together form a strong foundation for safe digital participation.

Finally, understanding data privacy laws highlights the broader responsibility of both individuals and organizations in protecting personal information. While regulations create standards and incentives for compliance, users play a crucial role by exercising rights, staying informed, and adopting safe practices. Together, legal frameworks and proactive user behavior foster a safer, more accountable digital ecosystem. Privacy is both a right and a responsibility, and understanding the law empowers individuals to safeguard their digital lives. Engaging with privacy laws strengthens not only personal security but also collective trust in the digital world.

CHAPTER .18

CYBERSECURITY IN THE CLOUD: SAFEGUARDING YOUR FILES

How to Securely Store, Share, and Access Your Files in Cloud Storage Platforms

Cloud computing has revolutionized the way individuals and organizations store and access data. By storing files in the cloud, users gain convenience, accessibility, and collaboration capabilities from any device with an internet connection. However, these advantages come with cybersecurity risks that must be carefully managed. Data breaches, unauthorized access, and misconfigured cloud services can expose sensitive information. Understanding cloud security principles is essential for safeguarding personal and professional files. Proactive strategies ensure that the convenience of cloud storage does not compromise data integrity or privacy.

Choosing a reputable cloud service provider is the first step toward secure file storage. Look for providers with strong security protocols, encryption standards, and a proven track record in protecting user data. Evaluate their compliance with regulations such as GDPR, CCPA, or HIPAA if handling sensitive information. User reviews, security certifications, and transparent privacy policies provide additional insights into reliability. Selecting a trusted provider reduces the likelihood of breaches and ensures that proper security practices are in place. A careful choice lays the foundation for safe cloud usage.

Encryption is a critical component of cloud cybersecurity. Many cloud providers offer encryption for data both in transit and at rest, protecting files from unauthorized access. Users should verify that strong encryption algorithms are employed and, when possible, enable client-side encryption for additional control. Encrypting files before uploading ensures that even if the cloud provider is compromised, the data remains unreadable without the proper key. Awareness of encryption practices empowers users to take active steps in protecting sensitive information. Encryption transforms cloud storage from a convenience into a secure extension of your digital environment.

Managing access controls is equally important for cloud security. Users should establish strong authentication measures, such as multi-factor authentication, for all accounts associated with cloud services. Limit file access to only authorized individuals and regularly review permissions to prevent unnecessary exposure. Organizational users should adopt the principle of least privilege, ensuring that employees have access only to files necessary for their roles. Regularly auditing access logs helps detect unusual or unauthorized activity. Proper management of access controls reduces the risk of internal and external breaches.

Backing up data remains a fundamental cybersecurity practice, even in the cloud. While cloud services often provide redundancy, users should maintain secondary backups on separate devices or platforms. This practice safeguards against accidental deletion, ransomware attacks, or provider-specific failures. Combining cloud storage with secure offline backups ensures that critical files remain accessible under all circumstances. A multi-layered approach to data storage balances convenience with security and resilience. Redundant backups are a proactive step in comprehensive cloud file protection.

Sharing files securely is another crucial consideration. Use secure links, expiration dates, and password protection when granting access to cloud files. Avoid sharing sensitive information via public or unencrypted links. Collaboration tools should offer granular permission settings to control viewing, editing, and downloading. Educating users about safe sharing practices prevents accidental exposure or misuse. Awareness of sharing risks enhances overall cloud security. Safe sharing ensures that files remain under your control, even when collaborating online.

Regularly updating cloud-connected devices and applications is essential. Outdated software can have vulnerabilities that cybercriminals exploit to access cloud-stored files. Enable automatic updates when possible and apply security patches promptly. Combined with strong passwords, encryption, and access management, this step creates a robust defense against unauthorized intrusion. Device security complements cloud provider protections and strengthens the overall cybersecurity posture. Maintenance and vigilance ensure that cloud storage remains a secure resource.

Understanding the shared responsibility model is crucial when using cloud services. While cloud providers manage the security of the infrastructure, users are responsible for protecting their data, managing access, and configuring security settings correctly. Misconfigured storage, weak passwords, or excessive permissions can expose sensitive files even if the provider's infrastructure is secure. Recognizing this distinction helps users take ownership of their part in cloud security. By understanding the shared responsibilities, individuals and organizations can reduce risk and prevent breaches. Awareness of these obligations ensures that both provider and user contribute to a secure cloud environment.

Strong authentication practices are essential for cloud account protection. Multi-factor authentication (MFA) provides a second layer of verification beyond passwords, significantly reducing the likelihood of unauthorized access. Consider using authentication apps or hardware tokens instead of relying solely on SMS codes, which can be intercepted. Regularly updating passwords and avoiding reuse across multiple services further strengthens account security. Authentication is the gateway to your cloud-stored files, and robust practices prevent attackers from gaining entry. Vigilance in authentication practices is one of the most effective ways to safeguard cloud data.

Monitoring and logging activity on cloud accounts is another key security measure. Many cloud platforms provide tools to track login activity, file access, and sharing events. Reviewing these logs regularly allows users to detect anomalies, such as logins from unexpected locations or unfamiliar devices. Promptly investigating suspicious activity can prevent data breaches before significant damage occurs. Organizational users should implement centralized logging and alerting systems for enhanced visibility. Active monitoring transforms reactive security into a proactive defense strategy. Awareness and timely response reinforce the safety of cloud environments.

Client-side encryption provides an additional layer of protection for sensitive files. By encrypting files before uploading them to the cloud, users maintain control over encryption keys, ensuring that even the cloud provider cannot access the content. This is particularly important for highly sensitive data, such as financial records, legal documents, or personal health information. Combining client-side encryption with provider-side encryption ensures that files remain protected both in transit and at rest. Understanding encryption options empowers users to make informed decisions about how to secure their information. Controlled encryption is a cornerstone of comprehensive cloud security.

Educating all users who interact with cloud-stored data is critical for reducing human error. Employees, family members, or collaborators should understand safe sharing practices, access management, and the importance of strong passwords. Regular training and reminders prevent accidental exposure due to negligence or misunderstandings. Cybersecurity is only as strong as the least-informed participant, so education strengthens overall protection. Encouraging informed behavior reduces the risk of breaches caused by social engineering or careless actions. Consistent awareness reinforces a culture of responsibility and safety in cloud usage.

Implementing tiered access and role-based permissions enhances security for collaborative environments. Not all users require full access to every file, and limiting privileges reduces the impact of potential compromises. Files can be segmented based on sensitivity, granting access only to authorized individuals. Role-based access control also simplifies auditing and monitoring. Organizations and individuals benefit from clearly defined responsibilities and limitations for cloud access. Properly managing permissions ensures that the principle of least privilege is applied consistently.

Regularly backing up cloud-stored data to independent systems is essential for resilience. While cloud providers often maintain redundancy, they are not immune to outages, ransomware, or accidental deletion. Maintaining local or alternative cloud backups ensures that critical files remain accessible under all circumstances. Testing backups periodically guarantees that they function correctly and can be restored when needed. This layered approach to storage safeguards against unforeseen disruptions. Resilient backup strategies complement strong cloud security practices.

Understanding the risks associated with cloud collaboration is critical for maintaining security. Shared folders, collaborative documents, and real-time editing features can expose files if access controls are not properly configured. Users should carefully manage who can view, edit, or download files and periodically review sharing settings. Avoid granting broad permissions to links or groups unless necessary. Mismanagement of collaborative features is a common source of accidental data exposure. Awareness and regular audits of shared content help maintain control over sensitive information.

Using secure devices to access cloud services is equally important. Devices that are compromised with malware or keyloggers can leak credentials, even if the cloud service itself is secure. Ensure that operating systems, browsers, and applications are up to date, and use antivirus software to detect potential threats. Avoid using public or unsecured devices for accessing sensitive files. Device security directly affects cloud account safety, creating a critical link in the cybersecurity chain. Safe device practices strengthen the overall protection of cloud-stored data.

Regularly reviewing and updating cloud account settings enhances security over time. Cloud providers often release new features, security options, and policies that can improve data protection. Users should stay informed and adjust configurations to take advantage of these updates. Periodic audits of permissions, encryption settings, and activity logs reduce the risk of undetected vulnerabilities. Keeping accounts current with best practices ensures continuous protection against evolving threats. Proactive account management is a simple yet effective way to prevent breaches and unauthorized access.

Awareness of phishing and social engineering attacks is vital for cloud security. Attackers frequently target users with deceptive emails or messages that appear to come from cloud providers, prompting them to enter credentials. Always verify the sender's authenticity and avoid clicking on suspicious links. Enabling multi-factor authentication adds an additional layer of protection, making it much harder for attackers to gain access. Educating all users who interact with cloud services minimizes the risk of falling victim to these tactics. Combining awareness with technological safeguards strengthens the overall cybersecurity posture.

Implementing data retention and lifecycle policies ensures that information is managed securely from creation to deletion. Files that are no longer necessary should be securely deleted to reduce exposure. Temporary or outdated files may become vulnerabilities if left accessible. Cloud providers often offer tools for automated retention management, which can help maintain compliance and minimize risk. Awareness of proper data lifecycle practices ensures that sensitive information does not remain unnecessarily exposed. Managing the full lifecycle of cloud data is essential for responsible digital stewardship.

Regular audits of cloud security settings are essential to identify potential vulnerabilities. Over time, default configurations, unused accounts, or forgotten shared files can create exposure points. Users should periodically review permissions, authentication settings, and encryption options to ensure that they align with best practices. Conducting regular security checks helps prevent unnoticed gaps that attackers could exploit. Organizations can implement automated tools to monitor compliance and alert administrators to suspicious activity. Vigilant auditing strengthens the integrity and confidentiality of cloud-stored data.

Multi-factor authentication (MFA) remains one of the most effective tools for protecting cloud accounts. Even if a password is compromised, MFA requires an additional form of verification, such as an authentication app or hardware token. Users should avoid SMS-based verification when possible, as it can be intercepted. MFA significantly reduces the likelihood of unauthorized access and adds a robust layer of protection for sensitive files. Encouraging MFA across all cloud accounts enhances overall security posture. Awareness and proper use of MFA are vital for mitigating common attack vectors.

Using client-side encryption tools provides users with ultimate control over file security. Before uploading files to the cloud, encrypt them using trusted software so that only authorized users with the encryption key can access the data. This ensures that, even if the cloud provider's systems are compromised, the files remain unreadable. Combining client-side encryption with provider-side encryption maximizes protection for sensitive information. Awareness of encryption options allows users to make informed choices about securing critical files. Encryption transforms the cloud into a secure extension of personal or organizational storage.

Secure sharing practices are essential for collaborative work in the cloud. Limit access to only those who need it, use password-protected links, and set expiration dates for shared files. Avoid sending sensitive information through public links or email without encryption. Educating collaborators about proper sharing protocols prevents accidental exposure. Organizations and individuals should adopt a culture of cautious sharing to protect sensitive information. Safe sharing practices preserve confidentiality while enabling effective collaboration.

Cloud security is ultimately a combination of technology, awareness, and disciplined practices. Users who understand how to configure accounts, manage access, and employ encryption can significantly reduce risks associated with cloud storage. Regularly auditing settings, monitoring account activity, and applying software updates further strengthen protections. Safe cloud usage also requires understanding the shared responsibility model, ensuring that both provider and user actively maintain security. Combining technical measures with informed habits transforms cloud storage into a reliable and secure tool for personal and professional use. Awareness and vigilance are the cornerstones of cloud cybersecurity.

Collaboration and education are critical components of maintaining security in cloud environments. Everyone who accesses cloud-stored files, from team members to family members, should understand secure sharing practices, strong password usage, and the importance of multi-factor authentication. Training and ongoing reminders prevent accidental data exposure caused by human error or negligence. A culture of security awareness within a household or organization ensures that cloud data remains protected across all devices and users. Knowledgeable users create an ecosystem where convenience and security coexist. Education complements technology to create a truly safe cloud environment.

Backup strategies enhance the resilience of cloud-stored data. While cloud services often provide redundancy, relying solely on the provider can leave users vulnerable to accidental deletion, ransomware, or service outages. Maintaining independent backups, either locally or on alternative platforms, ensures access to critical files under all circumstances. Testing backups periodically verifies their reliability and functionality. Redundant storage solutions provide peace of mind and an extra layer of defense. Combining cloud storage with secure backups creates a comprehensive approach to data protection.

Encryption and access control are the final pillars of effective cloud cybersecurity. Encrypting sensitive files, managing user permissions carefully, and monitoring access activity ensure that only authorized individuals can view or modify data. Even if a breach occurs, strong encryption and access restrictions minimize exposure and maintain confidentiality. Awareness of these principles allows users to take an active role in protecting their digital assets. Security is not passive; it requires continuous engagement and disciplined application of best practices. Protecting cloud data is an ongoing responsibility that rewards diligence with safety and reliability.

REFLECTION:

Reflecting on cloud security, I recognize that the convenience of accessing files from anywhere comes with serious responsibilities. Over the years, I have learned that vigilance, proper configuration, and proactive practices are far more effective than relying solely on provider assurances. Educating users, enforcing strong authentication, maintaining backups, and employing encryption have prevented potential breaches in my experience. Cloud security is not an abstract concept—it is a set of actionable habits that, when consistently applied, safeguard critical personal and professional information. Awareness, discipline, and technology together create a resilient and secure cloud environment.

"Security in the cloud is not about fear—it is about foresight, preparation, and consistent action."
— Unknown

CHAPTER .19

SECURING YOUR EMAIL: THE DIGITAL GATEWAY TO YOUR IDENTITY

How to Protect Your Email Accounts from Being Hacked and Used for Fraud

Email accounts are central to our digital lives, serving as gateways to social media, financial accounts, and personal communications. Because of their central role, email accounts are prime targets for cybercriminals. If compromised, attackers can access sensitive information, reset passwords for other accounts, and engage in identity theft or financial fraud. Protecting email accounts is essential for personal security and for preventing broader digital compromise. Awareness of common threats and best practices is the first step in safeguarding your email. Securing your email is not just about convenience—it is about protecting your identity and digital assets.

Choosing strong, unique passwords is critical for email security. Avoid common words, predictable sequences, or reuse of passwords across multiple accounts. A strong password should include a combination of letters, numbers, and symbols, and be at least twelve characters long. Using a password manager can help generate and securely store complex passwords, reducing the temptation to reuse or simplify them. Password strength is the first line of defense against unauthorized access. Strong, unique passwords make it significantly harder for attackers to gain control of your email account.

Enabling multi-factor authentication (MFA) adds a crucial layer of protection. Even if a password is compromised, MFA requires a second verification method, such as a code from an authentication app or hardware token. Avoid relying solely on SMS-based codes, as they can be intercepted. Many email providers support MFA, and enabling it dramatically reduces the risk of account takeover. Users should ensure MFA is enabled on all critical accounts linked to email. Multi-factor authentication transforms a single weak point into a layered defense system, enhancing security.

Recognizing phishing attempts is another key aspect of email security. Cybercriminals often send emails disguised as trusted sources, requesting login credentials, payment information, or personal data. These emails may appear urgent, threatening account suspension or financial consequences to provoke a quick response. Always verify the sender's email address, avoid clicking on suspicious links, and navigate directly to official websites. Educating yourself about phishing techniques prevents accidental compromise. Awareness and caution are essential in preventing attackers from exploiting trust.

Regular monitoring of account activity is vital for early detection of unauthorized access. Many email providers offer logs of recent login activity, including the device, location, and time. Reviewing this information regularly can alert users to suspicious activity before significant damage occurs. Immediate action, such as changing passwords and revoking active sessions, can prevent further compromise. Monitoring is a proactive measure that complements other security practices. Staying vigilant ensures that email accounts remain a secure hub for digital activity.

Organizing email accounts with security in mind also reduces risks. Avoid using a single email for all services, especially for sensitive financial or personal accounts. Consider creating separate accounts for personal communication, work, online shopping, and subscriptions. Segmenting accounts limits exposure if one account is compromised. Using alias or disposable email addresses for less critical services further reduces risk. Proper email organization strengthens security by containing potential breaches and limiting access to sensitive information.

Keeping devices and software up to date is essential for email security. Outdated operating systems, browsers, or email clients may contain vulnerabilities that attackers exploit to gain access. Enable automatic updates whenever possible and apply patches promptly. Using antivirus and anti-malware tools adds an additional layer of protection. Device security is directly linked to the safety of your email accounts. Ensuring up-to-date and secure devices creates a strong foundation for protecting your digital communications.

Email security is closely tied to recognizing and mitigating social engineering threats. Attackers often manipulate emotions, such as fear or urgency, to trick users into revealing credentials or clicking malicious links. Common tactics include fake account suspension notices, fraudulent payment requests, or impersonation of trusted contacts. Remaining skeptical of unsolicited messages and verifying their legitimacy is essential. Educating yourself and others who use your accounts helps prevent accidental disclosure of sensitive information. Awareness of social engineering attacks is a key step in maintaining email security.

Using encrypted email services or enabling encryption features in existing accounts adds a layer of confidentiality. Encryption ensures that messages can only be read by the intended recipient, reducing the risk of interception or tampering. Many providers offer end-to-end encryption or secure message options for sensitive communications. Users should consider encrypting emails containing financial, medical, or personal information. Encryption protects data during transit, especially when using public or untrusted networks. Incorporating encryption into daily email habits enhances privacy and reduces vulnerability.

Regularly reviewing email account settings strengthens security and reduces exposure to threats. Check forwarding rules, linked devices, third-party access, and security notifications. Malicious actors often create hidden forwarding rules or authorize external apps to gain access without your knowledge. Removing unnecessary connections and enabling security alerts improves control over your account. Staying proactive with account settings ensures that any unauthorized changes are detected and mitigated quickly. Consistent review of account configurations is a critical preventative practice.

Strong spam and filter management also helps maintain email security. Configure filters to block suspicious emails, mark potential phishing attempts, and segregate newsletters or promotional content. Avoid interacting with unverified senders, and do not click on unknown attachments or links. Proper filtering reduces exposure to malware and phishing campaigns that could compromise your account. Educating yourself about safe email practices and maintaining active filtering safeguards your inbox. Spam management complements authentication, encryption, and monitoring in a holistic security approach.

Backing up emails periodically ensures that important messages are preserved even in the event of account compromise or accidental deletion. Many email clients and services allow exporting emails to secure local storage or encrypted cloud backups. Regular backups provide a safety net, allowing users to restore critical information if access is lost. This practice is especially important for work-related correspondence, legal communications, or records containing personal data. Combining backups with strong authentication and monitoring provides a multi-layered approach to security. Redundancy and preparedness are essential components of email protection.

Educating yourself on the latest email threats is an ongoing necessity. Cybercriminals continually develop new techniques to bypass security measures, including sophisticated phishing schemes and malware attachments. Staying informed about emerging threats, software updates, and security best practices ensures that your defenses remain effective. Subscribe to security advisories, follow trusted cybersecurity resources, and attend relevant training sessions. Continuous learning allows users to anticipate and respond to new challenges. Knowledge and vigilance are essential for maintaining email security in an ever-evolving digital landscape.

Two-factor authentication (2FA) should be combined with recovery planning to ensure account continuity in the event of compromise. Even with strong authentication, accounts may become temporarily inaccessible due to lost devices or app errors. By maintaining updated recovery methods—such as backup codes, alternate email addresses, or trusted contacts—users can regain access without delay. Regularly reviewing these recovery options ensures they remain accurate and effective. Recovery planning complements proactive security measures, providing a safety net in emergencies. Being prepared for account recovery reduces stress and limits potential damage.

Phishing simulations and awareness exercises are effective for both individuals and organizations. Simulating phishing attacks helps users recognize suspicious emails, learn appropriate responses, and reinforce secure habits. Regular practice reduces the likelihood of falling victim to real attacks. Organizations benefit from incorporating phishing education into training programs, and individuals can test their own awareness through online resources or safe simulations. Knowledge gained from these exercises improves vigilance and decision-making. Experience with controlled simulations increases confidence in detecting and avoiding malicious attempts. Practicing safe behavior is as important as technical defenses.

Email clients and applications should be configured securely to minimize exposure. Disable automatic downloads of attachments or images from unknown senders, as these can carry malware or tracking scripts. Limit third-party access and ensure that integrated applications have proper permissions. Regularly reviewing connected apps and revoking access where unnecessary strengthens account security. Proper configuration ensures that the client or app does not inadvertently expose sensitive data. Technical settings complement behavioral precautions to create a comprehensive security posture.

Monitoring for compromised credentials outside your immediate email environment is also crucial. Tools like "Have I Been Pwned" allow users to check if their email address appears in data breaches. If a breach is detected, passwords should be updated immediately, and related accounts should be reviewed for unauthorized access. Early detection of compromised credentials reduces the potential impact of attacks on multiple accounts. Being proactive and using breach-monitoring tools helps maintain the integrity of your email and associated services. Vigilance beyond the inbox is an essential aspect of modern email security.

Segmentation of email usage improves security and minimizes exposure. Consider creating separate email addresses for financial accounts, personal communication, subscriptions, and online shopping. Isolating sensitive accounts reduces the risk of widespread compromise if one account is breached. Using disposable or alias emails for one-time interactions further limits exposure. Account segmentation is a simple but highly effective way to contain potential threats. Strategic management of multiple addresses enhances both privacy and security. Thoughtful separation prevents cascading vulnerabilities across digital accounts.

Email security is closely linked to recognizing and mitigating risks associated with public Wi-Fi and shared devices. Using unsecured networks can expose login credentials and sensitive messages to attackers who intercept communications. Whenever possible, access email accounts only from private, secure networks. If public Wi-Fi is necessary, use a trusted virtual private network (VPN) to encrypt your connection. Similarly, avoid logging into email accounts on shared or public devices unless additional precautions, such as temporary passwords and clearing browsing data, are used. Being mindful of the environment from which you access email is a crucial step in safeguarding sensitive information.

Regular software updates for email clients and connected devices are essential for maintaining security. Outdated applications can contain vulnerabilities that attackers exploit to gain unauthorized access. Enabling automatic updates ensures that critical patches are applied promptly, reducing exposure to malware or hacking attempts. Keeping browsers, operating systems, and mobile apps current complements other security practices like strong passwords and multi-factor authentication. Combined, these updates form a foundational defense against evolving threats. A disciplined approach to updating software strengthens the overall security of your email accounts.

Implementing proper email retention policies is another layer of protection. Avoid storing sensitive emails indefinitely, especially those containing personal, financial, or confidential information. Regularly archiving or securely deleting unnecessary messages reduces the potential damage if an account is compromised. Cloud-based email services often include tools for automated archiving and deletion, which can simplify this process. Understanding the lifecycle of your email messages helps maintain both privacy and compliance. Effective retention management reduces exposure while keeping critical information organized.

Educating others who have access to your email is equally important. Family members, colleagues, or assistants who handle your account must understand safe email practices. This includes recognizing phishing attempts, avoiding unsafe links or attachments, and adhering to multi-factor authentication protocols. Shared responsibility ensures that everyone interacting with the account contributes to security. Consistent communication and training reduce the risk of accidental breaches caused by human error. Informed users strengthen the resilience of email systems against cyber threats.

Email is the central hub for most of our online activities, which makes it an essential target for cybersecurity efforts. Securing your account protects not only your communications but also your financial data, social media accounts, and digital identity. By combining strong passwords, multi-factor authentication, encryption, regular monitoring, and cautious behavior, users create a robust defense against cyber threats. Proactive engagement with account settings, secure sharing practices, and device management ensures that your email remains safe and reliable. Security is an ongoing process, requiring vigilance, education, and a commitment to best practices. Treating email as the gateway to your digital life reinforces the importance of protecting it consistently.

A layered approach is the most effective way to secure email accounts. No single strategy is sufficient on its own. Strong authentication, device security, software updates, phishing awareness, and recovery planning all work together to minimize risk. Regularly reviewing account activity and access settings helps detect anomalies early. Segregating accounts by purpose, enabling encryption, and backing up messages further reduces exposure. Each layer strengthens the overall protection, creating a resilient environment against evolving threats.

User education and awareness are critical components of long-term email security. Cybercriminals continually develop new phishing techniques, malware, and social engineering tactics. Staying informed about these threats, understanding safe practices, and sharing knowledge with others are essential for maintaining a secure email environment. Awareness also empowers users to exercise caution, make informed decisions, and avoid risky behaviors. A well-informed user is a strong first line of defense. Security is as much about behavior and vigilance as it is about technology.

Recovery planning ensures that you can regain control if an account is compromised. Regularly updating recovery email addresses, security questions, and backup codes is essential. Testing these recovery options confirms they function correctly when needed. Prompt action during an incident, such as changing passwords and revoking unauthorized access, limits potential damage. A prepared recovery plan complements preventative measures and provides peace of mind. Combining preparation with proactive security practices completes a comprehensive email protection strategy.

REFLECTION:

Reflecting on securing email, I've realized that the account we often take for granted is actually the key to our entire digital presence. Over the years, I've witnessed accounts being compromised due to weak passwords, lack of awareness, or simple oversight. Implementing multi-factor authentication, monitoring activity, and educating users have proven to be the most effective defenses. Email security is not just a technical challenge; it is a matter of habit, discipline, and consistent vigilance. Treating your email as the cornerstone of your digital identity has transformed my approach to cybersecurity.

"Your email is the gateway to your digital life; protect it as you would your most valuable possession."
— Unknown

Chapter .20

The Risks of Data Breaches and How to Respond

What to Do When Your Personal Information Has Been Compromised in a Data Breach

Data breaches have become increasingly common in today's digital landscape, affecting individuals, businesses, and governments alike. A data breach occurs when unauthorized parties gain access to sensitive information, such as passwords, financial records, or personal identifiers. The consequences can range from identity theft and financial loss to reputational damage and long-term privacy risks. Understanding the risks associated with breaches is crucial for minimizing harm and taking timely action. Awareness of potential threats allows individuals to respond effectively and protect their digital identities. Data breaches are not just a technical issue—they are a personal and societal challenge that requires vigilance.

The first step after discovering a breach is to assess its scope. Determine which accounts, passwords, or personal information may have been exposed. Check notifications from the affected organization, and monitor official channels for details about the breach. Understanding the extent of exposure is crucial for prioritizing responses and mitigating potential damage. Individuals should maintain a record of the breach, including affected accounts and communications from the organization. A clear assessment provides a roadmap for taking immediate and effective action.

Changing passwords promptly is critical following a data breach. All affected accounts should have their passwords updated immediately, and any reuse of passwords across multiple platforms must be addressed. Using strong, unique passwords for each account prevents attackers from leveraging compromised credentials to access additional services. Password managers can assist in generating and securely storing complex passwords. Multi-factor authentication (MFA) should also be enabled where possible to add an additional layer of protection. Promptly changing credentials is one of the most effective ways to limit further exposure.

Monitoring financial and personal accounts is essential after a breach. Check bank accounts, credit cards, and online payment services for unauthorized transactions. Consider placing alerts on your accounts or using credit monitoring services to detect suspicious activity. If identity theft is suspected, contact financial institutions immediately to freeze or secure accounts. Proactive monitoring allows early detection of fraud and minimizes financial losses. Remaining vigilant over your accounts ensures that attackers cannot exploit compromised information for extended periods.

Reporting the breach to relevant authorities is another important step. Depending on your location and the type of data exposed, you may be able to notify regulatory agencies, consumer protection offices, or local law enforcement. Organizations like the Federal Trade Commission (FTC) in the U.S. provide guidance on responding to identity theft and breaches. Reporting not only helps protect yourself but also contributes to broader efforts to address cybercrime. Awareness of legal and regulatory resources empowers individuals to take action and seek assistance. Filing reports strengthens accountability and access to support.

Communication with affected institutions is critical for recovery. Contact service providers, employers, or financial institutions to understand their remediation procedures. Follow recommended steps for securing accounts, recovering lost access, and mitigating potential harm. Many organizations offer tools, hotlines, or guidance for breach response. Staying informed and cooperating with these processes ensures that remedial measures are effective. Collaboration between the individual and the organization reduces risk and accelerates recovery. Being proactive in communication strengthens resilience after a breach.

Preventive measures are equally important for minimizing future risks. Regularly update passwords, enable MFA, and review account security settings. Use encryption for sensitive files, maintain secure backups, and monitor your digital footprint. Awareness of phishing schemes, social engineering tactics, and suspicious communications helps prevent further compromise. Continuous vigilance and proactive habits are key to reducing vulnerability. Learning from a breach can improve long-term cybersecurity practices. Prevention complements reactive measures to create a comprehensive security strategy.

Understanding the types of data exposed in a breach helps determine the appropriate response. Breaches may involve passwords, credit card information, Social Security numbers, medical records, or personal identifiers. Each type of data requires specific actions to mitigate harm. For instance, compromised financial information may necessitate alerting banks and credit bureaus, while leaked personal identifiers might require monitoring identity theft services. Awareness of the nature of the breach ensures targeted and effective remediation. Assessing the type of data involved guides both immediate and long-term protective measures.

Identity theft is one of the most serious consequences of a data breach. Cybercriminals can use stolen information to open accounts, apply for loans, or commit fraudulent transactions in the victim's name. Early detection is crucial to prevent prolonged damage. Individuals should regularly check credit reports, set fraud alerts, and consider credit freezes when necessary. Vigilant monitoring can help identify unauthorized activity before it escalates. Awareness and prompt action reduce the risk of long-term identity-related problems. Protecting personal information is central to maintaining control over your digital identity.

Data breaches also often lead to phishing attempts targeting victims. Attackers exploit leaked information to craft convincing emails or messages that request additional sensitive data. Being aware that your information may have been exposed helps you recognize suspicious communications. Never respond to unsolicited requests for personal or financial information, even if they appear legitimate. Verification through official channels is essential before taking any action. Education and skepticism are powerful tools in mitigating secondary attacks following a breach. Remaining cautious prevents further exploitation of compromised data.

Securing all affected accounts is a vital next step. Change passwords for any service linked to compromised credentials, and consider updating security questions or authentication methods. Enable multi-factor authentication (MFA) wherever possible to add an extra layer of protection. Ensure that recovery options, such as alternate email addresses or backup codes, are current and secure. Systematically addressing each affected account prevents attackers from leveraging breaches across multiple platforms. Thorough remediation strengthens your overall cybersecurity posture. Accountability and diligence in securing accounts are key to recovery.

Documenting the breach and your response actions is essential for tracking and accountability. Maintain a record of communications with affected organizations, steps taken to secure accounts, and monitoring measures implemented. This documentation can be useful for reporting to authorities, insurance purposes, or legal proceedings. It also helps evaluate the effectiveness of your response for future incidents. A detailed record provides clarity and structure during a stressful situation. Awareness, organization, and documentation improve both recovery speed and long-term security planning.

Taking advantage of monitoring and alert services can help detect further misuse of compromised information. Credit monitoring services, identity theft alerts, and account-specific notifications provide early warnings of suspicious activity. These tools allow users to respond quickly before significant damage occurs. Many services offer automated alerts for unusual logins, changes to account settings, or new accounts opened under your name. Integrating monitoring into your digital security routine enhances situational awareness. Early detection is a powerful defense against the cascading effects of a breach.

Engaging with professional support when necessary strengthens your response strategy. Cybersecurity experts, identity theft resolution services, or legal advisors can provide guidance on complex cases. Particularly when sensitive information like financial records or medical data is compromised, professional assistance ensures that you take appropriate steps to mitigate harm. Support services can help communicate with institutions, recover accounts, and implement long-term protective measures. Leveraging professional resources adds expertise and reduces the likelihood of mistakes. Awareness of available support empowers individuals to respond effectively to breaches.

Learning from the breach is an essential step in strengthening future security. Analyze how the breach occurred, what vulnerabilities were exploited, and what preventative measures could have reduced exposure. Update passwords, review security policies, and implement stronger monitoring protocols. Awareness and adaptation turn a negative event into a catalyst for improved cybersecurity practices. Documenting lessons learned also benefits family members or colleagues who may share similar risks. Proactive reflection helps prevent similar incidents and fosters a culture of digital resilience.

Communicating the breach responsibly is also critical. Inform relevant parties such as banks, service providers, and even close contacts who may be affected. Transparency ensures that others can take precautions and prevents further exploitation of compromised information. Avoid sharing sensitive breach details publicly unless necessary, as this can expose additional vulnerabilities. Strategic and measured communication helps contain the impact and protects both yourself and others.

Awareness of responsible communication practices is an integral part of breach management.

Maintaining emotional resilience during and after a breach is often overlooked but equally important. Data breaches can cause stress, anxiety, and a sense of violation. Taking time to process the incident, seek support, and approach remediation methodically helps maintain composure and ensures effective decision-making. Cybersecurity is not just a technical matter; it involves managing human responses and emotions in high-stress situations. Awareness and emotional discipline allow individuals to act decisively and protect themselves. Resilience is a vital component of recovering from cyber incidents and preventing future mistakes.

Proactive prevention is the most effective strategy for minimizing the impact of data breaches. Regularly updating passwords, enabling multi-factor authentication, and reviewing account security settings reduce the likelihood of unauthorized access. Avoid reusing passwords across multiple accounts, and consider using a password manager to generate and store complex credentials. Maintaining secure backups of sensitive data ensures recovery if accounts or systems are compromised. Combining technological safeguards with informed user behavior creates a layered defense against breaches. Prevention is always more effective than remediation after the fact.

Understanding the legal and regulatory framework can help guide your response. Laws such as GDPR, CCPA, and others provide mechanisms for notification, compensation, and protection in the event of a breach. Reporting breaches to appropriate authorities can facilitate recovery and enforce accountability. Knowing your rights under these regulations empowers individuals to take informed action. Awareness of legal protections strengthens both your response strategy and your confidence in dealing with the incident. Legal frameworks provide a structured path for remediation and redress.

Employing threat detection tools and software enhances monitoring after a breach. Many cybersecurity solutions can alert users to suspicious logins, unusual file access, or compromised credentials. Using these tools in combination with manual account monitoring provides a comprehensive safety net. Technology enhances the speed and accuracy of detecting post-breach activity, reducing potential harm. Awareness of available cybersecurity tools allows users to act proactively rather than reactively. Integrating automated monitoring strengthens your overall breach response plan.

Education and ongoing awareness play a central role in mitigating future risks. Cybercriminals continuously develop new techniques, and understanding emerging threats helps users adapt their defenses. Regular training, awareness programs, and following trusted cybersecurity news sources keep you informed of potential vulnerabilities. Knowledge gained from education allows for more confident decision-making and reduces susceptibility to attacks. Awareness transforms a reactive approach into a proactive, preventative strategy. Continuous learning is essential for resilience in an evolving digital landscape.

Finally, fostering a culture of digital responsibility ensures long-term protection. Applying lessons learned from breaches, maintaining secure habits, and promoting awareness within families, workplaces, or communities strengthens collective cybersecurity. Sharing best practices, encouraging vigilance, and supporting those affected by breaches reinforces a proactive approach to online safety. Responsibility and diligence in personal and shared digital spaces prevent future incidents and enhance resilience. Awareness, preparation, and collective commitment create a safer, more secure digital environment for everyone.

CHAPTER .21

THE ROLE OF ARTIFICIAL INTELLIGENCE IN CYBERSECURITY

How AI Is Revolutionizing the Field of Cyber Defense and Enhancing Personal Data Protection

Artificial intelligence (AI) has emerged as a transformative force in cybersecurity, enabling faster and more accurate detection of threats. Traditional security measures rely heavily on predefined rules, which can leave gaps when new attack methods arise. AI systems, by contrast, can analyze massive datasets in real time, identify patterns of malicious behavior, and adapt to evolving threats. This proactive approach allows cybersecurity professionals to respond more quickly to potential breaches. For individuals, AI enhances personal data protection by automatically flagging suspicious activity across accounts, devices, and networks. Awareness of AI's capabilities highlights its potential as both a shield and a tool in the fight against cybercrime.

Machine learning, a subset of AI, plays a critical role in threat detection. By training algorithms on historical attack data, machine learning models can recognize unusual activity indicative of phishing, malware, or unauthorized access. These models improve over time as they process more data, becoming increasingly effective at predicting threats before they manifest. For personal use, AI-driven antivirus programs and email filters can detect suspicious links or attachments, reducing the likelihood of compromise. The adaptability of machine learning ensures that defenses evolve alongside attackers' strategies. AI empowers both organizations and individuals to stay one step ahead in cybersecurity.

Behavioral analytics is another AI application that enhances personal data protection. AI systems can learn normal usage patterns for accounts, devices, and networks, identifying deviations that may signal a cyber attack. For example, an unusual login from a foreign country or atypical file access can trigger immediate alerts. This real-time monitoring allows for rapid response, limiting potential damage. Individuals can benefit from AI-powered alerts that notify them of suspicious activities on their email, banking, or social media accounts. Behavioral analytics transforms reactive cybersecurity into a proactive, intelligent defense strategy.

AI also improves incident response and threat mitigation. Automated systems can isolate compromised devices, block malicious traffic, and deploy countermeasures without waiting for human intervention. This reduces the window of opportunity for attackers to exploit vulnerabilities. For personal cybersecurity, AI-driven solutions can recommend security updates, flag weak passwords, and guide users in improving account protections. By integrating AI into both detection and response, the overall resilience of digital systems is greatly enhanced. Awareness of AI's role in response helps users leverage technology to maintain data safety.

Despite its advantages, AI introduces new considerations and potential challenges. Attackers are increasingly using AI to develop sophisticated malware, phishing campaigns, and automated attacks. Individuals must remain vigilant and not rely solely on technology, as AI tools cannot replace informed behavior. Understanding the dual nature of AI—as a defensive and offensive tool—encourages balanced, proactive cybersecurity strategies. Education, awareness, and human judgment remain essential complements to AI-driven solutions. Combining intelligent technology with responsible practices ensures optimal protection of personal data.

The integration of AI with existing cybersecurity infrastructure enhances threat prediction and prevention. By analyzing global threat intelligence, AI systems can identify emerging attack trends and recommend preemptive measures. Individuals benefit when service providers leverage AI to safeguard accounts, detect anomalies, and block fraudulent activity. Machine learning models continually refine their understanding, improving detection and reducing false positives. Awareness of AI's predictive capabilities emphasizes the importance of using technology to supplement, not replace, user vigilance. Intelligent systems empower users to navigate the digital world with greater security and confidence.

AI also facilitates advanced authentication methods. Biometric recognition, behavioral verification, and adaptive security measures leverage AI algorithms to ensure that only authorized users gain access. These methods strengthen personal cybersecurity while providing convenience, reducing reliance on traditional passwords alone. Awareness of AI-enhanced authentication options allows users to choose stronger, more secure methods for protecting accounts. AI-driven verification is both a safeguard and a tool for improving the user experience in secure environments. Technology and convenience can coexist without compromising security.

AI-driven threat intelligence platforms enhance cybersecurity by collecting and analyzing vast amounts of data from multiple sources. These platforms can identify emerging malware, ransomware campaigns, and phishing schemes faster than human analysts alone. For individuals, services that integrate AI threat intelligence can alert users to unsafe websites, suspicious emails, or compromised accounts. The speed and scale of AI analysis provide an advantage against attackers who rely on automation to exploit vulnerabilities. Awareness of these platforms allows users to take advantage of AI-driven insights without needing deep technical expertise. Leveraging AI intelligence makes personal data protection more proactive and informed.

Automated anomaly detection is a key feature of AI in cybersecurity. By continuously monitoring user activity and network behavior, AI can flag unusual patterns that might indicate account compromise or data theft. For example, a sudden transfer of large files, multiple failed login attempts, or unusual device access can trigger instant alerts. These automated systems reduce reliance on users to notice suspicious behavior manually. Real-time anomaly detection empowers individuals to act quickly, mitigating potential damage. Integrating anomaly detection into daily digital routines strengthens overall security. Awareness of this capability reinforces the value of AI in protecting personal data.

AI also plays a critical role in malware analysis and prevention. Machine learning models can identify malicious code, even when it is newly created or disguised to avoid traditional antivirus detection. Behavioral analysis enables AI to recognize patterns indicative of ransomware, spyware, or trojans. Individuals benefit when their devices run AI-enhanced security software that continuously scans and neutralizes threats. Automated threat remediation minimizes response time, reducing the window of opportunity for attackers. Awareness of AI-driven malware defense empowers users to rely on advanced protections while maintaining safe habits. Technology complements vigilance to ensure comprehensive digital security.

Natural language processing (NLP), a subset of AI, improves phishing detection by analyzing the content of emails, messages, and websites. AI can identify suspicious language patterns, deceptive URLs, and fraudulent communication tactics. This capability allows security tools to flag potentially dangerous messages before users interact with them. NLP-powered filters help protect individuals from falling victim to sophisticated phishing campaigns. Awareness of AI-enhanced content analysis helps users understand how technology assists in identifying subtle threats. Combining human judgment with AI analysis increases confidence in navigating digital communications safely.

AI also contributes to adaptive authentication, which dynamically adjusts security measures based on user behavior and context. For instance, if a login attempt occurs from an unusual location or device, AI systems can require additional verification or temporarily restrict access. Adaptive authentication balances security with convenience, reducing unnecessary friction for trusted users while maintaining strong protections. Individuals benefit from AI-enabled safeguards without sacrificing usability. Awareness of adaptive authentication options allows users to make informed decisions about their security preferences. AI-driven adaptability strengthens digital defenses in real time.

AI-powered predictive analytics is transforming how cybersecurity professionals and individuals anticipate attacks. By analyzing historical attack patterns, AI models can forecast potential vulnerabilities and identify high-risk behaviors. This allows for proactive measures, such as updating software, strengthening passwords, or adjusting access controls before an attack occurs. For personal cybersecurity, predictive insights can suggest actions to secure accounts or detect unusual activity early. Awareness of predictive analytics empowers users to prevent problems rather than react to them. Predictive AI turns cybersecurity from a reactive process into a proactive, strategic discipline.

Incident response automation is another way AI enhances cybersecurity. Automated systems can isolate affected devices, block suspicious IP addresses, and implement predefined countermeasures immediately upon detecting threats. This reduces the window of opportunity for attackers and limits the potential damage from breaches or malware infections. Individuals benefit when AI tools manage low-level threats in real time, allowing them to focus on more complex security decisions. Awareness of automated response capabilities reinforces confidence in using technology to safeguard personal data. Combining human oversight with AI automation creates an efficient and effective defense system.

AI also strengthens vulnerability management by identifying weaknesses in software and systems before they are exploited. Machine learning algorithms can scan networks, devices, and applications to detect outdated software, misconfigurations, or security gaps. Individuals and organizations can prioritize remediation based on risk severity and likelihood of exploitation.

Awareness of AI-driven vulnerability assessment allows users to take preemptive steps to secure accounts, devices, and networks. Continuous scanning and risk assessment keep security measures up to date against evolving threats. Proactive vulnerability management ensures digital environments remain resilient.

The integration of AI into threat hunting improves the ability to uncover sophisticated or hidden cyber threats. AI systems can sift through enormous amounts of data to identify suspicious patterns, anomalies, and indicators of compromise that might go unnoticed by humans. This capability enables early intervention, reducing the potential impact of attacks. Individuals benefit from AI-powered threat hunting through enhanced monitoring of accounts, emails, and connected devices. Awareness of AI's threat hunting functions highlights how technology supplements human vigilance. Together, predictive, analytical, and detection capabilities allow for comprehensive threat management.

AI-driven anomaly detection extends beyond individual accounts to entire networks and connected devices. By monitoring traffic patterns, user behavior, and system interactions, AI can quickly identify potential intrusions or unauthorized activity. For individuals using smart devices or cloud services, this means suspicious activity can be flagged before significant damage occurs. Awareness of AI's network monitoring capabilities encourages proactive engagement with security tools. Continuous, automated observation allows users to respond to threats faster than manual monitoring alone. AI enhances both situational awareness and response efficiency, creating a more resilient digital environment.

Adaptive AI systems can tailor security measures based on evolving threats and user behavior. For example, if a user frequently accesses sensitive information from multiple devices, AI can dynamically adjust security protocols, such as requiring additional authentication or temporarily restricting risky actions. This balance between convenience and protection ensures that users remain secure without sacrificing usability. Understanding adaptive AI helps individuals make informed choices about enabling intelligent security features. Personalized defenses create stronger protection by aligning with individual usage patterns. AI-driven adaptation makes security smarter, faster, and more effective.

AI also supports proactive alerting and education for users. Security platforms can notify individuals of potential risks, suggest best practices, and guide them in securing accounts or devices. For example, AI can alert users if passwords are weak, reused, or have been compromised in a breach. These recommendations empower users to take immediate action and improve their cybersecurity hygiene. Awareness of AI-powered guidance enables individuals to actively strengthen their defenses. By combining alerts, recommendations, and automated safeguards, AI transforms users from passive observers into active participants in their own security.

Ethical considerations are crucial when integrating AI into cybersecurity. While AI can provide significant protection, it also raises concerns around data privacy, decision-making transparency, and potential bias. Users should be aware of how AI systems process personal data and ensure that security tools adhere to privacy regulations. Ethical deployment of AI ensures that protective systems do not inadvertently compromise user privacy. Understanding the ethical dimensions of AI encourages responsible use and informed consent. Awareness and ethical vigilance complement technological safeguards, promoting trust and security in AI applications.

AI is not a replacement for human vigilance but a force multiplier that enhances our ability to protect personal data. By combining automated detection, predictive analytics, anomaly recognition, and adaptive authentication, AI strengthens digital defenses across multiple layers. Individuals benefit from AI's real-time monitoring, threat intelligence, and actionable recommendations, which reduce the likelihood of account compromise or data theft. However, technology is only effective when paired with informed behavior, secure habits, and continuous awareness. A holistic approach integrates AI with proactive human oversight to maximize cybersecurity. Understanding the strengths and limitations of AI empowers users to leverage its capabilities effectively.

AI also democratizes cybersecurity by providing advanced protection to individuals and small organizations that may lack dedicated security teams. Cloud-based AI services, smart antivirus programs, and AI-enhanced email filters bring enterprise-level security to everyday users. These tools continuously learn from global threat data, improving their effectiveness over time. Awareness of accessible AI-powered security solutions allows individuals to take advantage of cutting-edge technology without deep technical expertise. Technology becomes an equalizer, offering robust defenses to anyone willing to adopt it responsibly. AI-enabled security is both sophisticated and user-friendly when applied thoughtfully.

Continuous learning is a key component of AI-driven cybersecurity. Machine learning models improve as they process more data, identifying previously unknown threats and reducing false positives. For individuals, this means that security tools become increasingly accurate over time, detecting attacks before they can cause significant damage. Awareness of AI's evolving capabilities encourages users to maintain engagement with security tools and updates. By staying informed and leveraging AI's learning potential, users strengthen their digital resilience. Continuous adaptation ensures that defenses remain effective against emerging cyber threats.

AI also enhances collaboration between users, organizations, and cybersecurity communities. Shared threat intelligence powered by AI helps identify new attack vectors, coordinate responses, and implement preventive measures globally. For individuals, this collective approach means that insights gained from widespread data contribute to personal protection. Awareness of community-driven AI solutions highlights the value of collaboration in cybersecurity. By participating in or relying on AI-assisted intelligence networks, users gain both knowledge and protection. Collective learning amplifies the effectiveness of individual security practices.

Reflection:

Reflecting on AI in cybersecurity, I have come to appreciate its role as both a protective shield and a proactive partner. Over the years, I've seen how intelligent systems can detect threats that humans might miss, provide actionable insights, and simplify complex security tasks. However, I have also learned that technology alone cannot guarantee safety; human judgment, awareness, and disciplined habits are essential. AI empowers us to navigate the digital world with confidence, but it is our responsibility to use it wisely and ethically. The combination of intelligent technology and informed human oversight creates the strongest defense against evolving cyber threats.

"Artificial intelligence strengthens our defenses, but vigilance, awareness, and responsible action turn protection into resilience."
— Unknown

CHAPTER .22

NAVIGATING INTERNET OF THINGS (IOT) SECURITY

How to Safeguard Your Smart Devices and Ensure They Don't Become a Gateway for Cybercriminals

The Internet of Things (IoT) connects everyday devices—from thermostats and cameras to smart refrigerators and wearable technology—to the internet. While these devices provide convenience and efficiency, they also create new attack surfaces for cybercriminals. Vulnerable IoT devices can be exploited to access personal networks, steal sensitive data, or even launch attacks on other systems. Awareness of the potential risks is the first step toward securing IoT devices. By implementing proper security practices, individuals can enjoy the benefits of connected technology without compromising privacy or safety. Understanding IoT security is essential in an increasingly connected digital world.

Changing default credentials is one of the most critical steps in securing IoT devices. Many devices come with factory-set usernames and passwords that are publicly documented, making them easy targets for attackers. Users should immediately update these credentials to strong, unique passwords. In addition, consider using a password manager to store complex credentials securely. Changing default login information prevents unauthorized access and reduces the likelihood of compromise. Awareness and immediate action transform IoT devices from vulnerable points into controlled, secure endpoints. Security begins with small but critical adjustments.

Firmware and software updates play a crucial role in IoT security. Manufacturers often release updates to patch vulnerabilities, improve performance, and enhance device security. Failing to apply updates leaves devices exposed to known exploits. Enable automatic updates whenever possible and regularly check for manual updates. Awareness of the importance of firmware maintenance ensures that devices remain resilient against emerging threats. Regular updates protect both the device and the broader network it connects to. Keeping software current is one of the simplest yet most effective security measures.

Network segmentation enhances protection for IoT devices. Placing smart devices on a separate network or VLAN isolates them from personal computers, smartphones, and sensitive data. This limits the impact of a potential compromise, preventing attackers from accessing critical accounts or information through a single device. Router settings can often be adjusted to create guest or isolated networks specifically for IoT devices. Awareness of network segmentation techniques allows individuals to contain risks effectively. Thoughtful network design strengthens both privacy and security. Segmentation ensures that a single compromised device does not jeopardize the entire network.

Device monitoring and logging are essential for detecting unusual activity. Many IoT devices offer logging features that record access attempts, firmware changes, or abnormal behavior. Regularly reviewing these logs allows users to identify potential breaches or suspicious actions early. Alerts and notifications from connected apps can also help monitor device status in real time. Awareness of monitoring tools ensures that anomalies are addressed before they escalate. Active oversight complements preventative measures, maintaining a secure IoT environment. Vigilance transforms passive devices into actively protected components of your digital ecosystem.

Privacy settings should be carefully reviewed on every IoT device. Many smart devices collect extensive personal data, from voice commands to location tracking. Users should disable unnecessary data collection, limit sharing, and configure privacy settings according to their comfort level. Understanding the types of data each device collects allows informed decisions about usage. Awareness of privacy risks prevents unintentional exposure of sensitive information. Configuring devices thoughtfully ensures that convenience does not come at the cost of personal privacy. Responsible data management strengthens both security and user confidence.

IoT devices often interact with cloud services, making cloud security a critical component of overall IoT protection. Data transmitted to and from the cloud should be encrypted both in transit and at rest. Strong authentication and access controls for cloud accounts prevent unauthorized access to sensitive information stored off-device. Awareness of cloud security measures helps users evaluate the safety of their IoT ecosystem. Many devices offer settings to limit cloud storage or restrict sharing to trusted platforms. Properly securing cloud connections reduces exposure and strengthens the overall security posture of connected devices.

Regular audits of connected devices are essential for maintaining IoT security. Users should periodically review all devices on their network, checking for unauthorized additions or outdated equipment. Remove devices that are no longer used, as they can remain vulnerable points of entry. Awareness of which devices are connected allows users to manage risks proactively. Routine audits also provide an opportunity to verify updates, review logs, and confirm privacy settings. Systematic evaluation ensures that no device becomes an overlooked weakness in your digital environment. Maintaining an accurate inventory of connected devices is foundational to proactive security.

Segregating administrative access is another critical consideration. IoT device management should be limited to trusted users, and administrative accounts should use strong, unique passwords.

Avoid sharing credentials, and enable multi-factor authentication where supported. Awareness of access control measures reduces the likelihood of unauthorized modifications or exploitation. Managing user privileges thoughtfully ensures that devices cannot be tampered with by unverified individuals. Proper access control maintains both device integrity and the security of the broader network.

Monitoring for unusual network traffic patterns is vital for detecting IoT security breaches. AI-based or automated monitoring tools can analyze data streams for irregularities, such as unexpected outbound connections or spikes in data usage. Alerts from these tools enable prompt investigation and mitigation. Awareness of traffic monitoring empowers users to identify potential attacks early. Combining automated monitoring with manual oversight strengthens detection capabilities. Being proactive in identifying anomalies reduces the likelihood of prolonged exposure or extensive damage. Vigilant observation ensures that threats are addressed before they escalate.

Educating all household or organizational members about IoT security practices enhances protection. Users should understand the risks, the importance of updates, strong passwords, network segmentation, and careful device placement. Shared awareness creates a culture of cybersecurity, reducing the chances of accidental compromise. Awareness of best practices ensures that every person interacting with IoT devices contributes to overall safety. Training and communication strengthen both technical defenses and behavioral safeguards. Collective vigilance multiplies the effectiveness of security measures.

Regularly reviewing manufacturer recommendations is also important for IoT safety. Device manuals often include security guidelines, firmware update instructions, and tips for safe usage. Following these recommendations ensures devices are configured correctly and maintained according to best practices. Awareness of manufacturer guidance complements broader security strategies and helps avoid misconfigurations. Taking the time to read and implement these instructions strengthens both device performance and security. Manufacturer-aligned practices support a proactive approach to cybersecurity.

IoT devices often collect sensitive personal information, making data privacy a critical aspect of security. Users should regularly review what data each device collects, how it is stored, and who has access. Minimizing unnecessary data collection reduces exposure in the event of a breach. Awareness of privacy settings and data flows allows users to make informed choices about device usage. Some devices allow anonymization or selective data sharing, which can further protect personal information. Proactive management of data collection strengthens both privacy and security for connected devices.

Implementing a layered defense strategy is crucial for IoT security. No single measure is sufficient; users should combine strong passwords, regular firmware updates, network segmentation, monitoring, and cloud security measures. Each layer compensates for potential weaknesses in others, reducing the overall risk. Awareness of a multi-layered approach helps individuals understand the cumulative effect of different protections. Layered security ensures that even if one safeguard fails, others remain in place to limit damage. Strategic integration of multiple defenses creates a resilient IoT environment. Comprehensive protection is achieved by combining technical, behavioral, and organizational measures.

Device decommissioning is another often-overlooked aspect of IoT security. When devices are no longer used, they should be properly reset to factory settings and, if possible, physically destroyed or securely recycled. Residual data left on devices can become an entry point for attackers. Awareness of proper decommissioning procedures ensures that devices do not pose future security risks. Following recommended steps for device disposal or transfer protects both personal information and network integrity. Responsible end-of-life management is an essential part of the IoT security lifecycle. Securing devices from installation to disposal ensures long-term protection.

Regularly reviewing and testing security configurations helps maintain IoT defenses over time. Devices may lose security efficacy due to software updates, changes in network architecture, or evolving cyber threats. Periodic testing of device access controls, network segmentation, and monitoring alerts ensures that security measures remain effective. Awareness of the need for ongoing evaluation prevents complacency and strengthens long-term protection. Documenting changes and reviewing configurations also helps identify trends or recurring vulnerabilities. Continuous assessment and adaptation keep IoT systems secure in a dynamic digital landscape.

User behavior is the final layer of IoT security. Individuals must be mindful of how they interact with devices, which networks they connect to, and the permissions granted to apps and services. Awareness and education on safe practices, including limiting remote access and avoiding untrusted applications, significantly reduce the risk of compromise. Behavioral vigilance complements technical safeguards to provide a comprehensive defense. Security-conscious habits, combined with monitoring and layered defenses, create a culture of safety around IoT devices. Responsible usage ensures that technology serves convenience without introducing unnecessary risk.

IoT ecosystems often include multiple interconnected devices, which increases both convenience and risk. A vulnerability in one device can potentially compromise others within the network. Awareness of device interconnectivity encourages users to apply security measures consistently across all devices, rather than focusing on a single point. Monitoring the interactions between devices helps identify unusual behavior, such as unexpected communications or data transfers. Implementing security policies that cover the entire IoT environment strengthens protection. A holistic approach ensures that interconnected devices do not inadvertently create vulnerabilities.

Segregating IoT devices from critical systems is another effective strategy. By placing smart devices on separate networks from computers containing sensitive information, users can limit the potential impact of a compromised device. Guest networks, VLANs, or firewalls can help isolate IoT devices. Awareness of network isolation techniques allows users to contain breaches and protect important data. Proper segmentation ensures that attackers cannot easily pivot from a vulnerable device to more critical resources. This approach balances connectivity with security, reducing the overall attack surface.

IoT security also relies on vigilant monitoring for firmware and software updates. Manufacturers frequently release updates to patch vulnerabilities, improve functionality, and enhance security. Users should enable automatic updates whenever possible, or schedule regular manual checks. Awareness of update practices ensures devices remain resilient against emerging threats. Skipping updates can leave devices exposed to exploits that are already well-known to attackers. Consistent maintenance protects both individual devices and the broader network they interact with.

Behavioral alerts and AI-enhanced monitoring can further strengthen IoT defenses. Some smart home systems now include AI-driven anomaly detection to identify suspicious behavior or device compromise. Alerts may include unusual traffic patterns, unexpected device actions, or attempts to access restricted areas. Awareness of AI monitoring capabilities encourages users to respond promptly to potential threats. Combining human oversight with intelligent alerts enhances detection and response speed. Proactive monitoring is essential for preventing small vulnerabilities from escalating into larger breaches.

IoT security is not a one-time task but an ongoing process that requires vigilance, maintenance, and adaptation. As new devices are added, networks change, and threats evolve, individuals must continuously evaluate and update their security practices. Awareness of this dynamic landscape encourages proactive behavior, ensuring devices remain protected over time. Regular audits, updates, and monitoring reinforce the effectiveness of technical safeguards and reduce the risk of exploitation. The combination of education, technological tools, and disciplined behavior creates a resilient IoT ecosystem. Understanding that security is a continuous journey rather than a fixed solution is essential for long-term protection.

Privacy management should remain a central focus when using IoT devices. Many smart devices collect, transmit, and store personal information, often without explicit user attention. Awareness of the data each device gathers, how it is stored, and who has access helps users make informed decisions about usage. Adjusting privacy settings, limiting unnecessary data collection, and securely managing accounts ensures that personal information remains under control. Proactive privacy management complements broader security strategies and minimizes exposure to cyber threats. Maintaining vigilance over personal data ensures IoT convenience does not come at the expense of security.

IoT devices often rely on cloud services for functionality, making secure cloud integration vital. Proper authentication, encryption, and restricted access to cloud platforms reduce the risk of data compromise. Awareness of cloud security best practices allows users to implement measures that protect sensitive information while maintaining device functionality. Regularly reviewing cloud account activity, storage permissions, and connected services strengthens the security of both individual devices and broader digital ecosystems. Cloud security and device security are intertwined, requiring a holistic approach for maximum protection. Coordinated attention to both ensures seamless and safe IoT operation.

Education and awareness extend beyond technical measures to user behavior. All individuals interacting with IoT devices should understand safe practices, including limiting remote access, avoiding untrusted applications, and monitoring for unusual activity. Awareness and communication create a culture of security that reinforces technical safeguards. Shared responsibility ensures that human error does not undermine the protection provided by devices, networks, and monitoring systems. Behavioral vigilance is the final layer of defense in a comprehensive IoT strategy. Combining education, technology, and responsible practices ensures a resilient and safe connected environment.

CHAPTER .23

WHAT TO KNOW ABOUT DIGITAL FOOTPRINTS AND TRACKING

How Your Online Activity Leaves Traces and How to Minimize Its Impact on Your Privacy

Every action taken online leaves a digital trace, collectively forming what is known as a digital footprint. From websites visited and social media posts shared to online purchases and app usage, this footprint is constantly growing. Digital footprints can reveal personal habits, interests, locations, and even sensitive information. Awareness of the data trail you leave is the first step toward protecting your privacy. By understanding how information is collected, stored, and shared, individuals can take measures to minimize exposure. Managing your digital footprint is essential for safeguarding personal information in the modern connected world.

Search engines and websites track user activity to optimize content, target advertisements, and collect data for analytics. This tracking can range from simple cookies to sophisticated behavioral profiling. Awareness of how websites and services monitor activity empowers users to make informed decisions about browsing and engagement. Tools like private browsing modes, browser extensions, and cookie management can help reduce unwanted tracking. Limiting unnecessary data sharing helps control the information available to advertisers, third parties, and potential cybercriminals. Thoughtful navigation of the web minimizes your digital footprint without sacrificing usability.

Social media platforms are a significant contributor to digital footprints. Every post, comment, photo, or location check-in adds to the publicly accessible record of your activity. Awareness of privacy settings, friend lists, and content visibility helps individuals control who sees their information. Avoid sharing unnecessary personal details, and regularly review past posts to ensure they align with your desired privacy level. Conscious participation on social media reduces vulnerability to identity theft, social engineering, and online profiling. Social media literacy is a critical component of effective digital footprint management. Responsible sharing ensures your online presence is secure and intentional.

Online purchases, subscriptions, and app usage also contribute to your digital footprint. Payment details, shipping addresses, and personal preferences are stored by service providers and can be targeted by attackers or used for profiling. Awareness of the information requested during transactions allows users to limit data exposure. Using secure payment methods, disposable email addresses, and minimal personal details can reduce the risks associated with commercial tracking. Careful consideration of what information is shared ensures financial and personal data remain protected. Protecting digital footprints extends beyond visibility into personal behavior—it safeguards sensitive information as well.

Searchable public records, forums, and online directories contribute additional layers to your digital footprint. Even seemingly innocuous participation can leave lasting traces that reveal personal information. Awareness of these sources allows individuals to take steps to minimize exposure, such as limiting public posts or requesting removal of personal details from directories. Understanding the permanence of digital content encourages cautious online behavior. Combined with careful social media and browsing practices, this awareness reduces vulnerability to cybercrime. Proactive management of publicly accessible information is essential for comprehensive privacy protection.

Device identifiers and app permissions also contribute significantly to digital footprints. Smartphones, tablets, and smart devices often transmit unique identifiers to apps and websites, which can be used to track usage patterns. Awareness of app permissions and the types of data collected empowers users to restrict access to sensitive information. Regularly reviewing app settings, disabling unnecessary permissions, and uninstalling unused apps reduces tracking exposure. These measures ensure that personal behavior and device data are shared only when necessary. Thoughtful device management strengthens privacy and limits unwanted digital traces.

Browser extensions and tracking blockers are powerful tools for controlling your footprint. Ad-blockers, anti-tracking extensions, and privacy-focused browsers can prevent the collection of browsing data by third-party trackers. Awareness of these tools allows users to selectively limit which websites or services can monitor activity. Combining multiple extensions and privacy settings can significantly reduce digital surveillance while maintaining the functionality of essential websites. Using these tools proactively reinforces user control over online behavior. Digital hygiene practices, like regular clearing of cookies and cache, further minimize traceable data. Active management ensures the digital footprint remains intentional rather than accidental.

Location tracking is another area where digital footprints can become extensive. Many apps and services request access to GPS or device location data, often without clear necessity. Awareness of when and why location data is collected helps users decide whether to grant access. Disabling unnecessary location permissions or using temporary location settings limits exposure to tracking. For social media, geotagging photos or posts should be managed carefully. Thoughtful handling of location data reduces the risk of targeted attacks, stalking, or privacy breaches. Controlling location information strengthens overall digital security and autonomy.

Search engine activity leaves traces that can influence targeted advertising and data profiling. Awareness of personalized search results, auto-suggestions, and ad targeting highlights how search behavior contributes to your digital footprint. Using private browsing, VPNs, or search engines that do not track queries can limit this exposure. Awareness of search behavior encourages more cautious querying and prevents unnecessary data collection. Controlling the visibility of search activity minimizes profiling and enhances personal privacy. By combining these strategies with responsible browsing habits, users can navigate the web more securely.

Minimizing digital footprints requires consistent behavioral awareness across all online activities. Conscious sharing, careful management of accounts and devices, use of privacy tools, and regular audits of personal information collectively reduce the risk of data exposure. Awareness is the foundation of proactive privacy management, ensuring that digital traces do not become liabilities. Thoughtful practices allow users to enjoy the benefits of online services without compromising personal security. Every action online should be considered in terms of its contribution to your footprint. Maintaining intentional, informed behavior strengthens long-term protection of personal data.

Cookies and tracking scripts play a central role in monitoring online activity. These small pieces of data are stored by websites to remember user preferences, but they can also be used to follow behavior across multiple sites. Awareness of how cookies function allows individuals to make informed decisions about accepting, rejecting, or managing them. Browser settings, cookie managers, and privacy extensions provide ways to control this tracking. Limiting third-party cookies reduces exposure to targeted advertising and data profiling. Thoughtful management of cookies ensures that browsing activity remains as private as possible.

Social engineering attacks often leverage digital footprints. Information collected from social media, public directories, and online activity can be used by attackers to craft convincing phishing emails, impersonation attempts, or other manipulative strategies. Awareness of what personal data is publicly accessible helps individuals anticipate and avoid potential threats. Limiting the amount of personal information available online reduces susceptibility to these attacks. Regularly reviewing privacy settings and minimizing exposure is key to mitigating risks. Being proactive in managing your digital footprint strengthens defense against social engineering. Knowledge and caution are critical in protecting personal information.

Search engine indexing also contributes to persistent digital footprints. Publicly available posts, comments, or forum activity can remain searchable for years. Awareness of the permanence of online content encourages users to think carefully before sharing personal details. Removing or anonymizing old posts and accounts can limit exposure. Maintaining control over what is visible on the web ensures that past actions do not become future liabilities. Understanding search engine indexing reinforces the need for conscious online behavior. Digital responsibility requires foresight and consistent monitoring.

Mobile apps and wearable devices generate extensive logs of activity, location, and personal preferences. Awareness of the data collected by these devices allows users to manage what information is shared. Reviewing app permissions, disabling unnecessary tracking features, and periodically clearing stored data reduce exposure. Thoughtful device management ensures that convenience does not come at the cost of personal privacy. Minimizing data collection at the source is often the most effective approach to managing digital footprints. Combining technical adjustments with behavioral awareness maintains personal control over sensitive information.

Digital footprint awareness also involves understanding data brokers and third-party aggregators. These companies collect, consolidate, and sell personal information obtained from online activity, public records, and purchases. Awareness of their practices allows individuals to opt-out where possible or limit the sharing of personal data. Taking steps to reduce exposure to data brokers complements broader privacy strategies. Vigilance in managing your digital presence ensures that personal information is not unnecessarily exploited. Controlling how and where data is shared strengthens overall privacy and minimizes digital vulnerabilities.

Regular audits of your online presence are essential for managing digital footprints effectively. Searching your name, reviewing social media accounts, and checking data broker listings can reveal what information is publicly available. Awareness of these exposures allows you to take corrective action, such as adjusting privacy settings or requesting removal of sensitive data. Periodic evaluation ensures that your digital footprint does not expand unnoticed over time. Proactive auditing fosters accountability and reinforces privacy-conscious habits. Maintaining a clear understanding of your online presence is key to long-term digital security.

Email accounts also contribute to digital footprints. Subscriptions, online purchases, and account registrations create records that can be exploited if compromised. Awareness of how your email activity is stored and tracked enables better management, such as unsubscribing from unnecessary newsletters and using separate accounts for different purposes. Minimizing exposure through email hygiene reduces the risk of identity theft and targeted attacks. Using aliases or disposable addresses for online registrations further limits traceable information. Thoughtful email management is a practical step in controlling your digital footprint.

Using privacy-focused browsers and search engines strengthens digital anonymity. Platforms that do not track searches or browsing history, combined with ad-blocking and anti-tracking extensions, reduce the collection of personal data. Awareness of these tools empowers users to make conscious decisions about their browsing habits. Layering privacy-focused solutions across devices and accounts maximizes effectiveness. Digital behavior combined with technology creates an environment where personal information is less vulnerable to monitoring. Awareness and action go hand in hand in minimizing tracking exposure.

VPNs (Virtual Private Networks) are another critical tool for managing your footprint. By encrypting internet connections and masking IP addresses, VPNs prevent external parties from linking online activity to specific devices or locations. Awareness of the proper use of VPNs allows users to maintain privacy when browsing, streaming, or using public Wi-Fi. Integrating VPNs into regular internet use adds an additional layer of protection against surveillance and tracking. Combining VPNs with other privacy measures ensures comprehensive defense against digital tracking. Consistent use of these tools strengthens control over personal information.

Lastly, cultivating intentional online behavior is essential for reducing your digital footprint. Every post, share, comment, or purchase contributes to the overall record of your activity. Awareness of the long-term implications of online actions encourages thoughtful engagement. Limiting unnecessary sharing, using strong privacy settings, and regularly reviewing accounts ensures that your footprint remains manageable. Responsible digital behavior combined with technical safeguards creates a secure online environment. Conscious choices in online activity are the most powerful tool for protecting personal privacy and data.

Understanding digital footprints is essential for both personal privacy and cybersecurity. Every online action, whether intentional or incidental, contributes to a growing profile that can be accessed by advertisers, cybercriminals, or even governments. Awareness of this fact empowers individuals to take control of the information they share and the traces they leave behind. Thoughtful use of privacy tools, careful management of accounts, and strategic behavior online reduce exposure and risk. Combining technical measures with disciplined habits ensures that your digital presence is intentional rather than vulnerable. Managing your footprint is not about eliminating all traces, but about minimizing unnecessary risks and retaining control.

Children and teens are particularly vulnerable to creating extensive digital footprints, often without realizing the long-term implications. Parents and guardians should educate younger users about responsible online behavior, privacy settings, and the potential consequences of oversharing. Awareness and guidance at an early age help build lifelong habits of caution and informed decision-making. Implementing parental controls, monitoring activity, and discussing online safety are effective strategies to protect children's digital footprints. Teaching digital responsibility ensures that young users grow up understanding the balance between connectivity and privacy. Education is a powerful tool in cultivating a safer digital generation.

Public Wi-Fi networks can also exacerbate risks related to digital footprints. Unsecured networks may expose browsing activity, login credentials, and personal data to third parties. Awareness of network security encourages users to take protective measures, such as using VPNs, avoiding sensitive transactions, and disabling automatic connections. Safe browsing practices minimize exposure when accessing online services on public networks. Combining network precautions with careful device management further reduces the risk of tracking or data compromise. Thoughtful awareness of network environments is essential in managing digital footprints.

Digital footprint management also extends to offline interactions that leave online traces. Credit applications, service subscriptions, and interactions with businesses can result in data being stored digitally. Awareness of these connections allows users to limit exposure, opt-out of unnecessary data collection, and request removal where possible. Being mindful of offline-to-online data flows strengthens overall privacy. Comprehensive digital footprint management involves both online activity and the digital traces generated indirectly. Vigilance across all sources of personal information ensures more complete protection of data and privacy.

CHAPTER .24

PROTECTING YOUR DATA DURING REMOTE WORK

Essential Security Measures for Telecommuters to Safeguard Personal and Corporate Data

Remote work has become increasingly common, offering flexibility and efficiency, but it also introduces unique cybersecurity challenges. Home networks, personal devices, and shared workspaces can all create vulnerabilities if not properly managed. Awareness of these risks is the first step toward establishing a secure remote work environment. Ensuring data protection requires a combination of technical safeguards, behavioral practices, and organizational policies. Individuals must take responsibility for both personal and work-related data security. Implementing proactive measures prevents small vulnerabilities from becoming costly breaches.

One of the most critical steps is securing home networks. Routers should be configured with strong, unique passwords, and firmware should be updated regularly. Network encryption, such as WPA3, provides an additional layer of protection for data transmitted over Wi-Fi. Awareness of potential threats, such as rogue devices or unsecured networks, encourages users to monitor activity and restrict access. Segmenting home networks to separate personal and work devices can further reduce exposure. Proper network security establishes a foundation for safe remote work. Vigilance at the network level prevents unauthorized access to sensitive data.

Device security is equally important for telecommuters. Laptops, smartphones, and tablets used for work must have updated operating systems, antivirus protection, and firewalls enabled. Awareness of potential malware, phishing attempts, or unauthorized access ensures users remain cautious in daily operations. Using device encryption protects data in the event of loss or theft. Password management, multi-factor authentication, and secure login practices strengthen defenses. A well-secured device is the cornerstone of remote work cybersecurity. Protecting hardware and software prevents breaches before they occur.

Cloud storage and collaboration tools are indispensable for remote work, but they also present potential vulnerabilities. Awareness of file-sharing permissions, access controls, and authentication requirements ensures data remains private and secure. Regularly reviewing who has access and minimizing unnecessary sharing prevents accidental leaks. Encrypting sensitive files before uploading to the cloud adds an extra layer of protection. Utilizing secure platforms with robust privacy policies ensures compliance with corporate and regulatory requirements. Proper management of cloud resources balances productivity with security, maintaining both efficiency and safety.

Behavioral vigilance is essential for all remote workers. Employees should be cautious with emails, links, and attachments to avoid phishing and social engineering attacks. Awareness of secure communication channels, such as encrypted messaging and VPN usage, reinforces data protection. Avoiding public Wi-Fi for sensitive tasks, locking devices when unattended, and logging out of accounts after use are practical measures that minimize risk. Conscious daily habits complement technical protections to create a comprehensive security posture. Responsible behavior in remote work environments reduces the likelihood of breaches and ensures the safety of both personal and corporate information.

Virtual Private Networks (VPNs) are essential tools for secure remote work. By encrypting internet traffic, VPNs prevent unauthorized parties from intercepting sensitive data transmitted over home or public networks. Awareness of VPN usage encourages employees to connect only through trusted servers when accessing corporate resources. Using a reliable VPN service ensures that communications remain confidential and reduces exposure to cyberattacks. VPNs are particularly important for accessing internal company systems, email servers, and file storage remotely. Integrating VPNs into daily remote work practices provides a critical layer of protection for both personal and organizational data.

Multi-factor authentication (MFA) strengthens remote access security. Requiring an additional verification step beyond a password—such as a code from an app or a biometric scan—significantly reduces the risk of unauthorized account access. Awareness of MFA options allows users to implement stronger defenses across email, cloud services, and corporate applications. Even if a password is compromised, MFA acts as a barrier against intrusion. Organizations should encourage or mandate MFA usage for all remote employees to standardize security practices. Combining MFA with strong password policies creates a robust security foundation. Multi-factor authentication is a simple yet powerful defense against credential-based attacks.

Regular software updates are critical for maintaining secure remote work environments. Operating systems, applications, and productivity tools often release patches to fix vulnerabilities that could be exploited by cybercriminals. Awareness of update schedules and automatic update settings ensures devices remain protected against known threats. Delaying or ignoring updates can leave critical security gaps exposed to attackers. Keeping all work-related devices current reduces the risk of malware, ransomware, and system exploits. Continuous maintenance of software and firmware is a practical and proactive approach to data protection. Updated systems provide the most resilient defense against evolving threats.

Secure file sharing and storage practices are essential for telecommuters. Awareness of the risks associated with sending sensitive files via unsecured email or public services encourages the use of encrypted communication channels. Cloud storage platforms should be selected based on security features, including end-to-end encryption and access control. Limiting file access to only authorized collaborators and using strong passwords for shared documents reduces potential exposure. Regularly reviewing and cleaning up shared files minimizes unnecessary risks. Thoughtful file management ensures that data remains confidential while maintaining collaborative efficiency. Secure sharing habits protect both personal and organizational information.

Endpoint monitoring is an important strategy for remote work security. Personal devices connected to corporate networks should be regularly scanned for malware, unauthorized software, and unusual activity. Awareness of endpoint security tools allows users to detect and respond to potential breaches quickly. Some organizations provide security software or management platforms to centralize monitoring and ensure compliance. For individuals managing personal devices, installing trusted antivirus programs and enabling alerts for suspicious activity is critical. Active endpoint management strengthens the overall security posture for remote work. Monitoring devices proactively reduces the likelihood of unnoticed intrusions or data compromise.

Creating separate work and personal accounts on devices enhances security for remote work. Mixing personal and professional accounts can inadvertently expose corporate data through shared applications, browser sessions, or cloud services. Awareness of account separation encourages disciplined usage of email, storage, and productivity tools. Configuring distinct profiles ensures that sensitive work files remain isolated from personal activity. This approach minimizes the risk of accidental data leaks and prevents malware from spreading between accounts. By maintaining clear boundaries, employees protect both organizational resources and their own personal information.

Physical security is often overlooked in remote work settings. Laptops, external drives, and other work devices should be stored securely when not in use to prevent theft or unauthorized access. Awareness of the importance of physical security includes locking devices, using privacy screens, and controlling access in shared spaces. Even with strong digital protections, physical compromise can render those measures ineffective. Secure storage and mindful placement of devices ensure that confidential data remains protected. Physical security complements digital safeguards, creating a comprehensive remote work defense strategy. Protecting hardware is as important as securing software and networks.

Backups are a critical component of remote work cybersecurity. Regularly saving copies of important files, either locally or in encrypted cloud storage, ensures that data can be recovered in case of loss or ransomware attacks. Awareness of backup procedures encourages employees to schedule consistent updates and verify restore capabilities. Combining automated backup solutions with manual checks increases reliability. Secure backups provide peace of mind and reduce the impact of accidental deletion, device failure, or malicious attacks. Data redundancy is a simple yet powerful tool in maintaining continuity and minimizing risk. Proper backup strategies protect the integrity and availability of critical information.

Educating employees and household members about security practices is essential for maintaining a safe remote work environment. Awareness of phishing scams, safe browsing habits, and secure communication techniques helps reduce human error, which is often the weakest link in cybersecurity. Consistent education reinforces the importance of vigilance and strengthens the overall security posture. Sharing best practices and creating clear guidelines ensures that all participants understand their responsibilities. Training combined with technical safeguards creates a culture of proactive security. Knowledgeable users act as a first line of defense, complementing digital protections.

Regularly reviewing and updating security policies is necessary to keep pace with evolving threats. Remote work introduces unique risks, and organizational guidelines should reflect current best practices, technologies, and potential vulnerabilities. Awareness of policy updates ensures that employees remain compliant and informed. Policies should cover areas such as device usage, network access, cloud storage, and incident reporting. Aligning behavior with policies reinforces security protocols and reduces exposure. Continuous policy evaluation maintains relevance and effectiveness in protecting sensitive data in remote work environments.

Remote work often involves the use of video conferencing and collaboration tools, which introduce additional security considerations. Awareness of meeting settings, such as password protection, waiting rooms, and participant permissions, helps prevent unauthorized access. Sensitive discussions and shared documents should be confined to secure platforms with end-to-end encryption. Avoiding public sharing links or unprotected recordings reduces the likelihood of data leaks. Proper configuration and disciplined usage ensure that communication remains private and professional. Thoughtful management of virtual collaboration tools protects both organizational and personal information.

Using strong authentication practices across all remote work platforms is crucial. Beyond multi-factor authentication, employees should employ complex passwords, password managers, and unique login credentials for each service. Awareness of password reuse risks encourages disciplined management across multiple accounts. Regularly updating passwords and monitoring login attempts enhances security. Strong authentication practices prevent unauthorized access even if credentials are compromised elsewhere. Combining password hygiene with multi-factor authentication and vigilant monitoring creates robust defenses for remote workers. Proper authentication is the foundation of secure access in distributed environments.

Monitoring for unusual activity is essential when working remotely. Users should pay attention to unexpected emails, login notifications, or system alerts that may indicate attempted breaches. Awareness of patterns in daily operations allows early identification of anomalies. Organizations often provide monitoring tools to detect suspicious activity across corporate accounts. Individuals should complement these tools with personal vigilance, such as checking account activity and enabling alerts. Timely recognition and response to anomalies reduce potential damage from cyber threats. Proactive monitoring reinforces all other security measures in a comprehensive remote work strategy.

Securing endpoints goes beyond devices to include peripheral tools such as printers, external drives, and IoT devices connected to the home network. Awareness of potential vulnerabilities in these peripherals helps prevent them from becoming points of compromise. Implementing access controls, updating firmware, and monitoring device behavior ensures that all connected tools are protected. Peripheral security prevents attackers from exploiting weak links in the remote work ecosystem. Combining endpoint management with network security creates a unified defense. Comprehensive attention to every device connected to the work environment is essential for minimizing risk.

Remote work security is a blend of technology, behavior, and awareness. Devices, networks, and cloud systems must be secured, but user habits ultimately determine the effectiveness of these measures. Awareness of threats, such as phishing, malware, and unsecured networks, encourages proactive behavior. Implementing strong passwords, multi-factor authentication, and VPNs ensures that digital communication remains private. Regular updates, backups, and endpoint monitoring reinforce these protections. Combining technology with vigilant habits creates a robust defense against cyber threats in remote work environments.

Communication and collaboration must also be conducted mindfully. Sharing sensitive information over unsecured channels or mismanaging access permissions can result in data exposure. Awareness of secure practices ensures that video conferences, file sharing, and messaging remain protected. Using encryption, password protection, and access restrictions provides both security and peace of mind. Educating all participants about secure practices strengthens the overall remote work ecosystem. Thoughtful collaboration prevents avoidable mistakes that could compromise both personal and organizational data. Security-conscious communication safeguards the integrity of all shared information.

Maintaining a proactive approach is key to remote work cybersecurity. Monitoring for unusual activity, auditing access, and staying informed about emerging threats empowers users to take action before breaches occur. Awareness of potential vulnerabilities, both technical and behavioral, allows for continuous improvement of security measures. Adopting a mindset of vigilance ensures that remote work remains safe, productive, and resilient. The integration of personal responsibility with organizational support creates a culture of security. Continuous evaluation and adaptation enhance long-term protection of sensitive data. Proactive habits are the backbone of a secure remote work environment.

Documentation and adherence to policies further reinforce remote work security. Awareness of company guidelines, compliance requirements, and best practices ensures that employees align their actions with organizational expectations. Properly documenting access, updates, and security incidents provides accountability and helps identify areas for improvement. Following structured procedures reduces human error and ensures consistent application of security measures. Policy adherence, combined with technological safeguards, forms a comprehensive approach to protecting data. Awareness and discipline translate security policies into practical, actionable behavior. Proper procedure adherence strengthens both compliance and personal accountability.

CHAPTER .25

THE DANGERS OF DATA COLLECTION AND HOW TO OPT-OUT

How Companies Collect and Use Your Data, and How to Limit or Refuse Their Access

Data collection has become a cornerstone of modern business, shaping marketing strategies, product development, and customer engagement. Companies track user behavior through websites, apps, purchases, social media interactions, and even offline activity. Awareness of these practices is essential to understand how personal information is being gathered, stored, and monetized. While some data collection is necessary for service functionality, excessive or unauthorized collection can pose privacy risks. By recognizing how data is collected, individuals can take steps to limit exposure and maintain control over their personal information. Informed users are empowered to make deliberate choices about what information they share.

Advertising networks and data brokers play a significant role in aggregating and selling personal data. Even seemingly harmless online interactions can be collected, combined with other sources, and used for profiling, targeting, or predictive analytics. Awareness of these systems helps users understand the breadth of data collection and potential implications. Opting out of data-sharing programs, adjusting privacy settings, and using privacy-focused tools can limit the amount of personal information circulating in these networks. Controlling access to your data reduces exposure to identity theft, unwanted advertising, and manipulation. Knowledge of the data ecosystem allows individuals to reclaim agency over their digital footprint.

Social media platforms often request extensive personal information for account creation and continued engagement. Awareness of what is shared, either voluntarily or through default settings, allows users to manage privacy effectively. Limiting the information visible to others, adjusting permissions, and regularly reviewing account activity minimizes potential risks. Opting out of personalized ads and location tracking further reduces data exposure. Proactive management of social media accounts protects both personal and professional identities. Thoughtful engagement ensures that social networks serve as tools for connection, not vectors for exploitation.

Many apps and online services request access to sensitive information, such as contacts, location, microphone, and camera. Awareness of these permission requests allows users to make informed decisions about which features to enable. Only granting necessary permissions and periodically reviewing app access limits potential misuse. Opting out of unnecessary data collection reduces the digital footprint and prevents unauthorized tracking. Mobile devices often provide tools to manage permissions, monitor activity, and disable background data collection. By actively managing app access, users can enjoy functionality without sacrificing privacy. Intentional oversight of app permissions is a key step in controlling personal data exposure.

Email communications and subscription services also contribute to the collection of personal data. Companies track open rates, click-throughs, and engagement patterns to build detailed user profiles. Awareness of these practices enables individuals to take control, such as unsubscribing from unnecessary lists, using disposable email addresses, or filtering marketing messages. Opting out of email tracking and marketing data collection reduces exposure to profiling and targeted campaigns. Implementing these measures creates a more controlled and private online experience. By combining careful email management with broader privacy practices, users can maintain a stronger hold over their personal information.

Many websites use tracking technologies such as cookies, pixels, and scripts to collect behavioral data. Awareness of these trackers empowers users to make choices about what information is shared during web browsing. Browser settings, ad-blockers, and privacy extensions can limit tracking by blocking third-party cookies or anonymizing activity. Opting out of tracking mechanisms prevents companies from building detailed profiles without consent. Combining technical tools with conscious browsing habits ensures that online activity remains more private. Proactive management of web tracking protects personal information and reduces targeted advertising exposure.

Location tracking is a particularly sensitive form of data collection. Smartphones, apps, and smart devices often transmit location information to service providers. Awareness of when and why location data is collected allows individuals to disable unnecessary tracking features. Opting out of location sharing, using location spoofing tools, or restricting app permissions reduces exposure. Thoughtful management of location data prevents profiling, unwanted marketing, and potential physical security risks. Controlling how location information is shared strengthens both privacy and personal safety. Awareness and action empower users to limit the impact of constant location monitoring.

Opt-out mechanisms provided by companies and governments are essential tools for controlling data collection. Many platforms offer settings to limit personalized advertising, data sharing with partners, or participation in analytics programs. Awareness of these options encourages users to actively manage their privacy preferences. Regulatory frameworks, such as GDPR and CCPA, provide legal avenues to restrict how companies handle personal data. Exercising these rights allows individuals to reclaim control over their information. Combining legal awareness with technical tools creates a powerful approach to minimizing data exposure. Informed decisions about opting out protect both privacy and autonomy in the digital ecosystem.

Privacy-focused tools, including VPNs, secure browsers, and encrypted communication apps, help limit data collection.

Awareness of these tools enables users to maintain anonymity and reduce unnecessary tracking. Using encrypted messaging, private search engines, and ad-blockers minimizes the amount of personal information shared online. Opting for privacy-enhancing technologies complements manual opt-out actions and strengthens overall security. Regularly updating and reviewing these tools ensures they remain effective against evolving tracking practices. Integrating technology and user awareness creates a resilient defense against pervasive data collection.

Behavioral habits play a critical role in controlling exposure to data collection. Awareness of what information is shared, with whom, and how often guides responsible online behavior. Limiting oversharing on social media, reviewing app permissions, and carefully managing online interactions reduce vulnerability. Opting out is most effective when combined with disciplined habits that prevent unnecessary data dissemination. Conscious decision-making ensures that personal information remains under individual control. Combining habits, tools, and opt-out strategies creates a comprehensive approach to protecting digital privacy.

Children and teens are especially vulnerable to data collection practices. Many apps, games, and social platforms target younger audiences, gathering information without full awareness of potential risks. Awareness of age-appropriate privacy settings, parental controls, and educational resources is crucial for protecting minors. Parents and guardians can opt out of unnecessary tracking, limit permissions, and monitor online interactions to reduce exposure. Teaching digital literacy from an early age helps children understand the consequences of sharing personal information. Guiding young users fosters safe habits that extend into adulthood.

Retailers and e-commerce platforms are major collectors of consumer data. Purchase history, browsing behavior, and loyalty programs provide detailed insights into customer preferences. Awareness of tracking techniques, such as cookies, rewards programs, and targeted ads, allows consumers to make informed choices. Opting out of marketing communications, minimizing data sharing, and using privacy-focused payment methods can limit exposure. Careful management of e-commerce activity prevents excessive profiling and reduces the risk of fraud. Conscious participation in online shopping balances convenience with personal privacy. Informed consumers reclaim control over their digital transactions.

Health and fitness apps also collect highly sensitive personal data. Step counts, location routes, dietary habits, and medical records can be transmitted to third parties if not properly managed. Awareness of privacy settings, data-sharing agreements, and app permissions is critical for maintaining confidentiality. Opting out of unnecessary data collection and using secure platforms minimizes the potential for misuse. Reviewing terms of service and understanding how data is processed empowers users to protect their health information. Protecting sensitive data in health apps preserves both privacy and personal security. Thoughtful management of wellness tools ensures that benefits do not come at the cost of exposure.

Data brokers aggregate information from multiple sources to create comprehensive profiles of individuals. Awareness of their role in the data ecosystem allows users to take corrective action. Many brokers provide opt-out procedures, allowing individuals to request removal from databases or limit information sharing. Utilizing these procedures helps reduce the risk of identity theft, unsolicited marketing, and profiling. Regular monitoring of personal information in broker databases ensures continued privacy. Taking proactive steps against data brokers is an essential part of a comprehensive digital privacy strategy. Control over your personal data starts with understanding who has access and asserting your rights.

Corporate transparency and privacy policies are essential for understanding how data is used. Awareness of privacy notices, terms of service, and user agreements helps individuals make informed decisions about sharing information. Opting out or restricting access based on policy guidelines allows users to maintain control over personal data. Regularly reviewing these documents ensures that users remain aware of changes in data collection practices. Knowledge of corporate obligations under privacy laws empowers individuals to exercise their rights effectively. Engaged and informed users are better equipped to navigate the complex landscape of data collection. Transparency combined with proactive action enhances digital security and privacy.

Browser settings play a crucial role in controlling online data collection. Many browsers allow users to disable third-party cookies, block trackers, and send "Do Not Track" signals to websites. Awareness of these features enables individuals to take full advantage of built-in privacy protections. Regularly reviewing and updating browser settings reduces exposure to tracking and profiling. Combining browser controls with ad-blockers and privacy-focused extensions further strengthens online anonymity. Thoughtful management of browsing behavior ensures that web activity remains private and secure.

Email services are another point where data collection occurs. Open rates, click-through links, and engagement metrics are monitored for marketing purposes. Awareness of these tracking techniques allows users to take preventive measures, such as using disposable email addresses, filtering marketing emails, and opting out of tracking. Secure email services with encryption provide additional protection for sensitive communications. Limiting data exposure through email reduces the potential for profiling, scams, and unsolicited contact. Combining secure email practices with broader privacy strategies enhances overall protection. Vigilance in email management is key to controlling personal data in digital correspondence.

Social media privacy settings must be regularly reviewed and updated. Platforms often change policies, default settings, and data-sharing practices, which can expose personal information if not monitored. Awareness of these updates ensures users can adjust privacy settings accordingly. Limiting who can view posts, tagging permissions, and location sharing reduces the amount of accessible data. Opting out of targeted advertising and data-sharing programs further protects personal information. Regular maintenance of social media accounts is essential to prevent inadvertent exposure. Active oversight of social platforms maintains a controlled and secure digital presence.

Legislation such as GDPR and CCPA provides tools for individuals to control data collection. Awareness of these legal frameworks allows users to exercise rights like access, correction, deletion, and opt-out of data sharing. Companies are required to provide mechanisms for individuals to manage their personal data under these laws. Opting out and exercising legal rights ensures compliance and strengthens personal privacy. Understanding your rights empowers you to actively participate in controlling the collection and use of your information. Combining technical tools with legal protections offers a comprehensive approach to limiting data collection. Knowledge of privacy law is a powerful ally in protecting personal information.

Behavioral awareness is the final and perhaps most important factor in managing data collection. Every click, form submission, and app download contributes to the information companies can gather. Awareness of the cumulative effect of online behavior encourages thoughtful, deliberate choices. Limiting unnecessary sharing, using privacy tools, and regularly auditing online accounts reduces the digital footprint. Proactive, mindful behavior complements technological and legal measures. By being conscious of actions and decisions online, users can maintain control over their personal information and reduce vulnerability to unwanted data collection.

Managing data collection effectively requires a combination of awareness, tools, and intentional behavior. Users must understand how their data is being collected, identify which platforms and services pose risks, and take proactive measures to limit exposure. Awareness of app permissions, browser settings, and privacy policies enables informed decision-making. Technical solutions such as VPNs, encrypted communications, and ad-blockers complement behavioral strategies. Opting out where possible reduces the amount of personal information available to third parties. Consistent vigilance ensures that privacy is maintained even as data collection methods evolve.

Regular audits of personal information are essential for controlling exposure. Searching your name online, reviewing social media accounts, and checking data broker listings provide insights into what information is publicly accessible. Awareness of these exposures allows you to take corrective action, such as adjusting privacy settings, deleting unnecessary accounts, or requesting removal from databases. Opting out of data collection programs and limiting data sharing reinforces privacy protections. Proactive monitoring prevents your personal information from being used without consent. Taking responsibility for your digital footprint strengthens both privacy and security.

Education is key to maintaining control over personal information. Awareness of evolving data collection methods, privacy-enhancing tools, and legal rights ensures users can respond effectively to new threats. Teaching friends, family, and colleagues about privacy practices multiplies the protective effect. Behavioral vigilance combined with technological solutions creates a strong defense against pervasive data collection. Opting out becomes a habit rather than an occasional action. Informed, consistent practices empower individuals to navigate the digital world safely.

Data collection is not inherently negative, but uncontrolled or unconsented collection can lead to exploitation. Awareness of how personal data is used helps users make deliberate choices about which services to trust. Opting out, limiting data sharing, and using privacy-focused platforms allow individuals to retain control over their information. Conscious management of data reduces vulnerability to identity theft, manipulation, and surveillance. Protecting personal data is an ongoing responsibility that requires diligence and proactive engagement. Balancing the benefits of technology with privacy safeguards ensures that users remain empowered.

CHAPTER .26

RANSOMWARE: HOW TO PREVENT AND RESPOND TO AN ATTACK

What Ransomware Is, How It Spreads, and How to Avoid Being Held Hostage by Cybercriminals

Ransomware is a type of malicious software designed to encrypt files or lock users out of their devices, demanding payment for restoration. Awareness of how ransomware operates is essential for both prevention and response. These attacks can spread through email attachments, malicious links, compromised websites, and unsecured networks. Understanding the various delivery methods allows users to recognize potential threats before infection occurs. Preventing ransomware requires a combination of technical safeguards, disciplined behavior, and backup strategies. Awareness and proactive measures dramatically reduce the risk of falling victim to these destructive attacks.

Keeping devices and software updated is one of the most effective ways to prevent ransomware. Security patches and updates close vulnerabilities that ransomware can exploit. Awareness of software lifecycle management, including operating systems, applications, and firmware, encourages timely installation of updates. Ignoring updates leaves systems susceptible to attacks that are well-documented and preventable. Combining updates with strong antivirus solutions provides a layered defense. Proactive maintenance significantly reduces the chances of ransomware infection. Consistent vigilance in updating systems ensures ongoing protection.

Email remains the primary vector for ransomware attacks. Awareness of phishing tactics, suspicious attachments, and unexpected links helps users identify potential threats. Verifying sender identity, avoiding downloads from unknown sources, and scanning attachments before opening are critical behaviors. Multi-factor authentication can limit the impact if credentials are compromised. Training and awareness programs for employees or household members further reduce susceptibility. Careful handling of emails transforms a high-risk channel into a manageable one. Vigilance in digital communications is a frontline defense against ransomware.

Regular backups are essential for mitigating the impact of ransomware. Awareness of the importance of multiple backup methods—local drives, network-attached storage, and encrypted cloud solutions—ensures data can be restored even if devices are compromised. Backups should be isolated from the primary network to prevent infection from spreading. Testing recovery procedures periodically confirms that backups are functional and reliable. Proactive backup strategies allow individuals and organizations to respond without succumbing to ransom demands. A well-structured backup plan transforms ransomware from a catastrophic event into a manageable inconvenience.

Immediate response strategies are critical when ransomware strikes. Awareness of signs of infection, such as unusual file extensions, system slowdowns, or ransom notes, enables swift action. Disconnecting affected devices from networks, preserving evidence, and contacting IT professionals or cybersecurity experts are essential first steps. Avoid paying the ransom, as it does not guarantee recovery and encourages future attacks. Reporting incidents to relevant authorities supports broader efforts to combat cybercrime. Understanding response procedures ensures that damage is minimized and recovery is efficient. Preparedness and knowledge transform panic into effective action.

Ransomware often exploits weak passwords and unsecured access points to infiltrate systems. Awareness of strong password practices and multi-factor authentication reduces the likelihood of unauthorized access. Using unique passwords for different accounts, regularly updating credentials, and avoiding password reuse strengthens defenses. Monitoring login attempts and alerts can help detect suspicious activity early. Combining strong authentication with user vigilance creates a robust barrier against ransomware intrusion. Preventing unauthorized access is a fundamental step in safeguarding digital assets.

Network security plays a vital role in defending against ransomware attacks. Awareness of potential vulnerabilities, such as unprotected Wi-Fi networks or misconfigured firewalls, guides preventive measures. Segmentation of networks, intrusion detection systems, and firewall management limit the spread of ransomware if an infection occurs. Regular monitoring and auditing of network traffic can identify suspicious behavior before it escalates. Educating users about safe network practices further reduces risk. A well-secured network acts as both a deterrent and a containment measure for ransomware threats. Proactive network management is key to minimizing exposure and damage.

Email filtering and security software are essential tools for preventing ransomware delivery. Awareness of filtering rules, attachment scanning, and threat detection capabilities ensures users leverage these tools effectively. Advanced antivirus programs can detect malicious code before execution, while sandboxing techniques can isolate suspicious files. Regular updates to security software maintain protection against evolving ransomware strains. Combining technical defenses with cautious behavior provides a strong layer of protection. Utilizing these tools effectively can prevent ransomware from ever reaching critical systems.

User education is one of the most effective defenses against ransomware. Awareness of phishing tactics, suspicious downloads, and social engineering techniques empowers individuals to make informed decisions online. Regular training and simulated exercises reinforce good practices and cultivate a security-conscious mindset. Users who understand the risks are less likely to inadvertently introduce ransomware into their environment. Continuous education complements technical measures, forming a holistic defense strategy. Informed behavior is a crucial factor in minimizing ransomware risk and ensuring long-term cybersecurity.

Ransomware attacks can target both individuals and organizations, highlighting the importance of preparedness. Awareness of potential attack vectors, response procedures, and recovery options ensures readiness. Establishing clear protocols for incident response, backup access, and communication reduces downtime and data loss. Coordinated planning between IT teams, management, and users strengthens resilience. Proactive preparation allows for rapid and effective responses when ransomware strikes. Combining awareness, technology, and planning transforms potential catastrophe into manageable recovery.

Remote work introduces additional risks for ransomware attacks, as employees access corporate resources from various networks and devices. Awareness of these risks encourages adherence to security best practices, including the use of VPNs, secure Wi-Fi, and updated devices. Segregating work and personal accounts, as well as applying endpoint security measures, reduces the likelihood of infection. Educating remote workers on recognizing suspicious activity ensures that threats are identified early. Implementing standardized security policies across all remote access points strengthens overall protection. Vigilance in remote environments is crucial for preventing ransomware from exploiting dispersed systems.

Mobile devices are increasingly targeted by ransomware, especially through apps and links in messages. Awareness of app permissions, downloads from untrusted sources, and suspicious SMS or email links is vital. Users should only install apps from reputable stores and verify authenticity before opening files or links. Mobile security solutions, including antivirus apps and regular updates, enhance protection. Combining cautious behavior with technology mitigates the risk of mobile ransomware infections. A comprehensive approach that includes both devices and behavior is essential in today's mobile-centric world.

Ransomware often leverages social engineering to trick users into initiating the attack. Awareness of phishing emails, fake alerts, and malicious links empowers individuals to resist manipulation. Users should verify sender identity, scrutinize unexpected messages, and avoid clicking on unknown links. Organizations can reinforce awareness through ongoing training and simulated phishing tests. Proactive vigilance against social engineering attacks significantly reduces ransomware incidents. Understanding attacker tactics allows users to respond with caution rather than reaction. Education and awareness are as critical as technical defenses in mitigating ransomware risk.

File access control limits ransomware's ability to encrypt critical information. Awareness of permissions, shared folder settings, and administrative privileges ensures that only necessary users can access sensitive data. Limiting access prevents ransomware from spreading uncontrollably across systems. Regular audits of file permissions and group access help maintain strict control over sensitive information. Combined with backups and endpoint security, access control forms a layered defense against ransomware attacks. Thoughtful configuration of access rights can prevent widespread data loss in case of infection.

Incident response planning is critical for minimizing ransomware damage. Awareness of a structured response plan, including isolation, communication, and recovery steps, ensures rapid action. Disconnecting infected devices, notifying IT or cybersecurity professionals, and preserving evidence for investigation are essential first steps. Avoiding payment of ransom demands and reporting the incident to authorities strengthens long-term resilience. Planning ahead reduces panic, preserves resources, and ensures data integrity. A comprehensive response plan transforms potential disaster into manageable recovery. Preparation and knowledge are the cornerstones of ransomware resilience.

Regular system monitoring and logging are crucial for early ransomware detection. Awareness of unusual file activity, unexpected encryption behavior, or system slowdowns can indicate an infection in progress. Implementing monitoring tools that track file changes and network activity allows for rapid identification of suspicious behavior. Employees should be trained to report anomalies immediately to IT or security teams. Early detection limits the damage caused by ransomware and allows for faster recovery. Combining vigilance with automated monitoring creates an effective detection and response framework.

Segmentation of networks can significantly limit ransomware's ability to spread. Awareness of the benefits of dividing networks into isolated segments prevents a single infection from compromising entire systems. By controlling communication between segments, organizations can contain attacks and protect critical resources. Implementing access controls and network segmentation policies reduces the potential reach of ransomware. Combining these structural defenses with proactive monitoring strengthens overall cybersecurity. Thoughtful network architecture acts as a barrier, giving security teams time to respond effectively. Containment strategies reduce risk and limit operational disruption during attacks.

Testing backup and recovery procedures is essential for ransomware preparedness. Awareness of the functionality and reliability of backups ensures that restoration can occur without paying ransom. Periodic drills and validation of recovery processes confirm that critical files can be restored quickly. Combining automated backup schedules with manual verification creates redundancy and confidence in recovery plans. Effective testing allows organizations and individuals to minimize downtime and data loss. A strong backup strategy, paired with tested recovery procedures, transforms ransomware from a catastrophic event into a manageable situation. Reliability and preparation are key components of resilience.

Cyber insurance can provide financial protection in the event of ransomware attacks. Awareness of policy coverage, limitations, and claim procedures ensures that organizations and individuals are prepared. While insurance does not prevent attacks, it can offset the financial consequences of data loss, system downtime, or ransom demands. Understanding the scope of coverage allows for informed decisions and proper risk management. Combining insurance with technical defenses, training, and backups creates a comprehensive security strategy. Being prepared for worst-case scenarios enhances overall resilience and peace of mind. Cyber insurance is a supplementary measure in a multi-layered defense plan.

Ransomware defense requires a holistic approach that combines prevention, detection, and response. Awareness, user education, secure behavior, technical tools, backups, and planning form a cohesive strategy. No single solution can eliminate ransomware risk entirely, but layered defenses significantly reduce exposure and impact. By integrating these measures into daily routines, organizations and individuals can maintain operational continuity and protect sensitive data. Vigilance, preparedness, and resilience are key to mitigating ransomware threats. A proactive mindset transforms potential vulnerability into empowerment and control.

Ransomware is not just a technological threat; it is also a test of preparedness, awareness, and response. Awareness of attack vectors, safe practices, and preventive measures empowers users to defend themselves effectively. Maintaining up-to-date systems, using strong authentication, implementing backups, and practicing safe behavior collectively reduce the risk of ransomware infection. A multi-layered approach ensures that even if one defense fails, others provide protection. By taking proactive steps, individuals and organizations can maintain control over their data and operations. Vigilance and preparation transform potential disasters into manageable challenges.

Response planning is just as important as prevention. Awareness of proper response steps—isolating infected systems, preserving evidence, notifying authorities, and engaging cybersecurity professionals—ensures that ransomware attacks are contained efficiently. Preparedness minimizes panic, data loss, and operational downtime. A structured, rehearsed approach ensures that both individuals and teams act decisively during crises. Regularly reviewing and updating response plans keeps them aligned with evolving threats. Knowing what to do before an incident occurs builds confidence and reduces the impact of ransomware attacks. Preparedness turns reactive fear into proactive control.

Collaboration between users, IT teams, and management strengthens ransomware resilience. Awareness of organizational policies, communication channels, and escalation procedures ensures that everyone acts in alignment. User vigilance complements technical safeguards and forms an integral part of a coordinated defense. By fostering a culture of cybersecurity awareness, organizations can reduce human error, which is often the weakest link in ransomware prevention. Collaboration and consistent enforcement of best practices create an environment where threats are less likely to succeed. Teamwork and shared responsibility enhance both prevention and recovery capabilities.

Recovery strategies must include both technical and operational considerations. Awareness of which systems and files are critical, the order of restoration, and the use of backups ensures a smooth recovery process. Documented recovery procedures provide clarity and reduce downtime. Practicing recovery drills strengthens confidence and reveals gaps in preparedness. Integrating technical, procedural, and human elements ensures that ransomware incidents are managed effectively. Recovery planning ensures continuity, maintains trust, and reduces the financial and operational impact of attacks. Thoughtful preparation allows recovery to be efficient and controlled.

CHAPTER .27

SECURING YOUR FINANCIAL DATA: PROTECTING BANK ACCOUNTS AND CREDIT CARDS

Steps to Take to Safeguard Your Financial Information and Detect Fraudulent Activities

Financial data is among the most sensitive information we possess, making it a prime target for cybercriminals. Awareness of the threats to bank accounts, credit cards, and online payment systems is essential for protecting your assets. Cybercriminals exploit weak passwords, phishing emails, unsecured devices, and malware to gain unauthorized access. Understanding these risks allows users to implement preventive measures that reduce the likelihood of theft. Proactive monitoring and cautious behavior ensure that your financial data remains secure. Safeguarding financial information is not optional—it is a critical aspect of personal and digital security.

Strong authentication is the first line of defense for financial accounts. Using complex, unique passwords for each account prevents unauthorized access even if one credential is compromised. Multi-factor authentication (MFA) adds an additional layer of protection by requiring a secondary verification step. Awareness of MFA options, such as SMS codes, authentication apps, or biometric verification, strengthens defenses. Avoiding password reuse and regularly updating credentials enhances security further. Combining strong passwords with MFA makes it significantly harder for attackers to compromise financial accounts. Vigilant authentication practices are essential for protecting sensitive financial data.

Monitoring account activity is a crucial aspect of financial security. Awareness of transaction alerts, unusual spending patterns, and login notifications enables early detection of fraudulent activity. Many banks and financial institutions provide email or SMS alerts for transactions above a certain threshold or from unusual locations. Reviewing statements regularly ensures that unauthorized transactions are identified promptly. Prompt reporting of suspicious activity can prevent further losses and expedite recovery. Combining active monitoring with strong authentication creates a proactive defense against financial fraud. Vigilance in observing account activity protects both money and peace of mind.

Secure online and mobile banking practices reduce exposure to cyber threats. Awareness of phishing emails, fake banking websites, and unsecured connections is critical when accessing financial accounts. Always access bank websites directly through trusted URLs and avoid clicking on links in unsolicited emails or messages. Using secure networks, avoiding public Wi-Fi, and enabling encryption where possible further protect sensitive information. Awareness of mobile app permissions and security features ensures safe banking on smartphones and tablets. Safe banking habits reduce the likelihood of unauthorized access and cybercrime. Maintaining digital caution is essential for financial security.

Credit card security extends beyond online accounts. Awareness of physical card handling, such as storing cards securely and immediately reporting lost or stolen cards, is essential. For online purchases, using secure payment methods, one-time card numbers, or virtual credit cards limits exposure. Avoid storing card information on multiple websites or devices unless necessary. Monitoring credit reports regularly helps detect identity theft or fraudulent activity early. Combining vigilance, secure practices, and monitoring safeguards financial health. Protecting credit card data is a continuous responsibility that requires awareness and proactive measures.

Two-factor authentication is particularly critical for protecting financial accounts. Awareness of potential threats, such as phishing attempts and credential theft, underscores the importance of MFA. Many banks and financial institutions now require or recommend additional verification steps beyond a password. SMS codes, authentication apps, or biometric verification provide an extra layer of security. Even if a password is compromised, these secondary measures prevent unauthorized access. Consistently using two-factor authentication significantly reduces the risk of financial fraud.

Fraud detection tools provided by banks can be highly effective if used properly. Awareness of features like transaction alerts, suspicious activity notifications, and real-time monitoring empowers account holders to respond quickly to potential breaches. Setting up customized alerts for unusual spending patterns or international transactions ensures that any unauthorized activity is identified promptly. Combining these tools with regular statement reviews reinforces protection. Quick action in response to alerts can prevent financial loss and limit the impact of fraud. Proactive use of fraud detection tools transforms banking from reactive to preventive.

Safe online shopping practices are essential for protecting credit card information. Awareness of secure website indicators, such as HTTPS, padlock symbols, and verified payment gateways, ensures that transactions are protected. Avoiding public Wi-Fi when making purchases, using strong passwords, and employing virtual credit cards or payment services adds additional layers of security. Being cautious about saving card details on websites minimizes exposure if the platform is compromised. Users who implement these practices reduce the risk of unauthorized charges and identity theft. Thoughtful online shopping habits safeguard financial information in everyday transactions.

Regularly reviewing credit reports helps detect early signs of fraud. Awareness of unexpected accounts, unauthorized loans, or unusual credit inquiries provides insight into potential identity theft. Checking reports from all three major credit bureaus ensures comprehensive monitoring. Opting for alerts from credit monitoring services adds another layer of vigilance. Promptly addressing discrepancies or suspicious activity minimizes financial damage. Maintaining a habit of monitoring credit health strengthens both security and financial resilience. Vigilance in credit reporting protects against long-term consequences of identity theft.

Educating oneself about common financial scams is critical for ongoing security. Awareness of phishing schemes, fake investment opportunities, lottery fraud, and impersonation tactics allows users to recognize and avoid these threats. Scammers often use urgency, fear, or deception to trick victims into sharing sensitive information. Practicing skepticism, verifying sources, and using official channels for verification reduces susceptibility. Combining knowledge with secure behaviors ensures that financial information remains protected. Continuous education about evolving threats keeps individuals one step ahead of cybercriminals. Informed users are empowered to defend their financial wellbeing effectively.

Mobile banking offers convenience but introduces unique security challenges. Awareness of potential threats, such as malicious apps, unsecured Wi-Fi, and phishing attempts via SMS, is essential for safe mobile banking. Using only official banking apps, keeping devices updated, and enabling screen locks are fundamental precautions. Multi-factor authentication adds an additional layer of protection, even on mobile devices. Users should avoid storing sensitive banking credentials in insecure apps or notes. Vigilance and careful app management ensure that mobile banking remains both safe and convenient.

Virtual credit cards and payment services provide added security for online transactions. Awareness of these tools allows users to minimize exposure of their actual card details. Temporary card numbers, disposable payment methods, and encrypted payment gateways reduce the risk of unauthorized charges. Limiting the number of merchants who store payment information further protects financial data. By using these options, users can complete online transactions with confidence and minimal risk. Employing virtual payment solutions complements strong authentication and monitoring practices for overall financial security.

Secure password management is critical for protecting bank accounts and credit cards. Awareness of the risks of password reuse, weak credentials, and easily guessable passwords drives the adoption of strong, unique passwords for each financial account. Using a reputable password manager simplifies maintaining complex passwords while ensuring security. Regularly updating credentials and avoiding sharing login details further reduce vulnerability. Combining password strength with two-factor authentication provides a robust barrier against unauthorized access. Effective password management is the foundation of financial cybersecurity.

Phishing scams continue to be a major threat to financial security. Awareness of deceptive emails, fake banking notifications, and fraudulent calls is essential for avoiding financial loss. Users should verify messages through official bank channels before providing any personal or financial information. Training oneself to recognize suspicious links, requests, and inconsistencies reduces the likelihood of falling victim to scams. Reporting attempted phishing attacks to banks or authorities helps protect others as well. Vigilance against social engineering is as important as technical safeguards in securing financial data.

Regular software and device updates help protect financial data from emerging threats. Awareness of vulnerabilities in operating systems, browsers, and banking apps highlights the importance of timely updates. Installing patches and updates reduces the risk of malware or exploits targeting financial accounts. Combining updated software with secure networks, multi-factor authentication, and user awareness forms a comprehensive security strategy. Staying current with software ensures that the most recent defenses are in place against evolving threats. Consistent attention to updates enhances the overall protection of bank accounts and credit cards.

Monitoring for unusual activity goes beyond just checking account balances. Awareness of subtle signs of fraud, such as small unauthorized transactions, repeated login attempts, or notifications from unfamiliar locations, can prevent more significant losses. Setting up automated alerts for transactions above a certain threshold ensures timely detection. Reviewing account activity regularly helps identify inconsistencies that may indicate compromise. Combining manual checks with automated monitoring strengthens overall security. Early detection allows for immediate action, reducing both financial and emotional impact.

Secure connections are essential for protecting financial information online. Awareness of the risks posed by public Wi-Fi or unsecured networks guides users to employ VPNs or encrypted connections. Accessing banking sites and financial apps over secure, trusted networks prevents interception of sensitive data. Avoiding the use of shared devices for financial transactions further mitigates risk. Combining secure networks with strong passwords and multi-factor authentication creates a robust defense. Conscious management of digital connections ensures that financial activity remains private and protected. Secure connections are a foundational aspect of safeguarding digital finances.

Physical security of financial instruments is equally important. Awareness of risks related to stolen wallets, lost cards, or compromised checkbooks encourages proactive measures. Keeping cards and checks in secure locations, immediately reporting loss or theft, and using secure storage for sensitive documents prevent unauthorized access. Shredding old statements or sensitive financial paperwork reduces exposure to identity theft. Combining physical security with digital protections ensures comprehensive financial safety. Taking simple, mindful steps to secure tangible financial assets complements online security practices. Physical vigilance prevents many forms of financial fraud before they occur.

Credit monitoring services provide an added layer of protection for financial data. Awareness of unusual credit activity, new accounts, or identity theft alerts allows for rapid response. Subscribing to monitoring services, either free or paid, helps detect fraud early and provides guidance for remediation. Coupling monitoring with proactive reporting and verification ensures minimal financial disruption. These services act as a safety net, complementing strong authentication, vigilant account management, and secure transactions. Regularly reviewing credit reports in tandem with monitoring tools strengthens the overall financial security framework. Monitoring enhances awareness and enables swift corrective action.

Financial literacy and awareness are crucial for long-term security. Understanding the risks, protective measures, and legal recourses empowers individuals to make informed decisions. Awareness of personal rights regarding banking, fraud reporting, and data protection ensures proactive defense against threats. Combining knowledge with behavioral practices, technical tools, and monitoring creates a resilient security posture. Consistency in vigilance, education, and proactive management fortifies defenses over time. Protecting financial data is an ongoing responsibility that integrates awareness, action, and informed decision-making. Financial literacy is both a shield and a guide for long-term security.

Securing financial data is a continuous process that combines awareness, vigilance, and proactive measures. Awareness of potential threats, including phishing, malware, and unsecured networks, drives the adoption of safe practices. Regular monitoring of accounts, strong authentication, and careful management of digital transactions help prevent unauthorized access. Combining technical tools with disciplined behavior strengthens defenses against fraud. Understanding the evolving tactics of cybercriminals allows individuals to stay ahead of threats. Consistent attention and informed decision-making create a resilient financial security posture.

Planning for potential financial breaches is essential. Awareness of incident response steps, such as reporting fraud, freezing accounts, and alerting credit bureaus, ensures rapid mitigation. Having emergency contacts for banks, credit card issuers, and cybersecurity resources enables swift action if an incident occurs. Combining preparation with strong preventive measures reduces the impact of any compromise. Practicing these steps and reviewing them periodically ensures readiness. Being prepared transforms potential panic into a controlled response. Proactive planning ensures that financial data remains as secure as possible even under adverse circumstances.

Education and self-awareness are critical components of long-term financial protection. Awareness of common scams, evolving threats, and new security technologies empowers individuals to make informed choices. Continuous learning, combined with application of best practices, reinforces overall defenses. Users who actively seek knowledge are less likely to fall victim to fraud. Integrating education with technical safeguards, secure behavior, and monitoring provides a comprehensive security approach. Informed users not only protect themselves but also influence safer practices within their families and communities.

Maintaining a culture of vigilance strengthens financial security across all digital and physical touchpoints. Awareness of personal and shared responsibility for safeguarding data ensures that both individual and collective assets are protected. Regularly revisiting security practices, monitoring accounts, and updating knowledge helps maintain high levels of protection. Combining consistent habits with proactive measures creates a resilient approach to financial security. Over time, disciplined attention transforms financial risk into manageable oversight. Security becomes not just a set of tools but a mindset integrated into daily financial activity.

CHAPTER .28

DIGITAL IDENTITY THEFT: HOW TO DETECT AND PREVENT IT

How to Protect Your Identity from Being Stolen and What to Do if It Happens to You

Digital identity theft occurs when cybercriminals gain unauthorized access to personal information, using it to commit fraud or impersonate the victim. Awareness of how identity theft happens is crucial for prevention. Personal information such as Social Security numbers, bank accounts, passwords, and health records can all be exploited. Cybercriminals use phishing emails, data breaches, malware, and social engineering to steal sensitive information. Understanding the methods used allows individuals to adopt proactive measures to protect themselves. Vigilance and informed habits form the foundation of digital identity protection.

Early detection is critical in minimizing the damage caused by identity theft. Awareness of warning signs, such as unfamiliar charges, suspicious emails, or unexpected account activity, enables prompt response. Regularly monitoring bank statements, credit card activity, and credit reports helps identify anomalies quickly. Using identity monitoring services provides additional layers of detection. The sooner suspicious activity is identified, the more effective mitigation measures will be. Proactive detection transforms a potentially devastating situation into a manageable problem.

Secure handling of personal information reduces exposure to identity theft. Awareness of what information is shared online, in emails, or through apps is crucial. Avoiding oversharing on social media and verifying website security before entering sensitive data limits potential risks. Using strong, unique passwords and multi-factor authentication protects accounts from unauthorized access. Awareness of phishing attempts and social engineering techniques further strengthens personal defenses. Combining secure digital habits with technical safeguards significantly reduces the risk of identity compromise.

Data breaches at companies and organizations are common sources of identity theft. Awareness of high-profile breaches and monitoring accounts linked to affected services is essential. Promptly changing passwords, enabling two-factor authentication, and reviewing account activity mitigates potential damage. Signing up for breach notification alerts allows timely action to protect personal data. Awareness of how breaches occur encourages proactive steps to minimize exposure. A combination of vigilance, technical measures, and timely action provides resilience against identity theft from external sources.

Recovery from identity theft requires structured and immediate action. Awareness of the necessary steps, such as reporting the theft to financial institutions, credit bureaus, and authorities, ensures swift mitigation. Placing fraud alerts or credit freezes prevents further unauthorized activity. Documenting all communications and monitoring affected accounts helps in resolving disputes. Promptly contacting relevant institutions reduces financial losses and restores control. Combining awareness, planning, and systematic action enables victims to regain security efficiently. Recovery is a structured process guided by knowledge, organization, and vigilance.

Passwords are the first line of defense against identity theft. Awareness of the risks associated with weak, reused, or easily guessed passwords drives the adoption of strong, unique credentials for each account. Using a reputable password manager helps manage complex passwords securely. Enabling multi-factor authentication adds an additional layer of protection against unauthorized access. Regularly updating passwords and avoiding sharing credentials ensures accounts remain secure. Strong password practices significantly reduce the risk of identity compromise.

Phishing attacks are a primary method for cybercriminals to steal personal information. Awareness of phishing tactics, such as fraudulent emails, fake login pages, and deceptive links, allows users to avoid being tricked. Always verifying sender identities and avoiding clicking on suspicious links protects sensitive information. Training oneself and family members on phishing recognition strengthens overall defenses. Combining cautious behavior with technical safeguards, like email filters and security software, creates a robust barrier against these attacks. Proactive vigilance against phishing prevents unauthorized access to personal accounts.

Monitoring credit reports and financial accounts is essential for detecting identity theft early. Awareness of irregularities, such as unfamiliar accounts, unexpected inquiries, or unusual transactions, can reveal potential compromise. Many credit bureaus provide free annual reports, and subscribing to credit monitoring services adds an extra layer of vigilance. Promptly addressing anomalies prevents escalation and financial damage. Combining monitoring with strong account security and immediate response forms a comprehensive identity protection strategy. Consistent observation of financial and credit activity strengthens early detection and prevention.

Social media and online presence management are key for protecting digital identity. Awareness of what personal information is publicly accessible reduces vulnerability to impersonation and social engineering attacks. Limiting shared details, reviewing privacy settings, and controlling connections on social platforms prevents data misuse. Avoiding oversharing and using caution when interacting with strangers online further mitigates risks. A conscious approach to online presence enhances overall security posture. Managing social media with intent protects against identity theft and digital exploitation.

Securing devices and networks is fundamental to preventing identity theft. Awareness of malware, key-loggers, and unsecured Wi-Fi networks informs safe digital behavior. Installing security software, enabling firewalls, and keeping operating systems updated reduces vulnerabilities. Avoiding public Wi-Fi for sensitive transactions and using VPNs when necessary protects data transmission. Physical security measures, such as device locks and encryption, further enhance protection. Combining technical and behavioral safeguards ensures personal data remains confidential and less susceptible to theft.

Identity theft can occur through compromised email accounts, which often serve as gateways to other sensitive information. Awareness of the importance of securing email accounts is crucial for preventing further exploitation. Enabling two-factor authentication, using strong passwords, and monitoring login activity reduces risk. Avoiding access to email on shared or public devices prevents unauthorized access. Regularly reviewing security settings and recovery options ensures accounts remain under your control. Securing email accounts acts as a foundation for broader digital identity protection.

Financial accounts require heightened vigilance against identity theft. Awareness of transaction patterns, unexpected charges, and unusual account activity allows early detection. Using alerts, notifications, and credit monitoring tools enhances situational awareness. Promptly reporting any suspicious transactions prevents further unauthorized activity and minimizes financial loss. Maintaining strong authentication and secure access practices further strengthens account protection. Consistent attention to financial accounts reduces exposure to identity theft and fraud. Vigilance is essential in safeguarding monetary assets.

Personal identification numbers (PINs) and security questions are often targeted by cybercriminals. Awareness of the risks of predictable or easily discovered information drives the use of secure, unique PINs and answers. Avoiding obvious choices, such as birthdays or common words, increases security. Storing this information securely and not sharing it unnecessarily reduces potential compromise. Combining secure PINs with multi-factor authentication adds another layer of protection. Careful management of these access points ensures that sensitive accounts remain secure. Protecting secondary security measures is as important as safeguarding passwords.

Medical and health information is increasingly digitized, making it vulnerable to identity theft. Awareness of how health records, insurance information, and prescription histories can be exploited informs protective strategies. Using secure patient portals, strong authentication, and privacy-conscious communication reduces exposure. Avoid sharing sensitive medical details unless necessary, and monitor accounts for unauthorized activity. Combining vigilance with encrypted communications and regular review of health accounts strengthens protection. Protecting health information preserves both privacy and identity integrity.

Recovery planning is critical in case digital identity is compromised. Awareness of necessary steps, such as reporting fraud, freezing credit, and contacting relevant institutions, enables rapid mitigation. Documenting incidents and maintaining communication records ensures that restoration efforts are organized and effective. Prompt action limits financial and personal damage. Recovery strategies should be regularly reviewed and updated to adapt to evolving threats. Combining awareness, preparation, and systematic action ensures that victims regain control efficiently and securely.

Educating oneself about emerging identity theft tactics is crucial for ongoing protection. Awareness of new phishing techniques, data breaches, and social engineering scams allows individuals to adapt their security practices. Following reputable cybersecurity sources, subscribing to alerts, and participating in training programs strengthens overall awareness. Combining knowledge with practical measures, such as secure passwords and vigilant account monitoring, creates a robust defense. Staying informed prevents complacency and ensures that protective strategies remain effective. Continuous learning transforms potential vulnerability into proactive security.

Secure device management is a critical factor in identity theft prevention. Awareness of malware, spyware, and unauthorized access encourages responsible use of computers, smartphones, and tablets. Installing security software, keeping operating systems updated, and encrypting sensitive files limits exposure. Avoiding public or shared devices for accessing personal accounts reduces the risk of compromise. Using device locks, secure authentication, and careful app management further strengthens protection. Thoughtful device management ensures that sensitive information remains under personal control.

Social media privacy is a key component of protecting digital identity. Awareness of what is publicly visible on profiles, posts, and connections helps prevent exploitation. Limiting personal information, adjusting privacy settings, and avoiding oversharing reduces opportunities for identity theft. Being cautious about friend requests, messages, and third-party app integrations further protects information. Combining careful online behavior with privacy settings provides layered protection. Maintaining control over online social interactions is essential to securing one's digital identity.

Data breach response is essential for mitigating identity theft risks. Awareness of breaches affecting personal accounts allows for timely action, such as changing passwords and enabling two-factor authentication. Reviewing affected accounts, monitoring credit reports, and placing alerts or freezes where appropriate reduces potential harm. Reporting incidents to relevant authorities ensures proper documentation and support for recovery. Combining rapid response with proactive monitoring strengthens resilience against identity theft. Swift, informed action transforms a breach from a potentially catastrophic event into a manageable challenge.

Behavioral habits play a significant role in preventing identity theft. Awareness of daily digital practices, such as careful email handling, password hygiene, and cautious online interactions, reduces exposure to threats. Developing a habit of skepticism toward unsolicited requests and maintaining organized security routines strengthens protection. Combining consistent behaviors with technical tools and monitoring ensures comprehensive defense. Mindful digital habits are as important as technology in securing personal identity. Over time, disciplined behavior forms the foundation of lasting digital safety.

Preventing digital identity theft requires a combination of awareness, vigilance, and proactive measures. Awareness of phishing schemes, weak passwords, data breaches, and social engineering attacks enables individuals to adopt effective security practices. Using strong, unique passwords, enabling multi-factor authentication, and monitoring accounts regularly reduces vulnerability. Securing devices, managing social media privacy, and employing credit monitoring services strengthens protection. Combining technical safeguards with disciplined behavior creates a comprehensive defense against identity theft. Proactive habits ensure that personal information remains under control and less susceptible to exploitation.

Recovery planning is just as important as prevention. Awareness of steps such as reporting fraud to financial institutions, contacting credit bureaus, and freezing compromised accounts ensures rapid mitigation. Documenting all communications and maintaining a record of actions taken supports efficient resolution. Prompt action reduces both financial and personal damage. Combining preparation with ongoing vigilance ensures that even if identity theft occurs, it can be addressed effectively. A structured response transforms potential chaos into a controlled recovery process.

Education and continuous learning are critical for long-term identity protection. Awareness of evolving cyber threats, new attack techniques, and recommended protective measures empowers individuals to adapt. Following cybersecurity news, participating in training, and updating personal security habits reinforce a proactive approach. Integrating knowledge with practical safeguards ensures that identity protection is comprehensive and resilient. Informed individuals are better equipped to anticipate threats and respond effectively. Continuous education transforms awareness into actionable security practices.

Collaboration and sharing knowledge also strengthen defenses against identity theft. Awareness of risks among family members, friends, and colleagues encourages responsible online behavior collectively. Educating others about phishing, secure password practices, and account monitoring multiplies the protective effect. Creating a culture of cybersecurity awareness helps prevent careless behavior that could expose sensitive information. Combining individual vigilance with collective awareness enhances overall safety. Shared knowledge and mutual support create a stronger defense against identity theft.

REFLECTION:

Reflecting on digital identity theft, I've realized that awareness and proactive habits are the most powerful tools for protection. Understanding threats, securing accounts, and monitoring activity empower individuals to maintain control over their personal information. I've observed that continuous learning, combined with disciplined digital behavior, greatly reduces the likelihood and impact of identity theft. Protecting digital identity requires a holistic approach that integrates technical safeguards, personal vigilance, and education. Knowledge, preparation, and consistency transform vulnerability into resilience. By cultivating these habits, individuals can navigate the digital world with confidence and security.

"Your identity is your most valuable asset; protect it with awareness, vigilance, and action."
— Unknown

CHAPTER .29

THE IMPORTANCE OF BACKUP AND DISASTER RECOVERY

Why Regular Backups and a Recovery Plan Are Crucial in Case of Cyber Incidents.

Backups are an essential component of any cybersecurity strategy, providing a safety net in case of system failures or data loss. Awareness of potential threats, such as ransomware, hardware failures, or accidental deletion, highlights the necessity of regular backups. Creating copies of critical files and storing them securely ensures that data can be restored when needed. Both individuals and organizations benefit from adopting consistent backup practices. Combining multiple storage methods, such as local drives, network-attached storage, and cloud solutions, strengthens protection. Regular backups reduce the risk of permanent data loss and provide peace of mind.

Disaster recovery planning extends beyond simple backups, encompassing strategies for restoring systems and operations after an incident. Awareness of potential disruptions, from cyber attacks to natural disasters, informs the creation of a comprehensive recovery plan. Establishing recovery priorities, identifying critical systems, and documenting procedures ensures that recovery efforts are efficient. Testing recovery plans regularly confirms that they are effective and identifies areas for improvement. A well-prepared plan minimizes downtime and ensures continuity of operations. Combining backup strategies with structured recovery planning creates resilience against unexpected events.

Choosing the right backup methods depends on data type, volume, and access requirements. Awareness of options such as full, incremental, and differential backups allows users to select the most appropriate strategy. Cloud-based backups offer convenience, offsite protection, and scalability, while local backups provide rapid access and control. Combining multiple approaches ensures redundancy and reduces the risk of total data loss. Encryption of backup data adds an additional layer of security, preventing unauthorized access. Thoughtful selection and management of backup solutions are key to long-term data protection.

Automating backup processes enhances consistency and reliability. Awareness of scheduling tools, backup software, and automated workflows ensures that data is regularly copied without relying on human intervention. Regular monitoring of backup logs confirms successful completion and identifies errors. Automation reduces the chance of missed backups, which could leave critical data unprotected. Combining automation with manual oversight strengthens overall data integrity. Consistent, reliable backups form a core pillar of cybersecurity and disaster recovery strategies.

Recovery planning should also include communication strategies for incidents affecting multiple stakeholders. Awareness of who needs to be informed, from employees to clients or family members, ensures timely and accurate dissemination of information. Clear communication helps manage expectations, maintain trust, and coordinate response efforts. Documenting responsibilities and establishing contact protocols reduces confusion during crises. Integrating communication planning with technical recovery procedures provides a holistic approach to incident management. Effective communication complements technical solutions to ensure that recovery is orderly and efficient.

Regular testing of backup files ensures that data can actually be restored when needed. Awareness of potential corruption, incomplete backups, or outdated versions emphasizes the need for periodic verification. Running test restores confirms the integrity of backup files and verifies that procedures function as intended. Identifying and correcting issues during testing prevents unpleasant surprises during real incidents. Combining regular testing with monitoring and reporting strengthens the reliability of backup systems. A proactive approach to testing ensures that data recovery is swift and dependable when emergencies occur.

Offsite and cloud backups protect against localized disasters. Awareness of risks such as fire, theft, or physical damage underscores the importance of storing copies in separate locations. Cloud storage offers scalable, geographically diverse solutions that maintain accessibility even when local systems fail. Local backups complement cloud solutions, providing quick restoration without relying solely on internet access. Combining offsite and local strategies creates redundancy, reducing the likelihood of total data loss. Thoughtful placement of backups ensures resilience against both digital and physical threats.

Versioning and retention policies help maintain the most relevant and recoverable data. Awareness of the need to store multiple versions of files protects against accidental deletions or ransomware encryption. Retention policies determine how long backups are kept and which versions are prioritized for restoration. This balance between storage capacity and recovery requirements ensures that essential data is always available. Combining versioning with regular backups adds a layer of security against unexpected changes or corruption. A well-designed backup retention plan ensures operational continuity and mitigates potential losses.

Training individuals on proper backup and recovery procedures is essential for effectiveness. Awareness of roles, responsibilities, and execution steps ensures that backups are performed consistently and restoration is handled efficiently. Employees or household members should understand the tools, schedules, and verification steps involved in backup processes. Periodic refresher sessions reinforce best practices and address evolving threats. Combining education with automation and monitoring enhances overall reliability. Knowledgeable participants ensure that backup systems function as intended and support disaster recovery objectives.

Backup security is critical to prevent unauthorized access or tampering. Awareness of encryption, secure storage, and access control safeguards sensitive data from breaches. Both cloud and local backups should employ robust security measures, including password protection, encryption, and restricted access. Regular audits of backup permissions and logs ensure ongoing protection. Combining secure storage practices with consistent monitoring prevents data compromise and supports compliance with privacy regulations. Protecting backup data is an integral part of an overall cybersecurity and disaster recovery strategy.

Ransomware attacks highlight the critical need for robust backup systems. Awareness of ransomware's ability to encrypt live files and demand payment underscores the importance of isolated, secure backups. By maintaining offline or versioned copies of critical data, users can restore systems without succumbing to ransom demands. Combining proactive backups with disaster recovery plans ensures rapid operational recovery. Regularly updating backup strategies to reflect emerging threats strengthens resilience. Preparedness transforms ransomware incidents from catastrophic losses into manageable recovery events.

Automated backup solutions reduce human error and increase consistency. Awareness of potential oversight, such as missed manual backups or incorrect file selection, highlights the benefits of automation. Scheduled backups, coupled with monitoring alerts, ensure that critical data is consistently protected. Automation allows IT teams or individuals to focus on other security measures without sacrificing data protection. Combining automation with periodic verification balances efficiency and reliability. Thoughtful implementation of automated systems improves the overall effectiveness of backup strategies.

Integration with broader cybersecurity measures enhances recovery capability. Awareness of the interdependence between security tools, such as firewalls, antivirus programs, and backup systems, informs a holistic approach. Ensuring that backups are compatible with disaster recovery procedures streamlines response during incidents. Coordinating recovery with security monitoring and incident response plans minimizes downtime and data loss. Combining proactive defenses with tested recovery procedures creates a resilient digital environment. Integrated strategies improve both prevention and recovery outcomes.

Documenting backup and disaster recovery procedures ensures clarity and efficiency. Awareness of detailed steps, responsible personnel, and tools involved prevents confusion during crises. Clear documentation supports consistent execution, enables new team members to follow protocols, and facilitates audits or compliance checks. Periodically reviewing and updating documentation ensures alignment with evolving systems and threats. Combining documentation with training and testing improves overall preparedness. Well-documented procedures provide a roadmap for rapid and effective recovery.

Scalability is essential as data volume grows over time. Awareness of storage needs, file growth, and evolving digital infrastructure informs decisions about backup capacity and technology. Scalable solutions, whether cloud-based or on-premises, accommodate increasing demands without sacrificing performance. Regularly reviewing storage requirements ensures that backups remain efficient, secure, and cost-effective. Combining scalability with automation and monitoring maintains consistent protection as data environments expand. Planning for growth ensures that backup and recovery strategies remain effective long-term.

Disaster recovery planning should include prioritization of critical systems and data. Awareness of which files, applications, and processes are essential allows for an efficient restoration sequence. Establishing recovery time objectives (RTO) and recovery point objectives (RPO) guides decision-making during a crisis. Prioritizing high-impact systems ensures that operations resume quickly and with minimal disruption. Combining planning with thorough testing and monitoring enhances the effectiveness of recovery efforts. Thoughtful prioritization reduces downtime and mitigates the impact of cyber incidents or system failures.

Communication plans are integral to effective disaster recovery. Awareness of who needs to be informed, including employees, clients, vendors, and authorities, ensures timely and coordinated response. Clear communication protocols prevent confusion, support collaboration, and maintain trust during recovery operations. Combining communication planning with technical recovery steps improves overall efficiency. Documented contact lists and predefined messaging templates streamline notifications during emergencies. Effective communication, alongside robust technical procedures, enhances the organization's ability to recover quickly.

Periodic drills and simulations strengthen readiness for cyber incidents. Awareness of potential failure points and recovery challenges allows teams to practice response in a controlled environment. Simulations help identify gaps in procedures, evaluate resource allocation, and improve coordination. Combining drills with feedback and updates ensures continuous improvement of backup and recovery strategies. Practicing recovery scenarios prepares individuals and teams for real-world events. Rehearsals foster confidence, reduce errors, and improve response time during actual incidents.

Legal and regulatory compliance often requires proper backup and disaster recovery measures. Awareness of relevant data protection laws, industry standards, and contractual obligations ensures that backup procedures meet required criteria. Documentation, testing, and secure storage of backups support compliance efforts. Combining regulatory awareness with proactive technical and behavioral practices minimizes legal and financial risks. Maintaining compliance also reinforces trust with clients, partners, and stakeholders. Adhering to regulatory requirements strengthens both security and credibility.

A culture of continuous improvement ensures backup and recovery systems remain effective. Awareness of emerging threats, new technologies, and evolving organizational needs drives periodic reassessment. Updating backup strategies, recovery plans, and staff training ensures alignment with current risks and operational demands. Combining learning, testing, and adaptation cultivates resilience in the face of change. Continuous evaluation enhances efficiency, reliability, and confidence in disaster recovery capabilities. A proactive approach to improvement transforms backup and recovery from a reactive necessity into a strategic advantage.

Backup and disaster recovery are essential for maintaining control over your digital environment. Awareness of potential threats, from cyberattacks to hardware failures, underscores the importance of preparation. Regularly backing up data, testing restoration procedures, and maintaining clear recovery plans ensures that critical information is never permanently lost. Combining technical safeguards with organizational processes creates a resilient framework for data protection. Consistent attention to backups transforms potential crises into manageable events. Preparedness and vigilance are key to safeguarding information and sustaining operational continuity.

A proactive mindset strengthens both personal and organizational recovery capabilities. Awareness of vulnerabilities encourages ongoing evaluation and refinement of backup strategies. Planning ahead, documenting procedures, and training individuals or teams ensures that recovery can be executed efficiently. Combining preparedness with vigilance reduces the impact of unexpected events and accelerates restoration. Recovery is not merely reactive; it is a strategic measure that protects both assets and confidence. Taking proactive steps transforms uncertainty into control and resilience.

Education and training play a crucial role in effective disaster recovery. Awareness of the tools, responsibilities, and processes involved empowers individuals to act decisively during incidents. Regular drills, refresher courses, and updates on emerging threats ensure that everyone involved is prepared. Combining education with practical implementation reinforces consistency and reliability. Knowledgeable participants execute recovery strategies effectively, minimizing downtime and data loss. Cultivating a culture of continuous learning ensures that backup and recovery practices remain robust over time.

Integration with broader cybersecurity practices amplifies the effectiveness of backup and recovery. Awareness of how backups complement antivirus programs, firewalls, and access controls ensures a cohesive defense. Coordinating backup strategies with threat detection and incident response plans reduces overall risk. Combining technical defenses with structured recovery protocols provides a comprehensive security posture. Resilience emerges from the synergy of prevention, monitoring, and recovery measures. Integration strengthens both proactive and reactive capabilities, safeguarding data and operations comprehensively.

Chapter .30

How to Spot and Avoid Malware and Spyware

How Malicious Software Can Compromise Your Data, and How to Prevent Its Installation

Malware and spyware are malicious programs designed to infiltrate your systems, steal sensitive information, or disrupt operations. Awareness of the different types of malware, including viruses, trojans, ransomware, and key-loggers, is critical for prevention. These threats can enter through email attachments, infected downloads, compromised websites, or external devices. Understanding how malware operates enables users to recognize suspicious activity early and take action. Combining vigilance with proactive security measures reduces the likelihood of infection. Protecting systems against malware is a fundamental aspect of maintaining digital safety.

Recognizing symptoms of malware infection is an essential first step in mitigation. Awareness of unusual system behavior, such as slow performance, unexpected pop-ups, or unauthorized software installation, can indicate compromise. Frequent crashes, modified files, or unusual network activity are additional warning signs. Monitoring for these symptoms allows users to respond promptly and limit damage. Combining observation with proper diagnostic tools enhances early detection. Early recognition increases the chances of successful removal and prevents further exploitation.

Safe browsing practices reduce exposure to malware and spyware. Awareness of risky websites, malicious ads, and unverified downloads guides safer online behavior. Avoiding clickbait, scanning links before opening, and downloading software only from trusted sources minimizes infection risk. Using browser security features and keeping software updated further strengthens protection. Combining cautious browsing habits with technological safeguards ensures a lower likelihood of compromise. Consistent attention to online behavior significantly reduces malware exposure.

Email remains a major vector for malware distribution. Awareness of phishing attempts, suspicious attachments, and unknown senders is essential for email safety. Verifying sender identities, avoiding unsolicited attachments, and using email filters reduces risk. Combining email vigilance with endpoint security, such as antivirus programs, provides layered protection. Educating oneself and others about email-based threats improves organizational and personal cybersecurity. Careful email management prevents many malware infections before they occur.

Regular software updates and patch management are vital defenses against malware. Awareness of vulnerabilities in operating systems, applications, and plugins informs timely updates. Cybercriminals exploit outdated software to gain unauthorized access, install malware, or exfiltrate data. Enabling automatic updates, reviewing security patches, and removing unsupported applications strengthens defenses. Combining software hygiene with safe browsing, email caution, and security software creates a comprehensive approach to malware prevention. Staying current ensures that known vulnerabilities are addressed before they can be exploited.

Antivirus and anti-malware software form a critical line of defense against malicious programs. Awareness of reputable software options, regular scans, and real-time protection ensures that malware is detected and neutralized early. Configuring software to automatically update virus definitions keeps defenses current against emerging threats. Combining software protection with safe online practices reduces the likelihood of infection. Even sophisticated malware can often be blocked or contained when comprehensive security tools are in place. Layered defenses strengthen overall resilience against malware and spyware.

Behavioral awareness helps prevent accidental malware installation. Awareness of suspicious downloads, unfamiliar email attachments, and unsolicited prompts encourages cautious behavior. Avoiding pirated software, cracked programs, or unverified mobile apps reduces exposure to hidden threats. Combining vigilance with proper system permissions and user account controls minimizes the risk of accidental installation. Educating users about the tactics cybercriminals use to distribute malware enhances their ability to avoid infection. Awareness and careful action are as important as technical safeguards in preventing malware attacks.

Network security is another critical factor in preventing malware spread. Awareness of unsecured Wi-Fi networks, unencrypted connections, and open ports highlights potential vulnerabilities. Using firewalls, VPNs, and secure Wi-Fi passwords protects against unauthorized access. Monitoring network traffic for anomalies can identify compromised systems early. Combining network security with device-level protection ensures comprehensive malware defense. A secure network environment reduces both exposure and impact of potential malware infections.

Social engineering techniques are often used to trick users into installing malware. Awareness of tactics such as fake tech support calls, phishing messages, or deceptive pop-ups empowers individuals to respond cautiously. Verifying the legitimacy of requests before taking action prevents accidental compromise. Combining skepticism with proper verification procedures protects against both digital and human-targeted attacks. Education on social engineering strengthens the overall cybersecurity posture. Recognizing manipulation attempts is key to avoiding malware installation.

Regular system backups provide an additional layer of protection against malware and spyware. Awareness of the risks posed by ransomware and destructive malware emphasizes the importance of maintaining up-to-date backups. Should an infection occur, restoring clean copies of files minimizes data loss and reduces downtime. Combining backup practices with robust malware defenses ensures continuity in both personal and professional environments. Proactive backup strategies transform potential disasters into recoverable events. Consistency in both prevention and recovery safeguards critical data against malicious software threats.

Educating all users about malware risks strengthens overall defense. Awareness of common attack methods, suspicious file types, and deceptive online behaviors empowers users to recognize threats early. Training on safe email practices, secure downloads, and cautious browsing habits minimizes accidental infections. Combining education with technical safeguards, such as antivirus programs and firewalls, creates a robust layered defense. Continuous awareness and reinforcement of security principles improve overall resilience. Knowledgeable users become active participants in malware prevention rather than passive targets.

Mobile devices require special attention due to their widespread use and portability. Awareness of the risks associated with mobile apps, public Wi-Fi, and phishing messages helps prevent malware infections. Installing trusted apps only, keeping the operating system updated, and using mobile security software reduce vulnerabilities. Enabling device encryption and secure lock screens adds additional layers of protection. Combining mobile security practices with general cybersecurity habits ensures that smartphones and tablets remain safe. Vigilance on mobile platforms is essential, as these devices often contain sensitive personal and financial information.

Ransomware is one of the most destructive forms of malware, demanding special attention. Awareness of ransomware delivery methods, such as malicious email attachments or compromised websites, guides safe practices. Maintaining offline and cloud backups, enabling strong authentication, and avoiding suspicious downloads reduce the risk of paying ransom or losing data. Combining preventative measures with a prepared response plan ensures that systems can be restored quickly if an infection occurs. Knowledge of ransomware behavior and recovery techniques transforms a potentially catastrophic event into a manageable situation. Preparedness is the key to mitigating ransomware impact effectively.

Browser security is critical for preventing malware from entering systems through web activity. Awareness of malicious ads, unverified downloads, and insecure websites informs safer browsing practices. Enabling browser security settings, blocking pop-ups, and using content filters reduces the likelihood of infection. Avoiding clicking on unknown links, especially in unsolicited messages, strengthens defense. Combining safe browsing with antivirus and firewall protection creates multiple layers of security. Vigilance during online activity prevents malware from exploiting common web vulnerabilities.

Regular monitoring and maintenance of devices are essential for malware prevention. Awareness of unusual system behavior, such as slowed performance, frequent crashes, or unexpected network activity, allows early detection of infections. Running periodic scans, reviewing security logs, and updating software maintain system health. Combining consistent monitoring with proactive education and technical defenses reduces the risk of long-term compromise. Preventive maintenance ensures that malware, spyware, and other threats are identified and neutralized before causing major damage. Routine vigilance protects both data and system integrity.

Using sandboxing and virtual environments can minimize malware risk. Awareness of isolating untrusted files or applications in a controlled environment prevents infections from spreading to the main system. Testing suspicious programs safely allows users to evaluate risks without compromising critical data. Combining sandboxing with antivirus tools and monitoring practices enhances overall protection. This approach is particularly useful for advanced users or organizations handling potentially risky downloads. Isolation strategies act as an additional layer of defense against malware and spyware threats.

Email attachments and downloads remain one of the most common infection vectors. Awareness of potentially malicious file types, such as executable (.exe) or macro-enabled documents, helps prevent accidental installation. Verifying the sender and scanning attachments with security software ensures safe handling. Avoiding auto-download features and educating users about phishing and malware-laden emails further mitigates risk. Combining cautious behavior with technical safeguards strengthens email security. Vigilance in handling attachments protects both personal and organizational systems.

Network segmentation enhances protection against malware spread. Awareness of which devices or systems are critical helps prioritize network security measures. Isolating sensitive systems from general-use networks reduces the impact of potential infections. Firewalls, VLANs, and access controls further limit malware propagation. Combining segmentation with monitoring, intrusion detection, and endpoint security ensures comprehensive coverage. Strategic network management minimizes exposure and prevents localized malware from becoming a widespread problem.

Patch management is vital to reducing malware vulnerabilities. Awareness of software updates and security patches prevents attackers from exploiting known weaknesses. Regularly applying patches to operating systems, applications, and plugins closes security gaps. Combining patch management with real-time monitoring, antivirus software, and backup strategies ensures a multi-layered defense. Ignoring updates creates unnecessary risks that malware can exploit. Consistent patching strengthens overall system resilience against malicious software.

Behavioral monitoring can identify malware that bypasses technical defenses. Awareness of unusual user activity, network anomalies, or unexpected system processes can signal infection. Combining behavioral analysis with automated alerts and security tools enables early detection. Training individuals to recognize subtle signs of compromise enhances organizational security posture. Continuous vigilance ensures malware is addressed quickly and does not escalate. Monitoring behavior is an often-overlooked but critical layer of protection.

Preventing malware and spyware requires a holistic approach that combines technology, behavior, and education. Awareness of common infection vectors, suspicious files, and phishing tactics is essential. Using antivirus software, firewalls, secure networks, and sandboxing creates multiple layers of protection. Regularly updating software, monitoring system behavior, and practicing safe browsing reduce the likelihood of infection. Backups and recovery strategies ensure that data can be restored in case a threat bypasses preventive measures. A comprehensive approach transforms potential vulnerability into a resilient defense.

User education is equally critical for ongoing protection. Awareness of the tactics cybercriminals employ empowers individuals to recognize threats before they cause harm. Training on safe email practices, cautious downloads, and secure online behavior complements technical defenses. Combining education with monitoring, software tools, and proactive security habits strengthens overall resilience. Informed users act as the first line of defense against malware and spyware. Continuous learning ensures that security practices evolve alongside emerging threats.

Device and network hygiene forms the foundation of malware prevention. Awareness of potential vulnerabilities, such as outdated operating systems, unpatched applications, and unsecured networks, guides protective measures. Regular maintenance, updates, and secure configuration reduce opportunities for exploitation. Combining vigilant device management with backup strategies, network security, and monitoring enhances overall digital safety. Consistent attention to system integrity prevents malware from gaining a foothold. Maintaining a clean, secure environment is a proactive defense against malicious software.

Proactive monitoring and incident response are vital to mitigating the impact of malware. Awareness of abnormal system behavior, unexpected network traffic, or unauthorized access enables early detection. Combining monitoring with rapid response protocols, such as quarantining infected systems and restoring from backups, minimizes damage. Preparing for incidents ahead of time ensures that threats are managed efficiently and effectively. This proactive approach transforms potential crises into controlled recovery scenarios. Vigilance and preparation are key to limiting the consequences of malware attacks.

Reflection:

Reflecting on malware and spyware prevention, I've learned that vigilance and layered defense are indispensable. Awareness of potential threats, combined with technical safeguards, informed behavior, and continuous learning, significantly reduces risk. I've observed that proactive monitoring, education, and robust backup strategies provide both protection and confidence. Preventing malware is not about a single tool or practice but a combination of habits, policies, and preparedness. Consistency, awareness, and adaptability are the most reliable safeguards against digital threats. By embracing these principles, individuals and organizations can navigate the digital landscape safely.

"Security is not a product, but a practice; protect yourself through knowledge, vigilance, and preparation."
— Unknown

CHAPTER .31

CYBER HYGIENE: BEST PRACTICES FOR EVERYDAY DIGITAL SAFETY

Incorporating Simple Habits into Your Routine That Will Significantly Improve Your Cybersecurity

Cyber hygiene refers to the regular practices and precautions that individuals take to maintain system health and protect digital information. Awareness of potential threats and common vulnerabilities informs these daily habits. Regularly updating software, installing security patches, and using strong authentication methods are core elements of cyber hygiene. Combining technical measures with disciplined behavior reduces the likelihood of breaches and data loss. Good cyber hygiene extends beyond personal devices to include cloud services, email, and social media accounts. Consistently applying these habits creates a foundation for long-term digital security.

Strong password management is a central aspect of effective cyber hygiene. Awareness of risks posed by weak, reused, or predictable passwords drives the adoption of strong, unique credentials for each account. Using password managers simplifies the creation and storage of complex passwords while maintaining security. Enabling multi-factor authentication adds an additional layer of protection. Regularly reviewing and updating passwords ensures continued protection against evolving threats. Consistent password discipline is one of the most impactful daily cybersecurity habits.

Regular monitoring and auditing of accounts support cyber hygiene. Awareness of unusual activity, such as unexpected login attempts, unauthorized transactions, or unusual emails, allows for early detection of potential threats. Setting up alerts, reviewing account statements, and auditing privacy settings provides insight into digital security status. Combining monitoring with proactive measures ensures timely mitigation of issues. This practice extends to both personal and professional digital environments. Vigilant oversight reduces vulnerability and strengthens overall cybersecurity posture.

Safe browsing and cautious online behavior are fundamental components of cyber hygiene. Awareness of phishing websites, malicious links, and untrusted downloads guides safer decision-making online. Using updated browsers, enabling security features, and verifying website authenticity reduce exposure to cyber threats. Combining behavioral caution with technical safeguards, such as antivirus software and firewalls, creates layered protection. Educating oneself and family members about online risks reinforces these practices. Maintaining disciplined browsing habits prevents many cyber incidents before they occur.

Device maintenance and security form another pillar of cyber hygiene. Awareness of malware, spyware, and unauthorized access informs responsible device management. Regular software updates, secure configuration, and device encryption reduce the risk of compromise. Avoiding public networks for sensitive tasks and monitoring connected devices enhances overall security. Combining technical protections with behavioral vigilance ensures comprehensive protection. Proper maintenance of both hardware and software sustains system integrity and minimizes security risks.

Email hygiene is essential for everyday cybersecurity. Awareness of phishing attempts, suspicious attachments, and unknown senders helps prevent malware and identity theft. Using spam filters, verifying sender authenticity, and avoiding unsolicited links protects sensitive information. Combining email vigilance with strong passwords and multi-factor authentication strengthens defenses. Educating users about common email threats enhances both personal and organizational security. Consistently practicing safe email habits reduces the risk of compromise.

Regular data backups are a cornerstone of cyber hygiene. Awareness of potential data loss from system failures, ransomware, or accidental deletion drives proactive backup practices. Using automated backups, cloud storage, and offline copies ensures that critical data remains recoverable. Combining backup routines with secure storage and encryption further protects information. Consistent backup habits minimize the impact of incidents and ensure continuity. Maintaining up-to-date backups transforms unexpected disruptions into manageable events.

Device authentication and access control are critical for maintaining cyber hygiene. Awareness of unauthorized access risks motivates the use of strong passwords, biometric verification, and access restrictions. Limiting administrative privileges and using separate accounts for different purposes reduces exposure. Combining authentication measures with monitoring tools and encryption safeguards sensitive data. Educating all users about access control best practices reinforces security. Consistently applying access restrictions strengthens both personal and organizational defenses.

Social media hygiene helps protect digital identity and privacy. Awareness of what information is publicly visible, who can access it, and how it can be misused guides responsible online behavior. Limiting personal information shared, managing privacy settings, and avoiding oversharing reduces vulnerability. Combining cautious social media use with strong account security, such as two-factor authentication, protects against identity theft. Regularly reviewing account activity and connections further enhances safety. Practicing social media hygiene ensures that personal information remains secure in an increasingly connected world.

Network security is a key component of everyday cyber hygiene. Awareness of risks posed by unsecured Wi-Fi, weak router passwords, and open ports informs protective measures. Using strong passwords, encryption, and firewalls on home and work networks reduces exposure. Combining network security with device-level protections ensures layered defense. Monitoring connected devices and network activity helps identify anomalies early. Maintaining secure networks protects all connected systems and preserves overall digital safety.

Regular software updates are fundamental to cyber hygiene. Awareness of vulnerabilities in operating systems, applications, and plugins highlights the importance of timely updates. Enabling automatic updates and reviewing patch notifications ensures that systems remain protected against known exploits. Combining updates with antivirus software and firewalls strengthens overall security. Neglecting updates creates openings for cybercriminals to exploit, making vigilance essential. Maintaining current software prevents threats from gaining a foothold in your digital environment.

Educating household members or employees reinforces cyber hygiene practices. Awareness of threats, safe online behavior, and system security measures empowers everyone to act responsibly. Conducting training sessions, sharing resources, and modeling good habits creates a culture of security. Combining education with practical safeguards improves compliance and reduces risk. Reinforcing cybersecurity awareness ensures that all users contribute to a safer digital environment. A well-informed community strengthens collective protection against cyber threats.

Safe download practices are crucial for maintaining system integrity. Awareness of the risks associated with unverified websites, file-sharing networks, and third-party apps guides safer decisions. Downloading only from trusted sources, scanning files with security software, and avoiding suspicious links prevents malware infections. Combining cautious download behavior with device and network protection ensures comprehensive security. Educating users about the potential consequences of unsafe downloads reinforces vigilance. Consistently practicing safe download habits preserves both system functionality and personal data.

Physical security complements digital cyber hygiene. Awareness of device theft, unauthorized access, and misplaced media emphasizes the need for physical safeguards. Using locks, secure storage, and controlled access prevents physical compromise of systems and sensitive information. Combining physical security with technical measures such as encryption and authentication ensures holistic protection. Regularly assessing physical security vulnerabilities strengthens overall cybersecurity posture. Protecting devices physically is as important as defending them digitally.

Incident response readiness is an essential aspect of cyber hygiene. Awareness of potential threats, unusual activity, and response protocols ensures quick mitigation of issues. Documenting procedures, assigning responsibilities, and testing response plans enhances preparedness. Combining technical tools with practiced human response reduces the impact of cyber incidents. Maintaining a culture of readiness allows individuals and organizations to recover quickly from unexpected security events. Cyber hygiene extends beyond prevention to include proactive preparation for potential incidents.

Password rotation and management are crucial for maintaining cyber hygiene. Awareness of the risks associated with stagnant or reused passwords motivates regular updates and the use of unique credentials for each account. Implementing password managers simplifies the creation, storage, and updating of strong passwords. Combining password hygiene with multi-factor authentication provides layered security. Regular audits of credentials ensure that outdated or compromised passwords are replaced promptly. Strong, dynamic password practices form the foundation for protecting digital identities.

Regular auditing of connected devices enhances security awareness. Awareness of all devices accessing networks, accounts, or cloud services helps identify unauthorized connections. Disconnecting unknown or unused devices and reviewing access logs reduces the risk of compromise. Combining auditing with authentication controls and network monitoring strengthens defenses. Educating users to recognize and report unusual devices promotes proactive security. Consistent device auditing prevents unnoticed vulnerabilities and maintains a secure environment.

Email security protocols play a critical role in daily cyber hygiene. Awareness of suspicious emails, phishing attempts, and malicious attachments informs safe practices. Using spam filters, verifying sender authenticity, and avoiding unsolicited downloads reduces infection risk. Combining careful email management with broader security measures ensures that sensitive information remains protected. Educating users about email-based threats enhances collective cybersecurity posture. Vigilant email habits are an ongoing and necessary component of digital safety.

Cloud storage hygiene is essential in modern digital routines. Awareness of who has access to files, permissions granted, and the security features of cloud platforms informs responsible usage. Using encryption, strong authentication, and regular access audits reduces the likelihood of data breaches. Combining cloud hygiene with local backups ensures redundancy and reliability. Regularly reviewing shared content and permissions prevents accidental exposure of sensitive information. Maintaining disciplined cloud practices protects both personal and organizational data.

Cyber hygiene also encompasses behavioral awareness when interacting online. Awareness of social engineering tactics, oversharing, and risky digital behavior guides safer choices. Limiting personal information exposure, verifying requests, and avoiding impulsive clicks strengthens security. Combining cautious online behavior with technical safeguards creates layered protection. Educating oneself and others about common attack methods reinforces cyber hygiene habits. Thoughtful digital behavior complements technical defenses and reduces the risk of compromise.

Maintaining consistent cyber hygiene requires discipline, awareness, and regular assessment. Awareness of daily routines, potential vulnerabilities, and emerging threats informs proactive behaviors. Combining technical safeguards, such as updated software, firewalls, and antivirus programs, with responsible digital habits reduces the risk of cyber incidents. Regularly reviewing passwords, device access, and online activity ensures ongoing protection. Educating household members, colleagues, or employees reinforces these practices and promotes a culture of security. Over time, consistent attention to cyber hygiene creates a resilient digital environment.

Integrating backups and recovery plans into daily routines further strengthens cyber hygiene. Awareness of the importance of regularly backing up data ensures that accidental loss or malware incidents can be mitigated quickly. Using cloud services, offline storage, and encrypted backups guarantees multiple layers of protection. Combining preventive measures with recovery readiness ensures that critical data remains accessible and secure. Preparedness transforms potential disruptions into manageable situations. Cyber hygiene is not only about prevention but also about resilience and recovery.

Monitoring and responding to unusual digital activity is a key habit in daily cybersecurity. Awareness of irregular account behavior, suspicious logins, or unexpected system changes allows early intervention. Combining monitoring with automated alerts, periodic reviews, and incident response procedures ensures timely mitigation. Consistently practicing this vigilance prevents minor issues from escalating into major breaches. Behavioral awareness complements technical measures to maintain a secure digital environment. By staying alert, users can detect and respond to threats effectively.

Education and continuous learning support long-term cyber hygiene. Awareness of emerging threats, best practices, and evolving technologies ensures that habits remain relevant and effective. Participating in training, following cybersecurity news, and sharing knowledge with others fosters a proactive mindset. Combining ongoing education with disciplined routines strengthens both individual and organizational cybersecurity. Knowledge empowers users to anticipate and avoid risks rather than react after incidents occur. Continuous learning ensures cyber hygiene evolves alongside the digital landscape.

CHAPTER .32

PROTECTING YOUR BUSINESS'S DATA: ESSENTIAL SECURITY PRACTICES FOR ENTREPRENEURS

Steps Small Business Owners Should Take to Safeguard Their Customers' and Employees' Data

Protecting business data is a critical responsibility for entrepreneurs, as breaches can damage reputation, finances, and customer trust. Awareness of common threats, including ransomware, phishing, and insider attacks, is essential for developing a strong security posture. Implementing robust technical safeguards, such as firewalls, antivirus software, and secure networks, provides the first layer of defense. Combining these measures with clear policies, employee training, and regular audits ensures comprehensive protection. Business data includes customer information, financial records, intellectual property, and operational details—all of which must be secured. A proactive approach to data security is fundamental to sustainable business growth.

Creating a comprehensive data security policy establishes expectations and guidelines for employees and contractors. Awareness of the types of data your business handles informs policy development. Policies should address password management, device usage, access controls, and acceptable use of company systems. Combining clear documentation with training and enforcement ensures that employees understand their responsibilities. Regularly reviewing and updating policies keeps them relevant as threats evolve. Well-defined policies create a foundation for disciplined and consistent data protection across the organization.

Securing networks and devices is critical to prevent unauthorized access. Awareness of potential vulnerabilities, such as unsecured Wi-Fi, outdated routers, or unpatched systems, informs preventative measures. Using strong passwords, encryption, and network segmentation reduces risk. Combining device security with employee training and endpoint protection ensures that both hardware and software are safeguarded. Regular monitoring of network traffic and system logs helps detect suspicious activity early. Network and device security form the backbone of a small business's cybersecurity strategy.

Employee training and awareness are essential for maintaining a secure business environment. Awareness of phishing, social engineering, and insider threats ensures that staff can recognize and respond to potential security risks. Conducting regular cybersecurity workshops, distributing best practice guidelines, and reinforcing safe behavior fosters a culture of vigilance. Combining technical safeguards with well-informed employees significantly reduces the likelihood of breaches. Consistent training ensures that everyone in the organization becomes an active participant in protecting sensitive data. Knowledgeable staff are a business's strongest defense against cyber threats.

Data backup and disaster recovery planning are vital for business continuity. Awareness of potential incidents, from ransomware attacks to hardware failures, informs backup strategy and recovery protocols. Regular automated backups, offsite storage, and encrypted cloud solutions ensure data can be restored quickly and securely. Combining preventive security measures with a tested disaster recovery plan minimizes downtime and financial loss. Employees should be trained in recovery procedures to respond effectively during incidents. Proactive backup and recovery strategies safeguard business operations and preserve customer trust.

Access control is a fundamental aspect of business data security. Awareness of who has access to sensitive files, databases, and systems helps prevent unauthorized usage. Implementing role-based access controls ensures that employees can only access the data necessary for their tasks. Combining access management with strong authentication methods, such as multi-factor authentication, further secures critical information. Regular audits of user accounts and permissions identify potential vulnerabilities before they are exploited. Effective access control reduces the risk of insider threats and external breaches.

Encryption is a key tool for safeguarding sensitive business data. Awareness of the risks posed by unencrypted files, emails, and communications highlights the importance of protecting information in transit and at rest. Using strong encryption protocols for customer records, financial data, and internal communications prevents unauthorized access. Combining encryption with secure storage solutions and access controls strengthens overall data security. Regularly updating encryption standards ensures protection against evolving threats. Encrypting critical business information mitigates the impact of breaches and builds customer confidence.

Secure software management reduces vulnerability to cyber attacks. Awareness of outdated software, unpatched applications, and insecure third-party programs informs responsible IT practices. Implementing automatic updates, regular patching, and careful vetting of new software minimizes risk. Combining software management with antivirus, firewalls, and endpoint protection creates a layered security strategy. Periodic software audits ensure that applications remain compliant with security policies. Maintaining secure software environments protects both business operations and customer data.

Monitoring and logging are essential for detecting suspicious activity in real-time. Awareness of potential anomalies, unusual logins, or unexpected system changes allows for rapid intervention. Implementing centralized logging, intrusion detection systems, and alert mechanisms enhances the ability to identify threats early.

Combining monitoring tools with trained personnel ensures that alerts are investigated promptly. Regular review of logs helps identify patterns, assess vulnerabilities, and strengthen defenses. Effective monitoring reduces the impact of breaches and improves overall security posture.

Vendor and third-party management is critical for maintaining secure business operations. Awareness of potential risks from suppliers, contractors, or cloud providers informs due diligence and security assessments. Establishing agreements, security requirements, and monitoring protocols ensures that third-party partners meet the company's standards. Combining internal security measures with third-party oversight reduces exposure to external threats. Regular reassessment of vendor security practices helps maintain compliance and trust. Strong third-party management safeguards both internal systems and customer data.

Implementing regular cybersecurity audits strengthens a business's overall defense posture. Awareness of existing vulnerabilities, misconfigured systems, and outdated policies informs corrective action. Conducting internal and external audits, vulnerability scans, and penetration tests identifies weak points before they are exploited. Combining audit results with remediation plans ensures that security gaps are addressed systematically. Regular auditing promotes accountability and maintains a proactive approach to cybersecurity. By identifying and mitigating risks early, businesses reduce exposure to costly breaches.

Employee accountability is a critical factor in securing business data. Awareness of roles, responsibilities, and the potential impact of negligence encourages compliance with security policies. Establishing clear guidelines, reporting protocols, and disciplinary measures fosters responsible behavior. Combining accountability with training, monitoring, and recognition of good practices reinforces a culture of vigilance. Encouraging employees to take ownership of data security strengthens the organization's overall resilience. Accountability ensures that security is not only the IT department's responsibility but a shared organizational priority.

Incident response planning prepares businesses for timely and effective mitigation of cyber threats. Awareness of potential attack scenarios, such as ransomware, phishing, or insider breaches, informs response strategies. Developing a formal incident response plan, assigning responsibilities, and conducting tabletop exercises enhances preparedness. Combining technical measures with clear communication channels ensures swift action during incidents. Periodic review and updating of response plans keeps them relevant to evolving threats. Preparedness minimizes downtime, financial loss, and reputational damage.

Employee training on cybersecurity best practices is a continuous necessity. Awareness of social engineering, phishing, password hygiene, and secure device usage empowers staff to make safer decisions. Conducting regular workshops, simulations, and knowledge checks reinforces learning and keeps security top of mind. Combining education with monitoring and feedback encourages compliance and proactive behavior. Well-trained employees act as an additional layer of defense against cyber threats. Continuous training ensures that human factors do not become a weak link in business security.

Maintaining secure backups is essential for business continuity. Awareness of the risks posed by data loss due to hardware failure, ransomware, or accidental deletion informs backup strategies. Using automated, encrypted, and redundant backups ensures that critical business data can be restored quickly. Combining backup practices with disaster recovery planning guarantees operational resilience. Periodic testing of backup integrity ensures reliability during emergencies. Secure backups protect both organizational operations and customer trust, forming a critical component of a robust security framework.

Implementing endpoint protection strengthens defenses for all devices used in the business environment. Awareness of threats targeting laptops, smartphones, and tablets emphasizes the need for security software, firewalls, and real-time monitoring. Combining endpoint protection with regular updates, patch management, and secure configurations ensures comprehensive device security.

Employee training on safe device usage complements technical measures and reduces the risk of human error. Monitoring endpoints for unusual activity allows rapid response to potential breaches. Endpoint security ensures that every device accessing company systems contributes to overall data protection.

Data classification and handling procedures reduce the risk of exposing sensitive information. Awareness of the varying levels of confidentiality, sensitivity, and criticality of data informs proper storage, access, and sharing practices. Implementing labeling, encryption, and access restrictions ensures that high-value information receives the highest level of protection. Combining classification with employee training and monitoring reinforces responsible data handling. Regular reviews of data storage and sharing practices prevent accidental leaks or misuse. Proper data handling safeguards customer trust, regulatory compliance, and business reputation.

Secure communication practices are vital for protecting business interactions. Awareness of risks in email, messaging apps, and video conferencing tools guides safe practices. Using encryption, secure networks, and authenticated platforms ensures that communications remain confidential. Combining secure communication with employee training on phishing and impersonation attacks strengthens overall cybersecurity. Monitoring communication channels for anomalies allows early detection of threats. Protecting the integrity and privacy of business communications prevents breaches and safeguards sensitive information.

Developing a culture of cybersecurity awareness ensures long-term protection. Awareness of potential threats, company policies, and best practices encourages responsible behavior at all levels. Combining formal training programs with daily reminders, simulations, and recognition for good practices reinforces security as a shared responsibility. Leaders should model vigilant behavior and support continuous improvement in cybersecurity habits. Engaging employees in security initiatives fosters accountability, vigilance, and proactive protection. A strong security culture complements technical measures and ensures sustainable data protection.

Regularly reviewing and updating security measures is essential to stay ahead of evolving threats. Awareness of emerging vulnerabilities, new attack vectors, and regulatory changes informs timely adjustments to security protocols. Combining continuous evaluation with testing, audits, and employee feedback ensures that security remains effective. Updating technical controls, policies, and training materials keeps defenses current and relevant. Proactive security management reduces the likelihood of successful attacks and strengthens resilience. Maintaining a dynamic approach to security ensures ongoing protection of business and customer data.

Cybersecurity for small businesses is an ongoing commitment, not a one-time project. Awareness of threats, evolving attack methods, and the value of business data informs continuous protection strategies. Combining technical safeguards, employee training, and policy enforcement creates a robust security posture. Regular audits, monitoring, and updates ensure that defenses remain effective against new vulnerabilities. Backup and recovery procedures guarantee operational continuity in case of incidents. By integrating these practices into daily operations, businesses can protect both their assets and their reputation.

Incident preparedness is crucial for minimizing the impact of cyber threats. Awareness of potential attack scenarios, response protocols, and communication strategies ensures timely and effective action. Combining prepared incident response with employee awareness, monitoring tools, and secure backups strengthens resilience. Practicing response plans through simulations and drills identifies gaps and improves readiness. Swift, coordinated action reduces downtime, prevents data loss, and maintains customer confidence. Proactive preparation transforms potential crises into manageable events.

Employee engagement reinforces the organization's cybersecurity posture. Awareness of the human element in security emphasizes the need for regular training, reminders, and encouragement. Combining education, clear policies, and positive reinforcement cultivates a security-conscious workforce. Encouraging employees to report suspicious activity and recognize potential threats makes them active defenders. Accountability and vigilance at all levels strengthen the organization's defenses. A well-informed and engaged team is one of the most valuable assets in preventing breaches.

Vendor and partner management ensures that external relationships do not introduce vulnerabilities. Awareness of security standards, compliance requirements, and potential risks from third parties informs contractual agreements and monitoring practices. Combining internal security measures with oversight of partners reduces exposure to external threats. Regular reassessment of third-party practices maintains alignment with business security goals. Effective vendor management protects both operational integrity and customer data. Vigilance over external connections prevents weak links from undermining overall cybersecurity.

CHAPTER .33

THE ROLE OF CYBERSECURITY IN PROTECTING HEALTHCARE DATA

How to Keep Your Health Information Secure in an Increasingly Digital Healthcare Environment

Healthcare data is among the most sensitive types of personal information, making it a prime target for cybercriminals. Awareness of the risks, including ransomware attacks, phishing, and insider threats, is essential for both patients and healthcare providers. Protecting electronic health records (EHRs), patient databases, and medical devices requires comprehensive technical safeguards. Combining encryption, access controls, and regular monitoring ensures that health data remains confidential and intact. Regulatory compliance, such as HIPAA in the United States, establishes legal obligations for protecting patient information. Maintaining cybersecurity in healthcare is both a moral and legal responsibility, safeguarding trust between patients and providers.

Secure access management is critical for protecting healthcare data. Awareness of who has access to sensitive patient information informs the implementation of role-based access controls. Using strong authentication methods, including multi-factor authentication, prevents unauthorized access. Combining access control with logging and audit trails ensures accountability and traceability. Regularly reviewing permissions and removing inactive accounts minimizes vulnerabilities. Proper access management ensures that only authorized personnel can view or modify critical health information.

Encryption plays a vital role in securing healthcare communications and records. Awareness of the risks of unencrypted transmissions, such as emails or portable storage, guides protective measures. Encrypting data both at rest and in transit prevents unauthorized interception and tampering. Combining encryption with secure key management and strict access policies strengthens overall data protection. Regularly updating encryption protocols ensures alignment with emerging threats. Effective encryption maintains the confidentiality and integrity of sensitive medical information.

Training healthcare staff on cybersecurity best practices is essential for reducing human error. Awareness of phishing, social engineering, and unsafe device usage empowers personnel to recognize and respond to threats. Conducting regular workshops, simulated attacks, and ongoing education reinforces secure behavior. Combining training with technical safeguards such as firewalls, antivirus software, and intrusion detection systems reduces vulnerabilities. Staff who understand the importance of cybersecurity contribute actively to protecting patient information. Continuous training helps create a culture of security within healthcare organizations.

Backup and disaster recovery are critical for maintaining access to healthcare data. Awareness of potential ransomware attacks, accidental deletions, and system failures emphasizes the need for regular backups. Implementing secure, encrypted, and redundant backups ensures that critical patient information can be restored quickly. Combining backups with disaster recovery planning minimizes downtime and protects patient care continuity. Periodically testing recovery procedures ensures reliability and effectiveness. Preparedness ensures that healthcare operations remain uninterrupted during cyber incidents or system failures.

Medical devices and connected healthcare systems require strong cybersecurity measures. Awareness of vulnerabilities in devices such as insulin pumps, pacemakers, and imaging equipment informs preventive strategies. Regular software updates, device encryption, and network segmentation help prevent unauthorized access or tampering. Combining device security with employee training and monitoring ensures comprehensive protection. Monitoring network activity and device performance allows early detection of anomalies. Securing medical devices safeguards both patient safety and sensitive data.

Cloud storage and data sharing in healthcare demand careful management. Awareness of risks associated with storing patient data in cloud environments guides secure practices. Using encrypted connections, strong authentication, and access controls protects cloud-based health information. Combining cloud security with regular audits and backups ensures redundancy and reliability. Periodic review of third-party cloud providers ensures compliance with regulations and data protection standards. Proper cloud management ensures that patient data remains both accessible and secure.

Incident response planning is vital in healthcare cybersecurity. Awareness of potential breaches, ransomware, or insider threats informs response protocols. Developing formal incident response plans, assigning responsibilities, and conducting regular drills enhances preparedness. Combining technical safeguards with clear communication channels ensures that incidents are mitigated swiftly. Periodic review and updating of response plans maintain relevance as new threats emerge. Effective incident response protects patient information and ensures continuity of care.

Regulatory compliance drives many healthcare cybersecurity practices. Awareness of laws such as HIPAA, GDPR, and other regional privacy regulations ensures that organizations meet legal obligations. Implementing policies, training, and technical measures in alignment with these regulations reduces the risk of fines and reputational damage. Combining compliance efforts with proactive security practices ensures both legal and practical protection. Continuous monitoring and auditing confirm adherence to regulatory requirements. Regulatory compliance is a key pillar of patient data security and organizational accountability.

Patient engagement and education also enhance healthcare cybersecurity. Awareness of how patients can protect their own health data, such as using secure portals, strong passwords, and cautious email behavior, reduces exposure. Educating patients on recognizing phishing attempts, verifying communications, and protecting mobile health apps strengthens overall security. Combining patient awareness with institutional safeguards creates a comprehensive defense. Informed patients are active participants in protecting their own information. Patient engagement complements organizational security practices for a more resilient healthcare ecosystem.

Monitoring and logging play a critical role in healthcare data protection. Awareness of unusual system activity, unauthorized access attempts, or data modifications allows early intervention. Implementing centralized logging, intrusion detection systems, and automated alerts ensures rapid response to potential threats. Combining monitoring with staff training and incident response plans strengthens the organization's resilience. Regularly reviewing logs helps identify vulnerabilities and patterns that may indicate security gaps. Proactive monitoring reduces the likelihood of breaches and protects patient trust.

Secure communication between healthcare providers is essential for maintaining confidentiality. Awareness of risks in emails, messaging apps, and telehealth platforms informs protective measures. Using encryption, secure channels, and authenticated platforms ensures that sensitive medical information remains private. Combining secure communication with staff training and monitoring prevents interception or misuse of data. Periodic audits of communication practices confirm adherence to security standards. Protecting communication integrity safeguards both patient privacy and the quality of care.

Physical security is often overlooked but remains crucial for healthcare cybersecurity. Awareness of unauthorized physical access to servers, devices, and storage areas informs preventive measures. Using locks, access controls, surveillance, and secure storage minimizes the risk of physical breaches. Combining physical security with technical safeguards, such as encryption and authentication, ensures comprehensive protection. Educating staff about the importance of physical security complements digital measures. A secure physical environment supports the integrity and confidentiality of sensitive health information.

Vulnerability management reduces the risk of exploitation in healthcare systems. Awareness of software bugs, outdated devices, and unpatched applications guides timely updates and fixes. Conducting regular vulnerability scans, penetration tests, and patch management ensures that weaknesses are addressed proactively. Combining vulnerability management with monitoring, employee training, and incident response enhances overall resilience. Consistent assessment and mitigation of vulnerabilities minimize opportunities for cybercriminals. Effective vulnerability management maintains the reliability and security of healthcare operations.

Collaboration between IT teams, healthcare staff, and management is essential for holistic cybersecurity. Awareness of each group's responsibilities and communication needs ensures coordinated protection efforts. Combining technical expertise, operational knowledge, and administrative oversight strengthens defenses against cyber threats. Regular meetings, shared protocols, and cross-department training enhance coordination and responsiveness. Engaging all stakeholders fosters a culture of cybersecurity and accountability. A collaborative approach ensures that patient data is protected across all levels of healthcare operations.

Third-party vendor management is critical in protecting healthcare data. Awareness of the security practices of suppliers, cloud providers, and service partners ensures that external relationships do not introduce vulnerabilities. Conducting due diligence, requiring security certifications, and monitoring compliance reduces the risk of data breaches from third parties. Combining internal cybersecurity measures with rigorous vendor oversight strengthens overall protection. Regular reassessment of vendor practices ensures alignment with organizational security policies. Effective vendor management protects both patient information and the organization's reputation.

Telehealth services introduce unique cybersecurity challenges. Awareness of risks associated with remote consultations, patient portals, and online communication guides protective measures. Using secure platforms, encryption, and strong authentication for both providers and patients reduces exposure. Combining technology safeguards with staff training and patient education ensures safe telehealth interactions. Monitoring telehealth systems for unusual activity allows early detection of potential breaches. Proper telehealth security maintains trust, privacy, and compliance in modern healthcare delivery.

Incident reporting and response protocols are essential for minimizing the impact of cyber threats. Awareness of how and when to report suspected breaches ensures rapid mitigation. Combining technical safeguards, staff awareness, and a formal response plan enables a coordinated reaction to security incidents. Regular drills, updates, and feedback improve the effectiveness of response strategies. Effective reporting and response protect patient data, reduce downtime, and maintain trust. Prompt action ensures that healthcare organizations can manage crises efficiently and responsibly.

Patient privacy policies guide secure handling of healthcare data. Awareness of regulations, consent requirements, and ethical considerations informs policy development. Implementing clear guidelines for data collection, storage, sharing, and disposal ensures compliance and protects patients. Combining policy enforcement with staff training and technical safeguards strengthens overall security. Periodic review of privacy policies ensures relevance and alignment with evolving regulations. Strong privacy policies build trust, ensure accountability, and reduce the risk of breaches.

Continuous improvement is essential for healthcare cybersecurity. Awareness of emerging threats, new technologies, and changing regulations guides ongoing adaptation. Combining regular training, audits, system updates, and policy revisions ensures that cybersecurity practices remain effective. Monitoring trends, learning from incidents, and implementing best practices strengthen resilience. Engaging all stakeholders in continuous improvement fosters a culture of vigilance and responsibility. Maintaining a proactive mindset ensures the long-term protection of sensitive healthcare data.

Maintaining healthcare cybersecurity requires a holistic approach that integrates technology, policy, and human behavior. Awareness of threats, vulnerabilities, and regulatory obligations informs a proactive security strategy. Combining technical safeguards, staff training, and continuous monitoring ensures that patient information remains protected. Regular audits, backups, and incident response planning further enhance resilience. Engaging both employees and patients in security practices strengthens the overall defense posture. A comprehensive approach transforms cybersecurity from a reactive necessity into a proactive foundation for healthcare trust.

Patient engagement is a crucial element in protecting healthcare data. Awareness of how patients manage their own data, such as through secure portals or mobile health applications, reduces exposure. Educating patients on safe digital behavior, recognizing phishing attempts, and protecting login credentials complements organizational safeguards. Combining patient awareness with institutional security measures creates a comprehensive protective framework. Informed patients contribute actively to maintaining the confidentiality and integrity of their health information. Empowering patients enhances the overall security culture within healthcare organizations.

Ongoing staff training ensures that healthcare personnel remain vigilant against evolving threats. Awareness of social engineering, ransomware, phishing, and device security encourages proactive behavior. Conducting regular workshops, simulations, and knowledge assessments reinforces cybersecurity principles. Combining education with monitoring and technical safeguards reduces human error, which is often the weakest link in security. Continuous reinforcement of training ensures that staff remain competent and confident in responding to threats. Skilled and informed personnel are essential to safeguarding sensitive healthcare data.

Regular review and updating of policies, procedures, and technology is key to long-term healthcare cybersecurity. Awareness of emerging threats, technological advances, and changes in regulatory requirements ensures that defenses remain effective. Combining ongoing evaluation with timely updates to security measures, access controls, and staff training strengthens resilience. Documenting improvements and lessons learned promotes accountability and continuous growth. Maintaining a culture of adaptability ensures that patient information remains secure amidst an ever-changing threat landscape. Proactive evolution is essential for sustained cybersecurity in healthcare.

Reflection:

Reflecting on the future of cybersecurity, I've realized that technology alone cannot guarantee protection. Awareness, adaptability, and strategic foresight are equally important for long-term resilience. I've seen that organizations and individuals who embrace continuous learning, proactive innovation, and ethical practices maintain stronger defenses. Cybersecurity is a dynamic field, and the ability to anticipate change, adopt emerging solutions, and cultivate human expertise will define success. Preparing for the future requires a holistic approach that integrates technology, education, and responsibility. By staying informed and agile, we can protect our digital lives and thrive in an ever-evolving cyber landscape.

"The best defense against tomorrow's cyber threats is knowledge, adaptability, and a commitment to continuous improvement today."
— Unknown

CHAPTER .34

THE FUTURE OF CYBERSECURITY: TRENDS YOU NEED TO KNOW

Exploring Emerging Cybersecurity Technologies and How They Will Shape Personal Data Protection

The landscape of cybersecurity is evolving rapidly, driven by advancements in technology and increasingly sophisticated threats. Awareness of emerging trends, such as artificial intelligence (AI), quantum computing, and advanced threat intelligence, is crucial for staying ahead. These technologies have the potential to both enhance defense mechanisms and introduce new vulnerabilities. Combining awareness with proactive adoption of cutting-edge security tools allows individuals and organizations to maintain robust protection. Continuous learning and adaptability are essential as threats evolve in complexity and scope. Preparing for the future requires foresight, vigilance, and a willingness to innovate in cybersecurity strategies.

Artificial intelligence is transforming the way cybersecurity threats are detected and mitigated. Awareness of AI-driven tools, including predictive analytics, automated threat detection, and behavioral analysis, provides new defensive capabilities. Combining AI with human oversight allows organizations to respond more quickly and accurately to attacks. However, AI can also be exploited by attackers to develop more sophisticated attacks, highlighting the need for careful implementation. Integrating AI responsibly enhances situational awareness, reduces response time, and strengthens overall security posture. AI represents a powerful ally in the ongoing battle against cyber threats.

Quantum computing presents both opportunities and challenges for cybersecurity. Awareness of quantum capabilities, particularly in encryption and data processing, informs preparation for future threats. Quantum technology may render traditional encryption vulnerable, requiring the development of quantum-resistant algorithms. Combining research, testing, and proactive adoption of quantum-safe protocols ensures continued protection of sensitive information. Organizations and individuals who monitor quantum advancements can mitigate risks before they become critical. Preparing for the quantum era ensures that data remains secure against future computational breakthroughs.

The rise of Internet of Things (IoT) devices creates new security considerations. Awareness of the potential vulnerabilities in connected devices, from smart homes to industrial systems, is essential for risk management. Implementing device authentication, network segmentation, and monitoring minimizes exposure to cyberattacks. Combining IoT security with broader cybersecurity strategies ensures holistic protection of personal and organizational data. As IoT adoption continues to accelerate, vigilance in securing these devices becomes increasingly important. Proactively addressing IoT risks prevents minor vulnerabilities from escalating into widespread security issues.

Cloud computing and remote work continue to reshape cybersecurity strategies. Awareness of risks associated with cloud storage, collaborative platforms, and telecommuting informs secure configuration and usage. Implementing strong access controls, encryption, and regular monitoring protects sensitive information in distributed environments. Combining cloud and remote work security with endpoint protection and employee training creates a multi-layered defense. As businesses and individuals increasingly rely on digital infrastructure, staying ahead of cloud-related threats ensures continuity and data protection. Adaptable strategies are critical to managing the evolving digital workspace.

Biometric security is becoming a cornerstone of modern cybersecurity practices. Awareness of technologies like fingerprint recognition, facial recognition, and behavioral biometrics highlights their potential to strengthen authentication. Combining biometric methods with traditional security measures, such as passwords and multi-factor authentication, enhances protection against unauthorized access. However, awareness of privacy concerns and potential vulnerabilities is necessary when implementing these technologies. Regular updates, monitoring, and careful management of biometric data ensure secure usage. Biometrics offer both convenience and robust security, shaping the future of identity verification.

Artificial intelligence-driven threat hunting is another emerging trend that changes how organizations detect and respond to cyber incidents. Awareness of machine learning algorithms that analyze patterns, detect anomalies, and predict attacks allows for faster mitigation. Combining automated threat intelligence with human expertise ensures comprehensive coverage and reduces false positives. Proactive AI monitoring helps organizations anticipate attacks before they escalate into serious breaches. Continuous refinement and adaptation of AI models keep detection capabilities current. AI-powered threat hunting represents a significant evolution in cybersecurity strategy.

Blockchain technology is also impacting data protection and secure transactions. Awareness of decentralized ledger systems allows organizations to utilize blockchain for secure record-keeping, identity verification, and transaction tracking. Combining blockchain with traditional security methods enhances data integrity and transparency. Implementing blockchain solutions requires careful planning, understanding regulatory implications, and ensuring interoperability with existing systems. The immutability and auditability of blockchain provide a reliable layer of security for critical information. As adoption grows, blockchain will become an increasingly important tool in protecting sensitive data.

The convergence of cybersecurity and regulatory compliance is shaping the future landscape. Awareness of evolving laws such as GDPR, CCPA, and other regional regulations informs proactive security practices. Organizations that combine compliance efforts with technological innovation reduce the risk of legal and financial penalties. Regular updates to policies, audits, and employee training ensure alignment with current requirements. Incorporating regulatory foresight into security planning strengthens resilience against both legal and cyber threats. Understanding and anticipating regulatory trends enhances long-term cybersecurity strategy.

Threat intelligence sharing and collaboration are becoming critical for defending against advanced attacks. Awareness of the benefits of information sharing among organizations, industry groups, and government agencies improves preparedness. Combining collaborative intelligence with internal monitoring allows for faster detection and mitigation of emerging threats. Participation in trusted networks and sharing anonymized threat data helps the entire community strengthen its defenses. Collaboration ensures that organizations do not face complex, evolving threats in isolation. Collective vigilance enhances the overall cybersecurity ecosystem.

The evolution of ransomware demands greater attention in the future of cybersecurity. Awareness of increasingly sophisticated ransomware attacks, including targeted campaigns against critical infrastructure and businesses, informs defensive strategies. Combining regular backups, network segmentation, and employee training helps mitigate the potential damage of these attacks. Implementing endpoint detection and response tools allows for faster identification and containment. Proactive planning, incident response exercises, and continuous monitoring reduce vulnerability to ransomware. Understanding the trajectory of ransomware threats ensures preparedness in an increasingly hostile digital landscape.

Artificial intelligence is also shaping predictive cybersecurity. Awareness of machine learning's ability to anticipate attack patterns allows organizations to take preventive measures before incidents occur. Combining predictive analytics with real-time monitoring enhances both proactive defense and rapid incident response. Continuous model training and data validation ensure predictive accuracy and reliability. Organizations that adopt AI for prediction gain a strategic advantage in defending against cyber threats. Predictive cybersecurity will play a critical role in reducing response times and preventing breaches.

Privacy-enhancing technologies (PETs) are becoming increasingly important for protecting personal data. Awareness of tools such as differential privacy, homomorphic encryption, and secure multiparty computation allows for secure data analysis without exposing sensitive information. Combining PETs with existing cybersecurity measures ensures compliance with privacy regulations and strengthens data confidentiality. Organizations that implement these technologies can perform analytics and research while maintaining robust privacy safeguards. Awareness and adoption of PETs are essential for balancing innovation with privacy protection. Privacy-first approaches are shaping the future of secure data usage.

The growing importance of cybersecurity education and workforce development cannot be overlooked. Awareness of the global shortage of skilled cybersecurity professionals highlights the need for training programs and continuous education. Combining formal education, certifications, and hands-on experience helps build the next generation of cybersecurity experts. Organizations that invest in workforce development strengthen internal defenses and foster a culture of vigilance. Continuous learning ensures that professionals remain capable of countering evolving threats. Education and talent development are critical to sustaining cybersecurity resilience in the future.

The integration of security into software development, known as DevSecOps, is redefining cybersecurity practices. Awareness of the benefits of embedding security throughout the development lifecycle improves system resilience. Combining secure coding practices, automated testing, and continuous monitoring ensures vulnerabilities are addressed early. Integrating security into development accelerates deployment while maintaining robust protection. Regular evaluation and adaptation of DevSecOps processes ensures alignment with evolving threats. DevSecOps exemplifies the shift toward proactive, built-in security for the digital future.

Zero-trust architecture is emerging as a fundamental principle in modern cybersecurity. Awareness of the concept—that no user or device is automatically trusted—guides secure network design. Implementing identity verification, access segmentation, and continuous monitoring minimizes exposure to potential breaches. Combining zero-trust principles with multi-factor authentication and endpoint security strengthens defenses. Regularly reviewing trust policies and access privileges ensures the model remains effective. Zero-trust provides a proactive framework to secure digital assets in a rapidly evolving threat landscape.

Automation and orchestration are revolutionizing cybersecurity operations. Awareness of how automated threat detection, response workflows, and security orchestration tools improve efficiency enables organizations to act faster. Combining human oversight with automation ensures critical decisions are guided by expertise while routine processes are expedited. Automation reduces response times, enhances accuracy, and frees personnel to focus on complex threats. Continuous tuning and evaluation of automated systems maintain effectiveness. Leveraging automation ensures organizations can scale their defenses in line with growing digital complexity.

The convergence of cybersecurity with artificial intelligence continues to create both opportunities and challenges. Awareness of AI-driven attacks, such as deepfakes and automated phishing campaigns, informs defensive strategy. Combining AI-based defenses with human intervention ensures that organizations can respond to sophisticated threats effectively. Monitoring AI-generated threats and continuously refining security protocols helps maintain resilience. Responsible AI deployment includes ethical considerations, bias mitigation, and accountability. AI will be a defining factor in both offensive and defensive cybersecurity in the coming years.

Behavioral analytics is becoming a key tool for detecting anomalies and insider threats. Awareness of patterns in user behavior, system interactions, and access logs enables early identification of suspicious activity. Combining behavioral insights with real-time alerts, access controls, and employee education enhances security posture. Continuous monitoring ensures that deviations from normal behavior are investigated promptly. Organizations that leverage behavioral analytics can prevent breaches before significant damage occurs. Behavioral insights are critical for adapting defenses to increasingly subtle and sophisticated threats.

Regulatory evolution will continue shaping the cybersecurity landscape. Awareness of upcoming legislation, international standards, and evolving privacy frameworks ensures organizations remain compliant. Combining legal compliance with proactive security practices reduces risk while fostering customer trust. Regular policy updates, employee training, and monitoring ensure alignment with new regulations. Organizations that anticipate regulatory changes are better prepared to implement secure practices efficiently. Understanding the regulatory trajectory is crucial for long-term cybersecurity strategy and data protection.

As cybersecurity evolves, staying ahead requires a combination of technology, education, and proactive strategy. Awareness of emerging trends, from AI and quantum computing to zero-trust architecture and automation, ensures preparedness for the challenges ahead. Combining cutting-edge tools with skilled personnel and continuous monitoring provides robust protection. Organizations and individuals must adopt a mindset of adaptability, recognizing that threats are constantly evolving. Strategic foresight allows for preemptive measures rather than reactive responses. Preparing for the future strengthens resilience and maintains trust in an increasingly digital world.

Investing in cybersecurity research and innovation is essential for long-term protection. Awareness of technological advancements and potential vulnerabilities allows organizations to anticipate and mitigate risks. Combining research insights with practical implementation ensures that defenses remain relevant and effective. Continuous evaluation and adoption of new security measures safeguard sensitive data against emerging threats. Collaboration across industries, academia, and governments enhances collective knowledge and capability. Innovation is the driving force that ensures cybersecurity evolves alongside the threats it faces.

Workforce development and education will play a pivotal role in shaping the cybersecurity landscape. Awareness of the skills gap and the need for continuous training informs investments in learning programs. Combining formal education, professional certification, and hands-on experience strengthens organizational resilience. Encouraging a culture of lifelong learning ensures personnel can adapt to new technologies and emerging threats. Well-trained professionals are better equipped to detect, prevent, and respond to attacks. Investing in human capital is as critical as deploying advanced technologies.

Cybersecurity strategies must balance technological innovation with ethical considerations and privacy. Awareness of the implications of AI, behavioral analytics, and data collection informs responsible implementation. Combining robust security measures with transparency, ethical practices, and compliance maintains public trust. Proactive governance ensures that cybersecurity advances protect both organizations and individuals. Ethical cybersecurity practices reduce legal, reputational, and operational risks. A future-ready strategy integrates security, privacy, and ethical responsibility seamlessly.

Chapter .35

Cybersecurity for Seniors: Protecting Older Adults from Digital Threats

Why Seniors Are Prime Targets for Cyber Attacks and How to Safeguard Their Information

Seniors are increasingly targeted by cybercriminals due to a combination of limited technical knowledge and trust in digital communications. Awareness of the types of scams, such as phishing, fraud, and identity theft, is essential to protect older adults. Implementing basic cybersecurity practices, including strong passwords, secure devices, and careful online behavior, significantly reduces risk. Combining technical safeguards with education and support empowers seniors to navigate the digital world safely. Regular discussions about emerging threats and practical demonstrations help reinforce safe habits. Protecting seniors' data requires patience, understanding, and consistent guidance.

Education is key in empowering seniors to defend themselves online. Awareness of common threats, safe browsing practices, and secure communication helps seniors make informed decisions. Providing step-by-step guidance, workshops, and easy-to-follow resources builds confidence and competence. Combining education with regular reminders and supervised practice ensures that knowledge is applied consistently. Encouraging questions and fostering curiosity helps seniors engage actively in protecting their information. Well-informed seniors become their own first line of defense against cyber threats.

Strong password practices are essential for senior cybersecurity. Awareness of the dangers of weak, reused, or easily guessable passwords informs better habits. Using password managers or writing down secure passwords in a protected place helps seniors maintain complex credentials. Combining passwords with multi-factor authentication adds an extra layer of protection. Regularly reviewing and updating passwords prevents unauthorized access over time. Establishing strong password habits ensures that seniors' accounts and sensitive information remain secure.

Device security is another crucial aspect of protecting older adults online. Awareness of threats from malware, viruses, and unauthorized access guides safe device usage. Installing antivirus software, keeping systems updated, and avoiding suspicious downloads reduce the likelihood of compromise. Combining device security with safe network practices, such as using secure Wi-Fi, strengthens overall protection. Teaching seniors to recognize warning signs, such as pop-ups or unusual activity, encourages vigilance. Maintaining secure devices is foundational to safe digital engagement for older adults.

Scam awareness is vital for seniors navigating emails, calls, and social media. Awareness of phishing attempts, fraudulent messages, and deceptive websites helps prevent financial and identity theft. Teaching seniors to verify sources, avoid clicking unknown links, and report suspicious activity minimizes exposure. Combining education with technical safeguards, like spam filters and browser warnings, reinforces safe behavior. Encouraging open communication about potential threats helps seniors feel supported and confident. Awareness, education, and vigilance work together to protect seniors from cybercriminals.

Social media safety is a critical component of senior cybersecurity. Awareness of oversharing personal information, friend requests from strangers, and malicious links helps seniors navigate platforms safely. Teaching them to adjust privacy settings, limit public visibility, and verify connections reduces exposure. Combining education with practical demonstrations and ongoing support ensures consistent application of safe practices. Regularly reviewing accounts with seniors helps identify vulnerabilities and reinforces good habits. Safe social media use protects both personal information and digital reputation.

Email security is essential for preventing scams and phishing attacks. Awareness of suspicious messages, unexpected attachments, and fraudulent links guides safe email behavior. Teaching seniors to verify senders, avoid clicking unknown links, and report phishing attempts reduces the risk of compromise. Combining email education with spam filters, secure email settings, and regular monitoring strengthens protection. Periodic discussions about new scam tactics ensure that seniors remain vigilant. Effective email practices are a cornerstone of senior digital safety.

Online shopping requires special attention to cybersecurity for older adults. Awareness of fake websites, unsecured payment portals, and phishing offers helps prevent financial loss. Teaching seniors to use trusted websites, secure payment methods, and strong passwords ensures safer transactions. Combining safe shopping practices with device security, antivirus protection, and secure networks reduces risk. Encouraging seniors to verify seller information and read reviews promotes informed decisions. Responsible online shopping habits safeguard both financial and personal information.

Tech support scams are a common threat to seniors. Awareness of unsolicited calls, pop-ups, or messages claiming technical issues helps prevent manipulation. Teaching seniors to avoid granting remote access or providing sensitive information to unknown callers is essential. Combining education with verification practices, such as contacting official support channels, ensures legitimate assistance. Regular reminders and open communication reinforce vigilance. Avoiding tech support scams protects seniors from financial and data-related harm.

Digital literacy programs empower seniors to confidently engage with technology. Awareness of basic cybersecurity principles, device operation, and safe online behavior builds competence.

Providing hands-on learning, clear instructions, and ongoing mentorship ensures seniors can apply their knowledge effectively. Combining digital literacy with continuous support fosters confidence, independence, and safe online engagement. Encouraging seniors to explore technology while remaining cautious strengthens both skills and security. Education is the foundation for lifelong digital safety.

Mobile device security is increasingly important as seniors adopt smartphones and tablets. Awareness of risks from apps, downloads, and unsecured Wi-Fi networks guides safe usage. Teaching seniors to install apps only from trusted sources, enable automatic updates, and use strong device passwords reduces vulnerability. Combining mobile security with antivirus software and careful network practices strengthens protection. Regularly reviewing device settings and app permissions ensures that personal information remains private. Secure mobile device habits allow seniors to enjoy technology safely and confidently.

Banking and financial account security is critical for older adults. Awareness of online banking scams, fraudulent transactions, and phishing attacks protects financial assets. Teaching seniors to use strong, unique passwords, two-factor authentication, and secure banking apps enhances account safety. Combining vigilance with technical safeguards, such as monitoring alerts and regularly reviewing statements, reduces exposure. Encouraging seniors to report suspicious activity promptly ensures swift response. Protecting financial information provides peace of mind and prevents costly losses.

Protecting health information is essential as seniors increasingly use digital healthcare tools. Awareness of risks associated with patient portals, telehealth services, and digital medical records is key. Teaching seniors to use secure passwords, encrypted connections, and verify portal authenticity ensures privacy. Combining technical security with guidance on safe online interactions strengthens data protection. Regularly reviewing access logs and sharing tips on safe digital healthcare practices reinforces vigilance. Safeguarding health information preserves privacy and builds confidence in digital health tools.

Creating a trusted support network enhances senior cybersecurity. Awareness of the importance of family, friends, or caregivers in providing guidance helps seniors navigate technology safely. Encouraging open communication about suspicious messages, unusual device behavior, or confusing online activity ensures timely intervention. Combining support networks with structured education and practical demonstrations strengthens seniors' digital confidence. Trusted advisors act as both a safety net and a source of encouragement. Collaboration ensures seniors remain secure while maintaining independence online.

Regularly updating knowledge and skills is vital for sustained cybersecurity. Awareness of evolving threats, scam tactics, and technological changes keeps seniors informed. Providing ongoing education, practical exercises, and reminders reinforces learning and prevents complacency. Combining continuous learning with vigilant habits and trusted support ensures seniors adapt to new challenges safely. Empowering seniors with updated knowledge fosters resilience against emerging cyber threats. Lifelong learning is essential for seniors to remain confident and protected in a digital world.

Phishing awareness is a cornerstone of senior cybersecurity. Awareness of deceptive emails, messages, and social media links enables seniors to recognize and avoid scams. Teaching them to verify sources, avoid clicking unknown links, and report suspicious communications strengthens protection. Combining phishing education with spam filters, safe browsing habits, and technical safeguards reduces risk. Regularly discussing new phishing trends helps seniors stay vigilant against evolving tactics. Proactive awareness empowers seniors to protect their personal and financial information online.

Secure password management is essential for protecting seniors' accounts. Awareness of the dangers of weak or repeated passwords guides the adoption of strong, unique credentials. Introducing password managers, secure storage methods, and regular updates ensures safety across multiple accounts. Combining good password habits with multi-factor authentication adds an extra layer of protection. Periodic reviews of password security reinforce consistent practices. Strong password management is a simple yet effective tool for safeguarding sensitive digital assets.

Internet safety habits reduce exposure to online threats. Awareness of suspicious websites, pop-ups, and unsecured networks helps seniors navigate the web safely. Teaching safe browsing, avoiding downloads from unknown sources, and verifying links promotes responsible online behavior. Combining digital hygiene practices with antivirus software and regular system updates strengthens overall security. Encouraging seniors to adopt safe habits gradually reinforces confidence and competence. Consistent internet safety practices reduce the likelihood of cyber incidents.

Email and messaging security is critical for preventing scams. Awareness of suspicious attachments, links, and unexpected messages helps seniors avoid phishing and malware. Teaching verification methods, careful communication, and reporting procedures enhances protection. Combining email security education with technical safeguards, such as spam filters and secure email providers, strengthens defense. Regularly reviewing communications ensures vigilance and reduces risk. Safe email and messaging practices protect seniors from common cyber threats.

Device maintenance and updates ensure continued security. Awareness of outdated operating systems, apps, and software vulnerabilities informs best practices. Teaching seniors to enable automatic updates, install security patches, and maintain device hygiene ensures robust protection. Combining maintenance practices with regular backups and monitoring strengthens resilience. Routine care and updates help prevent exploitation of known vulnerabilities. Well-maintained devices provide a reliable foundation for secure digital engagement.

Building confidence in digital technology is crucial for senior cybersecurity. Awareness of potential threats, combined with practical training and ongoing support, empowers older adults to navigate the online world safely. Encouraging gradual learning, providing clear guidance, and offering patient assistance ensures that seniors develop competence without fear. Combining knowledge with technical safeguards, strong passwords, and secure devices fosters independence and confidence. Regular reinforcement through practice and discussion strengthens habits and reduces mistakes. Confident seniors are more likely to engage safely and avoid falling victim to cyber threats.

Creating a trusted support system reinforces senior cybersecurity. Awareness of the benefits of family members, caregivers, or community programs in guiding seniors ensures proactive protection. Encouraging open communication about suspicious activity, unusual messages, or device concerns enables timely intervention. Combining support networks with structured education and practical demonstrations strengthens both knowledge and security. Trusted advisors provide both guidance and reassurance, empowering seniors to embrace technology safely. Collaboration enhances resilience while maintaining autonomy in digital engagement.

Encouraging continuous learning is vital for adapting to evolving threats. Awareness of new scams, security updates, and emerging technologies keeps seniors informed and prepared. Providing ongoing education, refresher courses, and hands-on practice reinforces skills. Combining continuous learning with technical safeguards ensures that seniors remain vigilant against cyber threats. Lifelong learning fosters both confidence and protection in the digital environment. By staying informed, seniors can enjoy technology safely while minimizing risk.

Developing practical routines supports long-term cybersecurity habits. Awareness of the importance of regular password updates, secure device usage, and cautious online behavior ensures consistent protection. Encouraging seniors to schedule periodic reviews of accounts, devices, and communications reinforces vigilance. Combining structured routines with education, monitoring, and support builds sustainable habits. Practical habits make cybersecurity manageable and reduce the likelihood of errors. Structured routines provide seniors with a sense of control and security in the digital world.

CHAPTER .36

THE DARK WEB: WHAT IT IS AND HOW TO PROTECT YOURSELF

How the Dark Web Works and How You Can Safeguard Your Information from It

The dark web is a hidden layer of the internet where anonymity is prioritized, often used for illegal activities. Awareness of its existence and the risks associated with it is essential for personal and organizational security. While the dark web itself is not inherently illegal, it hosts marketplaces for stolen data, illicit goods, and cybercrime tools. Understanding the distinction between the surface web, deep web, and dark web helps users navigate safely. Combining knowledge with proactive measures such as monitoring and protection safeguards sensitive information. Awareness and caution are key to avoiding exposure to the dark web's dangers.

Cybercriminals exploit the dark web to trade stolen data, including login credentials, financial information, and personal identifiers. Awareness of how data breaches feed these marketplaces highlights the importance of cybersecurity hygiene. Implementing strong passwords, multi-factor authentication, and regular monitoring reduces the likelihood that personal information will be compromised. Combining proactive security measures with vigilance in digital activities minimizes exposure. Periodically checking for compromised credentials and monitoring online accounts strengthens defenses. Staying informed about dark web trends allows individuals to respond effectively to potential risks.

Regular monitoring of personal information is an essential defense against dark web threats. Awareness of services that scan for leaked emails, credit cards, and other sensitive data helps identify exposure quickly. Combining monitoring with rapid remediation, such as changing passwords and alerting financial institutions, reduces potential damage. Educating users on recognizing suspicious activity ensures timely responses to compromised data. Ongoing vigilance is critical to maintaining security in an environment where stolen information is constantly traded. Continuous monitoring empowers individuals to protect their digital identity proactively.

Strong password management and encryption practices limit the value of personal information if it is exposed. Awareness of weak passwords, repeated credentials, and unsecured communications informs protective measures. Using unique, complex passwords and enabling encryption on sensitive data ensures that even if data is leaked, it remains inaccessible. Combining password management with multi-factor authentication further strengthens security. Regularly updating credentials and using secure communication channels minimizes the risk of unauthorized access. Properly implemented, these measures make personal information far less appealing to dark web actors.

Avoiding risky online behavior reduces the chance of personal data reaching the dark web. Awareness of phishing attacks, unsecured websites, and oversharing on social media informs safer digital habits. Teaching users to verify sources, avoid suspicious downloads, and limit personal data exposure strengthens defenses. Combining safe behavior with technical safeguards, such as antivirus software and firewalls, creates multiple layers of protection. Periodic reviews of online activity and privacy settings maintain security over time. Proactive online behavior is a critical component of defending against dark web threats.

Understanding the tools used to access the dark web is essential for awareness and safety. Awareness of technologies such as Tor, I2P, and VPNs helps users differentiate legitimate privacy tools from illicit activity. While these tools provide anonymity, they can also expose inexperienced users to hidden marketplaces and criminal forums. Combining safe use of privacy tools with knowledge of risks ensures responsible internet behavior. Educating oneself about the purpose and limitations of these technologies reduces the likelihood of accidental exposure. Awareness and caution are critical when dealing with networks designed to obscure identity.

The role of anonymized cryptocurrency in dark web transactions cannot be overlooked. Awareness of how digital currencies, particularly Bitcoin and other altcoins, facilitate untraceable exchanges informs protective strategies. Cybercriminals often rely on cryptocurrency to buy and sell stolen data, making financial vigilance essential. Combining secure payment practices with awareness of suspicious transactions reduces risk. Regularly monitoring financial accounts and enabling alerts can help detect unusual activity linked to dark web misuse. Understanding the financial mechanisms of the dark web strengthens overall cybersecurity readiness.

Monitoring for compromised data is an ongoing necessity. Awareness of services that track stolen credentials and personal information on the dark web helps individuals respond quickly to threats. Using these monitoring services allows for rapid action, such as password changes and account alerts, minimizing potential damage. Combining monitoring with proactive security measures strengthens overall protection. Regularly reviewing online accounts and credit reports ensures that any unauthorized activity is caught early. Vigilance and timely action are crucial for safeguarding personal and financial information.

Dark web risks extend beyond personal data to include organizational intelligence. Awareness of how company information, intellectual property, and employee credentials can be sold on dark web markets is essential for business cybersecurity. Implementing strong internal policies, access controls, and encryption reduces the likelihood of organizational data being compromised. Combining employee training, monitoring, and incident response ensures a comprehensive approach. Periodic audits and threat intelligence assessments help organizations stay ahead of potential breaches. Protecting both personal and organizational information minimizes the impact of dark web threats.

Education and awareness are the most effective defenses against dark web threats. Awareness of common tactics, the consequences of breaches, and safe digital behavior empowers individuals to make informed choices. Combining education with technical safeguards, continuous monitoring, and responsible online habits creates a robust protective framework. Encouraging proactive engagement with cybersecurity knowledge ensures that users remain vigilant. Staying informed about emerging dark web trends and vulnerabilities strengthens long-term defenses. Knowledge and vigilance remain the most reliable tools for safe navigation of the digital world.

Incident response planning is critical when dealing with potential exposure from the dark web. Awareness of the steps to take if personal or organizational information is compromised allows for rapid mitigation. Implementing a clear response plan, including notifying affected parties, changing passwords, and monitoring accounts, reduces the impact of breaches. Combining incident preparedness with technical safeguards and regular monitoring strengthens resilience. Periodically reviewing and updating response plans ensures they remain effective against evolving threats. A structured approach to incidents helps prevent panic and limits damage.

Businesses must take proactive steps to safeguard their information from dark web exploitation. Awareness of internal vulnerabilities, employee credentials, and third-party exposure guides comprehensive security strategies. Implementing access controls, encryption, and employee training reduces the risk of sensitive information reaching illicit marketplaces. Combining preventative measures with monitoring and threat intelligence allows early detection of potential compromises. Regular audits and testing of security systems ensure defenses remain robust. Proactive organizational measures minimize exposure and maintain trust in the digital ecosystem.

The use of threat intelligence feeds helps organizations track dark web activity. Awareness of marketplaces, forums, and data breaches allows companies to act swiftly when sensitive information appears online. Combining intelligence feeds with automated alerts, monitoring, and human analysis ensures timely responses to emerging threats. Proactive engagement with threat intelligence strengthens cybersecurity posture and reduces vulnerability. Regularly updating threat databases and cross-referencing with internal systems enhances detection accuracy. Leveraging dark web intelligence transforms reactive defense into proactive security management.

Password hygiene remains crucial in the fight against dark web exploitation. Awareness that reused or weak passwords can be sold and abused underscores the importance of strong credentials. Using unique, complex passwords for each account, combined with multi-factor authentication, significantly reduces the risk of compromise. Combining secure passwords with regular monitoring and immediate remediation practices ensures ongoing protection. Educating users about password risks and safe practices fosters a culture of vigilance. Strong password management is one of the simplest and most effective defenses against dark web threats.

Legal and regulatory considerations are vital in managing dark web risks. Awareness of laws regarding data breaches, privacy, and cybercrime informs responsible security practices. Combining compliance with proactive monitoring, reporting, and risk mitigation ensures both legal adherence and robust protection. Organizations that integrate regulatory awareness into cybersecurity planning reduce liability and enhance public trust. Periodic review of regulations, policies, and security practices ensures continued alignment with legal requirements. Legal and regulatory mindfulness complements technical defenses for comprehensive protection.

Secure communication is essential for minimizing exposure to the dark web. Awareness of encrypted messaging, secure email, and protected file-sharing tools reduces the risk of sensitive information being intercepted. Combining secure communication with strong authentication, device security, and careful online behavior ensures comprehensive protection. Regularly reviewing security settings and updating software further strengthens defenses. Educating both individuals and employees on secure communication protocols reinforces a culture of vigilance. Effective communication practices are a foundational layer of defense against dark web threats.

Limiting data exposure online is a proactive defense strategy. Awareness of oversharing personal details, social media information, and online accounts helps reduce the attractiveness of your information to cybercriminals. Combining minimal data disclosure with privacy settings, monitoring, and cautious online behavior lowers the risk of being targeted. Regularly auditing digital footprints and removing unnecessary personal data strengthens security. Educating users about the consequences of data exposure empowers informed decision-making. Controlled information sharing significantly reduces the probability of compromise via the dark web.

Cybersecurity tools and services play a significant role in dark web protection. Awareness of services that scan for stolen credentials, monitor account activity, and provide alerts helps mitigate risks. Combining these tools with technical safeguards, such as antivirus programs, firewalls, and encryption, creates layered defense. Regularly updating tools, monitoring alerts, and responding promptly ensures maximum effectiveness. Educating users on proper use of these services enhances protection. Leveraging specialized tools allows individuals and organizations to stay one step ahead of potential threats.

Regular audits and assessments strengthen resilience against dark web threats. Awareness of vulnerabilities, outdated credentials, and potential data leaks informs targeted security improvements. Combining routine audits with monitoring, incident response planning, and staff training ensures a proactive security posture. Periodically testing defenses helps identify weaknesses before they are exploited. Continuous assessment fosters a culture of vigilance and continuous improvement. A commitment to regular evaluation maintains robust protection against evolving risks.

Collaborating with cybersecurity experts enhances understanding and defense against dark web threats. Awareness of expert resources, advisory services, and industry collaboration provides insight into emerging risks. Combining professional guidance with internal policies, technical safeguards, and user education strengthens overall resilience. Regular consultations, threat briefings, and training sessions help individuals and organizations adapt to new challenges. Collaboration ensures that defenses remain current and effective. Expert engagement transforms reactive measures into proactive, strategic cybersecurity practices.

Understanding the risks and realities of the dark web empowers individuals and organizations to take informed action. Awareness of its purpose, the types of activities it hosts, and the methods used to access it allows for better preparation. Combining technical safeguards, secure online behavior, and ongoing education creates a strong defense against potential threats. Regular monitoring, incident response planning, and threat intelligence further enhance protection. Proactive engagement with cybersecurity practices ensures that exposure to the dark web is minimized. Knowledge and vigilance remain the most effective tools for mitigating risk.

Implementing multi-layered security measures strengthens defense against dark web exploitation. Awareness of password management, encryption, secure communications, and monitoring services ensures comprehensive protection. Combining these measures with user education and responsible online behavior reduces the likelihood of sensitive data appearing on illicit marketplaces. Regular audits, updates, and training reinforce the effectiveness of security practices. A layered approach prevents single points of failure and enhances resilience. Multi-layered security is the cornerstone of a robust defense strategy.

Organizations must adopt policies to protect both employees and business-critical information. Awareness of internal vulnerabilities, third-party exposure, and regulatory requirements guides proactive measures. Combining policies with technical safeguards, monitoring, and continuous training ensures that sensitive information remains protected. Periodic review and adjustment of security policies keeps defenses aligned with emerging threats. Organizations that integrate dark web awareness into cybersecurity planning minimize risk and maintain stakeholder trust. Policy-driven protection complements technology in achieving comprehensive security.

Personal vigilance is equally important for individual protection. Awareness of phishing, oversharing, weak passwords, and suspicious communications empowers users to make safe choices. Combining cautious behavior with technical safeguards like encryption, antivirus software, and monitoring services ensures robust personal security. Regularly reviewing accounts, credentials, and online footprints reinforces safe practices. Developing habits of mindfulness and skepticism online reduces vulnerability to cybercriminal activity. Personal responsibility and informed behavior are critical defenses in a world where the dark web thrives.

CHAPTER .37

ETHICAL HACKING: HOW WHITE HAT HACKERS HELP PROTECT YOUR DATA

What Ethical Hackers Do and How They Contribute to Strengthening Cybersecurity Measures

Ethical hacking is the practice of intentionally probing systems to identify vulnerabilities before malicious hackers can exploit them. Awareness of this discipline highlights how proactive testing strengthens cybersecurity defenses. White hat hackers use the same tools and techniques as cybercriminals, but their purpose is to protect rather than harm. Combining ethical hacking with strong organizational policies ensures that weaknesses are discovered and remediated promptly. Regular security assessments guided by ethical hackers reduce the likelihood of breaches and data theft. Understanding the role of ethical hacking fosters respect for this critical component of modern cybersecurity.

Penetration testing is one of the primary methods used by ethical hackers. Awareness of how simulated attacks reveal vulnerabilities in networks, applications, and devices informs organizational security strategies. Conducting regular penetration tests helps identify weak points before they can be exploited by malicious actors. Combining technical assessments with employee training and policy adjustments ensures comprehensive protection. Documentation and follow-up on identified vulnerabilities create a continuous improvement cycle. Penetration testing bridges the gap between theoretical security and practical, real-world defense.

Vulnerability assessments complement ethical hacking efforts. Awareness of software flaws, misconfigurations, and potential entry points allows organizations to prioritize remediation. Ethical hackers provide detailed reports that highlight risks and recommend actionable solutions. Combining assessments with patch management, access control, and monitoring ensures that vulnerabilities are addressed promptly. Regular reassessment keeps defenses current and minimizes the window of exposure. Vulnerability assessments transform hidden risks into manageable actions, strengthening cybersecurity posture.

Ethical hackers also play a role in social engineering awareness. Awareness of tactics like phishing, pretexting, and baiting helps organizations train employees to recognize and resist manipulation. White hat hackers often simulate social engineering attacks to test human vulnerabilities. Combining these simulations with awareness training and policy enforcement improves overall organizational resilience. Regular exercises ensure employees remain vigilant against evolving social engineering tactics. Human-centered testing is as critical as technical evaluation in comprehensive cybersecurity.

Bug bounty programs leverage ethical hackers to strengthen systems further. Awareness of platforms that reward the discovery of vulnerabilities encourages collaboration between organizations and independent security researchers. These programs provide incentives for identifying weaknesses in software, applications, and websites. Combining structured bug bounty initiatives with internal security measures expands the scope of protection. Proper management and communication ensure that findings are addressed effectively. Bug bounty programs exemplify how collaboration and responsible disclosure can enhance cybersecurity for all users.

Ethical hackers contribute to regulatory compliance and risk management. Awareness of legal requirements such as GDPR, CCPA, and industry-specific cybersecurity standards guides ethical hacking initiatives. Organizations that combine compliance objectives with proactive testing reduce exposure to legal penalties and reputational damage. Ethical hackers help identify gaps that could result in non-compliance, ensuring that security policies are effective and aligned with regulations. Regular audits and testing by skilled professionals strengthen governance and risk mitigation. Integrating ethical hacking into compliance strategies turns a potential liability into a proactive advantage.

Security awareness programs benefit from ethical hacking insights. Awareness of the ways systems and humans can be exploited allows organizations to design more effective training. Ethical hackers often simulate attacks to provide real-world scenarios for employees to recognize and respond to threats. Combining these exercises with continuous education reinforces safe practices and reduces risk. Feedback from ethical hacking activities informs policy adjustments and security improvements. Incorporating practical experience ensures that theoretical knowledge translates into actionable defensive behavior.

Red teaming is an advanced technique employed by ethical hackers to test organizational defenses. Awareness of red team operations, which mimic sophisticated attacker behavior, allows security teams to evaluate response readiness. Red teams simulate complex attacks, combining technical, social engineering, and physical intrusion methods. Combining red teaming with incident response planning and monitoring strengthens organizational preparedness. Post-assessment debriefings help identify weaknesses and recommend remediation. Regular red team exercises ensure that defenses remain robust against evolving threats.

Ethical hackers also provide guidance on secure system design. Awareness of secure coding practices, network architecture, and access control informs safer software and infrastructure development. By advising developers and IT teams, ethical hackers help embed security into systems from the outset. Combining proactive design principles with testing and monitoring reduces vulnerabilities and long-term risk. Ongoing collaboration ensures that emerging threats are addressed and mitigated promptly.

Security by design is a fundamental philosophy reinforced through ethical hacking expertise.

Collaboration between ethical hackers and IT security teams fosters continuous improvement. Awareness of the dynamic nature of cyber threats highlights the need for joint efforts. Ethical hackers share findings, recommend strategies, and provide insights that strengthen internal capabilities. Combining technical expertise, real-world testing, and continuous learning builds a resilient security culture. Organizations that embrace collaboration are better equipped to anticipate and counter attacks. Continuous engagement with ethical hackers ensures that security measures evolve alongside the threat landscape.

Ethical hackers play a crucial role in incident response and recovery planning. Awareness of potential attack scenarios allows organizations to develop detailed response protocols. By simulating breaches and analyzing system weaknesses, ethical hackers provide guidance on how to react efficiently during real incidents. Combining these insights with rehearsed incident response drills reduces downtime and mitigates damage. Continuous evaluation of response strategies ensures that lessons learned from simulations are applied effectively. Preparedness driven by ethical hacking strengthens resilience and confidence in managing cyber threats.

Penetration testing reports are valuable tools for decision-making. Awareness of the insights provided in detailed reports highlights risks that require immediate attention. Ethical hackers document vulnerabilities, attack pathways, and potential impact in a structured manner. Combining report analysis with prioritization of fixes ensures resources are allocated effectively. Regular review of penetration test results informs ongoing security improvements and strategic planning. Leveraging detailed reports turns discovered weaknesses into actionable steps for stronger cybersecurity.

Ethical hackers also assist in securing cloud environments. Awareness of cloud-specific vulnerabilities, such as misconfigured storage, insecure APIs, and weak authentication, informs protective measures. Conducting cloud penetration tests ensures that access controls, encryption, and monitoring are implemented correctly. Combining cloud security testing with continuous monitoring and policy enforcement strengthens defenses. Ethical hackers provide recommendations that help organizations adapt to the evolving complexities of cloud infrastructure. Securing cloud environments proactively prevents breaches that could compromise sensitive data.

Collaboration with external security communities amplifies the impact of ethical hacking. Awareness of industry forums, threat intelligence sharing, and collaborative research enhances collective knowledge. Ethical hackers contribute discoveries and methodologies that benefit a wider cybersecurity ecosystem. Combining insights from multiple sources ensures a broader understanding of emerging threats. Regular engagement with security communities fosters innovation, knowledge exchange, and rapid response. Ethical hacking extends beyond individual organizations, creating a safer digital environment for all.

Ethical hackers also focus on emerging technologies such as IoT, AI, and mobile applications. Awareness of vulnerabilities in connected devices, machine learning algorithms, and mobile software informs security strategies. Conducting ethical hacking assessments on these platforms ensures that risks are identified and mitigated early. Combining testing with secure development practices and user education strengthens overall cybersecurity posture. Proactive attention to emerging technologies helps prevent exploitation of novel vulnerabilities. Ethical hackers ensure that innovation does not outpace security readiness.

Ethical hackers help organizations strengthen human defenses through social engineering simulations. Awareness of tactics like phishing, pretexting, and baiting educates employees on potential manipulation attempts. Ethical hackers conduct controlled exercises to identify gaps in employee awareness and response. Combining simulation results with targeted training improves vigilance and reduces susceptibility to attacks. Continuous reinforcement ensures that employees maintain awareness and can respond appropriately in real-world scenarios. Human-centered testing complements technical defenses to create a well-rounded security strategy.

Ethical hacking promotes a culture of continuous improvement. Awareness of vulnerabilities is only valuable if it leads to actionable change. Ethical hackers provide recommendations that guide policy updates, technical enhancements, and employee education. Combining these insights with regular security audits ensures that organizations remain adaptive to evolving threats. Feedback loops established through ethical hacking activities encourage ongoing refinement of security measures. A culture that values proactive evaluation and learning strengthens defenses against future attacks.

The use of automated tools in ethical hacking increases efficiency and accuracy. Awareness of scanners, vulnerability assessment software, and penetration testing tools enables ethical hackers to identify issues quickly. Combining automated analysis with human judgment ensures comprehensive evaluation without overlooking subtle risks. Regular updates and configuration reviews of these tools maintain their effectiveness. Automation allows ethical hackers to focus on complex threats while maintaining consistent testing coverage. Leveraging technology enhances the precision and scope of ethical hacking efforts.

Ethical hackers contribute to strategic cybersecurity planning. Awareness of threat trends, attack vectors, and organizational vulnerabilities informs long-term decision-making. By collaborating with leadership and IT teams, ethical hackers help prioritize security investments and resource allocation. Combining technical assessments with strategic insights ensures that cybersecurity initiatives align with organizational goals. Periodic review of strategies based on emerging threats maintains resilience. Ethical hacking bridges the gap between tactical testing and overarching security planning.

Reporting and documentation are essential outputs of ethical hacking. Awareness of the importance of clear, actionable reports ensures that findings are understood and acted upon. Ethical hackers provide detailed documentation outlining vulnerabilities, potential impacts, and recommended remediation. Combining this information with follow-up verification ensures that identified weaknesses are effectively addressed. Regular documentation supports compliance, auditing, and continuous improvement initiatives. Proper reporting transforms ethical hacking from a technical exercise into a strategic asset for security enhancement.

Ethical hacking ultimately strengthens trust in digital systems and organizational integrity. Awareness of the role white hat hackers play in identifying vulnerabilities helps build confidence among users and stakeholders. Combining proactive testing, training, and continuous improvement ensures that systems are more secure and resilient against potential attacks. Regular engagement with ethical hackers fosters a culture of vigilance, learning, and accountability. Organizations that embrace ethical hacking demonstrate commitment to both security and the protection of sensitive information. This proactive approach ensures that cybersecurity is not merely reactive but strategically forward-looking.

Ethical hackers also drive innovation in security practices. Awareness of emerging threats and new attack methods informs the development of advanced defense strategies. By collaborating with IT teams, leadership, and security communities, ethical hackers help organizations anticipate and mitigate risks before they become critical issues. Combining technical expertise with strategic planning transforms potential weaknesses into opportunities for strengthening defenses. Continuous adaptation to evolving threats ensures sustained protection of personal, organizational, and sensitive data. Ethical hacking is therefore both a preventive and an innovative force in cybersecurity.

Training and mentoring are additional contributions of ethical hackers. Awareness of gaps in skills and knowledge among employees or IT staff highlights areas where targeted training is beneficial. Ethical hackers provide guidance, mentorship, and real-world examples to improve awareness and response capabilities. Combining education with practical exercises strengthens overall organizational resilience. Empowering staff to recognize and address vulnerabilities fosters a proactive security culture. Continuous knowledge transfer ensures that expertise is retained and applied effectively.

Collaboration between ethical hackers and other cybersecurity professionals enhances collective defense. Awareness of shared intelligence, threat analysis, and best practices ensures a broader understanding of emerging risks. By combining insights across teams, organizations can anticipate attacks and implement coordinated defensive measures. Regular communication and joint exercises improve response efficiency and effectiveness. Collaborative efforts make it harder for cybercriminals to exploit isolated weaknesses. Ethical hacking thrives in a cooperative environment, amplifying its impact across the digital ecosystem.

CHAPTER .38

THE PSYCHOLOGY OF CYBERCRIME: WHY HACKERS DO WHAT THEY DO

Understanding the Motives Behind Cybercrime and How This Knowledge Can Improve Your Defense

Cybercrime is driven by a complex mix of psychological, social, and economic factors. Awareness of these underlying motivations helps individuals and organizations anticipate potential threats. Some hackers are financially motivated, seeking monetary gain through fraud, ransomware, or theft of sensitive information. Others pursue recognition, challenge, or ideological goals, often engaging in hacktivism or digital protest. Combining knowledge of these motives with cybersecurity strategies allows for tailored defenses. Understanding the "why" behind attacks enhances the effectiveness of prevention and response measures.

The desire for financial gain is one of the most common drivers of cybercrime. Awareness of tactics like phishing, identity theft, and ransomware highlights the lengths criminals will go to obtain money. Attackers often exploit vulnerabilities in human behavior, such as trust or curiosity, to achieve their objectives. Combining financial literacy with strong cybersecurity habits, like secure banking practices and monitoring, reduces susceptibility. Regular education on emerging scams helps individuals stay ahead of evolving financial threats. By understanding the economic incentives behind cybercrime, users can better protect their resources.

Some hackers are motivated by personal challenge and intellectual stimulation. Awareness of these "white-hat-turned-black-hat" motivations shows that curiosity and problem-solving skills can be misapplied for illicit purposes. Attackers may target systems for the thrill of bypassing security measures or demonstrating their skills publicly. Combining robust technical safeguards with continuous monitoring limits opportunities for these types of intrusions. Encouraging responsible use of technical expertise in professional contexts can redirect talent toward ethical pursuits. Recognizing curiosity-driven attacks helps organizations anticipate unconventional tactics.

Ideology and social beliefs also drive cybercriminal behavior. Awareness of hacktivism and politically motivated attacks informs defensive strategies. Attackers may target organizations or individuals that contradict their beliefs, seeking to make a statement or disrupt operations. Combining knowledge of likely targets, motivations, and attack methods enhances preparedness. Monitoring for ideological threats, training employees, and implementing robust security measures reduce exposure. Understanding the social and ethical drivers behind cybercrime informs both technical defenses and strategic planning. Cybersecurity is not only technical—it is shaped by human psychology.

Some cybercriminals act out of revenge, resentment, or personal grudges. Awareness of insider threats and disaffected individuals helps organizations detect potential risks early. Attackers may exploit privileged access or insider knowledge to harm systems, steal data, or damage reputations. Combining access control, monitoring, and behavioral analysis mitigates the risk posed by disgruntled insiders. Regular communication, employee support programs, and ethical policies can reduce the likelihood of internal attacks. Recognizing the emotional and psychological drivers of cybercrime ensures a more comprehensive approach to security.

Social influence and peer pressure play a significant role in cybercriminal activity. Awareness of online communities, forums, and hacker networks helps explain why individuals engage in illicit behavior. Some hackers are drawn into illegal activity by peers who validate risky actions or provide guidance. Combining this knowledge with monitoring and threat intelligence allows organizations to anticipate group-driven attacks. Encouraging positive online communities and professional mentorship can redirect talent toward ethical cybersecurity practices. Understanding the social dynamics behind cybercrime helps prevent escalation and informs defensive strategies.

The thrill of anonymity motivates many cybercriminals. Awareness that digital environments allow attackers to hide their identity explains why some individuals take greater risks. The perceived invisibility can embolden behavior that would be unacceptable offline. Combining technical safeguards with monitoring, logging, and forensic readiness helps detect and attribute actions despite anonymity. Educating users and staff about the psychology of anonymity fosters vigilance against seemingly random or unprovoked attacks. Recognizing the influence of anonymity helps predict attacker behavior and design effective countermeasures.

Cybercrime can also be driven by opportunism. Awareness that attackers often exploit easily accessible vulnerabilities explains why even small oversights can have severe consequences. Opportunistic hackers take advantage of weak passwords, unpatched software, or exposed networks without prior planning. Combining preventative measures, such as patch management, secure configurations, and employee education, reduces the window of opportunity. Routine audits, monitoring, and rapid response protocols further limit exposure. Understanding opportunistic behavior reinforces the importance of consistent cybersecurity hygiene.

Psychological profiling of attackers aids in predicting future threats. Awareness of behavioral patterns, risk tolerance, and motivations allows security teams to prioritize defenses. Combining profiling with incident history, threat intelligence, and system monitoring enhances proactive security measures. Organizations can anticipate tactics, techniques, and likely targets by understanding hacker psychology. Integrating behavioral insights into cybersecurity planning strengthens both prevention and response. Knowledge of attacker psychology provides a strategic advantage in defending against sophisticated threats.

Ethical considerations also influence hacker behavior. Awareness that some individuals navigate a fine line between ethical and unethical actions helps organizations design policies and training. Combining understanding of ethical grey areas with clear expectations, oversight, and accountability reduces the likelihood of insider threats. Encouraging ethical decision-making and responsible use of skills fosters a culture of integrity. Recognizing the ethical motivations behind behavior contributes to holistic cybersecurity strategies. Psychology and ethics together shape both potential threats and effective defenses.

Fear and intimidation are often leveraged by cybercriminals to manipulate victims. Awareness of tactics like scare-ware, ransomware, and threatening emails explains why some individuals comply with demands quickly. Attackers exploit psychological pressure to bypass rational decision-making, increasing the likelihood of success. Combining education, awareness, and pre-planned response protocols helps victims resist manipulation. Training users to recognize fear-based tactics reduces susceptibility and empowers proactive action. Understanding the psychological tools of cybercriminals enables the design of stronger, human-centered defenses.

Some hackers are driven by boredom or the search for excitement. Awareness that curiosity and restlessness can manifest as digital mischief highlights why systems are often targeted seemingly at random. Opportunistic attacks may result from experimentation rather than financial or ideological motives. Combining strict access controls, monitoring, and rapid response mechanisms reduces risk from thrill-seeking behavior. Encouraging productive, ethical outlets for technical talent can redirect energy toward legitimate cybersecurity work. Recognizing these motivations helps predict potential attack patterns and allocate defensive resources efficiently.

The perception of low risk encourages many cybercriminals to act. Awareness that perceived anonymity, lack of enforcement, or weak security measures embolden attackers underscores the need for strong defenses. Combining deterrence measures, monitoring, and visible consequences for breaches decreases the likelihood of opportunistic attacks. Educating users and employees about the importance of cybersecurity reduces exploitable complacency. Continuous vigilance and proactive measures create an environment where cybercrime carries higher perceived risk. Understanding attacker risk assessment informs strategies that deter potential threats.

Cognitive biases play a role in both attacks and defenses. Awareness that hackers exploit human tendencies like overconfidence, authority bias, or trust helps organizations tailor protective measures. Similarly, defenders must be mindful of their own biases when assessing threats or designing security protocols. Combining knowledge of cognitive psychology with security practices enhances decision-making and reduces mistakes. Regular training and scenario-based exercises help identify and counter cognitive vulnerabilities. Psychological insights strengthen both proactive and reactive cybersecurity measures.

Motivation can change over time, influencing hacker behavior. Awareness that a financially motivated attacker may shift to ideological or revenge-driven motives highlights the dynamic nature of cyber threats. Combining continuous monitoring, threat intelligence, and adaptive security strategies ensures that evolving attacker motivations are addressed. Organizations and individuals must remain vigilant and flexible to respond to new threats. Understanding the fluidity of hacker psychology strengthens long-term preparedness. Dynamic strategies informed by psychological insights improve resilience and reduce vulnerability.

Cybercriminals often exploit emotional vulnerabilities, such as fear, greed, or empathy, to manipulate victims. Awareness of emotional triggers helps individuals recognize and resist phishing attacks, scams, and social engineering. Training users to pause, verify, and question unexpected requests reduces the effectiveness of these manipulative tactics. Combining emotional awareness with technical safeguards, like email filters and authentication, strengthens overall defense. Reinforcing emotional resilience through education empowers users to make rational decisions online. Understanding the emotional dimension of cybercrime improves both personal and organizational cybersecurity.

Social engineering leverages trust and relationships to gain unauthorized access. Awareness of tactics that exploit authority, familiarity, or helpfulness explains why even knowledgeable individuals can fall victim. Ethical hackers and cybersecurity educators use simulated attacks to train people to detect manipulation. Combining behavioral education with strict access policies and verification procedures mitigates risk. Continuous reinforcement of social engineering awareness helps maintain vigilance. Recognizing the interplay between psychology and cybercrime strengthens human-centered defenses.

Hackers may also be motivated by notoriety or the desire for recognition within online communities. Awareness of reputation-driven behavior highlights why some individuals engage in high-profile attacks or defacement. Technical safeguards combined with monitoring and rapid response limit opportunities for publicity-driven attacks. Organizations that understand these motivations can design effective deterrents and response strategies. Educating staff and users about potential exploit attempts prevents overexposure of sensitive data. Awareness of reputation-seeking behavior informs proactive risk management.

Insider threats often stem from dissatisfaction, resentment, or perceived injustice. Awareness of organizational dynamics that contribute to insider risks is critical for prevention. Implementing access controls, monitoring, and ethical workplace practices reduces vulnerability. Combining psychological insight with technical measures strengthens overall security posture. Encouraging open communication and feedback within organizations minimizes resentment-driven attacks. Understanding the internal human factors behind cybercrime complements external threat defenses.

Analyzing hacker motivations informs threat modeling and prevention strategies. Awareness of the psychological drivers behind cyber attacks enables security teams to anticipate tactics and prioritize protections. Combining intelligence from behavioral analysis, past incidents, and system monitoring creates more accurate risk assessments. Integrating these insights into policies, training, and technical safeguards enhances overall resilience. Regularly updating models based on new information ensures defenses evolve alongside threats. Understanding the psychology behind cybercrime empowers both proactive and reactive cybersecurity measures.

Understanding the psychology of cybercrime allows individuals and organizations to develop more effective defense strategies. Awareness of motivations, emotional triggers, cognitive biases, and social influences helps anticipate attacker behavior. Combining this psychological insight with technical safeguards, education, and monitoring strengthens resilience against cyber threats. Proactive strategies informed by human behavior reduce vulnerability and improve incident response effectiveness. Continuous learning about hacker psychology ensures that security measures remain adaptive and comprehensive. Knowledge of the "why" behind attacks empowers users to stay one step ahead of potential threats.

Organizations benefit from integrating psychological insights into cybersecurity planning. Awareness of both external and internal threats informs policies, training, and system design. Combining behavioral analysis with risk assessments, monitoring, and technical controls creates a holistic security approach. Encouraging a culture of vigilance, ethical behavior, and ongoing education strengthens defenses at every level. Regular evaluation of employee behavior, potential insider risks, and threat intelligence ensures preparedness. Understanding the human factors behind cybercrime enhances both prevention and recovery strategies.

Psychological awareness also supports user training and education. Awareness of common manipulation techniques, social engineering tactics, and emotional triggers allows for more engaging and effective cybersecurity programs. Combining practical simulations with education helps users recognize threats in real-world scenarios. Reinforcing these lessons through repetition and feedback ensures retention and application. Users who understand hacker psychology are better equipped to make informed, safe decisions online. Training with a psychological perspective enhances both individual and organizational security.

Behavioral insights can also guide technology design and policy creation. Awareness of human tendencies, such as overconfidence or routine behavior, informs the development of safeguards and user-friendly security tools. Combining technical solutions with behavioral understanding ensures that security measures are both effective and adopted consistently. Policies designed with psychology in mind address both compliance and practical usability. Continuous refinement of technology and policy based on human factors improves security adoption. Integrating psychology into design and governance strengthens defenses across the digital ecosystem.

CHAPTER .39

A DIGITAL AGE WITHOUT PRIVACY: THE LONG-TERM CONSEQUENCES

How a Lack of Privacy and Security Will Impact Society and What You Can Do to Prevent It

The erosion of privacy in the digital age presents profound societal challenges. Awareness of how personal data is collected, shared, and monetized reveals the potential for widespread surveillance and manipulation. Without proper protections, individuals lose control over sensitive information, leading to risks such as identity theft, financial loss, and reputational harm. Combining privacy awareness with secure practices, such as encryption and cautious data sharing, helps mitigate these risks. Governments, corporations, and individuals all have roles to play in preserving privacy. Understanding the long-term consequences of neglecting digital privacy is critical for informed participation in the modern world.

A society without privacy fosters a climate of constant surveillance. Awareness that governments and corporations can track online behavior, purchases, and communications underscores the need for vigilance. Combining technical protections, such as VPNs and secure messaging, with informed choices about platforms and services helps maintain a degree of personal autonomy. The psychological impact of constant monitoring can alter behavior, limit freedom of expression, and create self-censorship. Recognizing these effects emphasizes why protecting privacy is not just personal, but a societal imperative. Continuous advocacy and education support a culture that values and defends privacy rights.

Loss of privacy increases vulnerability to cybercrime and exploitation. Awareness of the ways attackers use exposed data—through phishing, identity theft, and financial fraud—demonstrates the practical dangers of poor digital hygiene. Combining strong cybersecurity practices, routine monitoring, and cautious online behavior reduces exposure. Organizations that fail to protect user data may inadvertently empower cybercriminals, creating widespread consequences. Ensuring that personal, corporate, and governmental systems are secure safeguards not just individual privacy but the broader digital ecosystem. Prioritizing security and privacy together forms the foundation for a resilient digital society.

The economic consequences of diminished privacy are significant. Awareness that personal data drives targeted advertising, credit scoring, and consumer profiling highlights the value of information. Companies that exploit unprotected data can gain an unfair advantage, while consumers may suffer financial and personal harm. Combining legal protections, corporate responsibility, and individual vigilance ensures a fairer and more secure marketplace. Ethical handling of data becomes essential to maintain trust and equitable access to services. Recognizing the financial stakes of privacy encourages both consumers and organizations to act responsibly.

Social and cultural implications arise when privacy is compromised. Awareness of how constant data collection can influence social interactions, political opinions, and cultural norms is crucial. The manipulation of information and targeted messaging can polarize communities and reduce collective trust. Combining awareness with critical thinking, media literacy, and secure communication fosters resilience against manipulation. Advocating for strong privacy policies and ethical digital practices helps protect social cohesion. Understanding the broader cultural impact of privacy erosion highlights the importance of proactive measures in the digital age.

The normalization of data collection can subtly influence behavior and decision-making. Awareness that online activities are constantly monitored highlights the psychological impact of living in a surveilled environment. Individuals may unconsciously alter their actions, opinions, or purchasing decisions based on perceived observation. Combining awareness with deliberate privacy measures, such as using secure browsers and minimizing personal exposure, helps maintain autonomy. Educating people about behavioral manipulation and targeted influence empowers informed choices. Understanding these psychological effects is critical to preserving personal freedom in a connected world.

Without privacy, the potential for misuse of personal information increases dramatically. Awareness of data breaches, unauthorized access, and corporate exploitation underscores the dangers of unprotected information. Combining strong cybersecurity hygiene, vigilant monitoring, and encrypted communication reduces the likelihood of exploitation. Societal norms around consent and personal boundaries may erode if privacy is continuously compromised. Advocating for strict regulations and transparent data practices protects both individuals and communities. Protecting personal information is a collective responsibility that ensures digital integrity and trust.

The rise of predictive analytics and AI amplifies privacy risks. Awareness that algorithms can infer habits, preferences, and vulnerabilities from minimal data demonstrates the hidden dangers of unregulated information use. Combining responsible AI development, privacy-conscious tools, and individual safeguards helps mitigate potential harms. Organizations must adopt ethical frameworks to govern AI applications and prevent discrimination or manipulation. Transparency in algorithmic decision-making protects societal trust and personal rights. Recognizing the intersection of technology and privacy prepares individuals for responsible digital engagement.

Digital footprints have long-lasting implications for reputation and opportunity. Awareness that online activity can be archived, shared, and exploited indefinitely emphasizes the importance of careful digital behavior. Combining cautious online engagement, data minimization, and content awareness reduces long-term risk. Employers, institutions, and social networks increasingly consider digital histories when making decisions, making privacy essential for professional and personal life. Teaching digital responsibility alongside technical safeguards reinforces accountability and prudent decision-making. Protecting one's digital footprint preserves autonomy and reduces vulnerability.

The absence of privacy can erode trust in institutions, technology, and society. Awareness that continuous monitoring and data misuse foster skepticism highlights the societal cost of ignoring privacy. Combining transparency, ethical practices, and robust security measures helps restore confidence. Educating the public about rights, protective tools, and responsible online behavior encourages a culture of accountability. Societal trust is strengthened when individuals feel secure and in control of their information. Prioritizing privacy is not only a personal safeguard—it is essential for the health of communities and the digital ecosystem.

The intertwining of privacy and freedom is increasingly evident in the digital era. Awareness that surveillance can influence expression, thought, and behavior underscores the fundamental importance of privacy rights. Individuals who feel constantly monitored may self-censor, limiting creativity, dissent, and personal growth. Combining privacy protections, secure communications, and responsible platform use helps maintain the space for free expression. Advocating for legal safeguards and transparent digital practices reinforces societal liberties. Preserving privacy is essential not only for personal security but for sustaining democratic values and social progress.

Erosion of privacy can exacerbate inequality and discrimination. Awareness that collected data may be used to profile, stereotype, or disadvantage certain groups highlights systemic risks. Combining ethical oversight, data anonymization, and inclusive policies helps mitigate the negative social impact. Organizations and governments must ensure that personal information is used fairly, protecting vulnerable populations. Understanding these dynamics enables individuals and policymakers to advocate for equitable treatment. Protecting privacy is thus intertwined with protecting fairness, justice, and societal well-being.

Children and future generations face heightened risks in a world with diminished privacy. Awareness that young people are particularly vulnerable to data exploitation, tracking, and manipulation emphasizes the need for proactive protection. Combining parental education, regulatory enforcement, and secure digital tools helps shield minors from harm. Teaching digital literacy from a young age fosters responsible, privacy-conscious habits that persist into adulthood. Protecting children's data ensures that the next generation can grow, learn, and explore safely online. Privacy safeguards today create a foundation for healthier digital experiences tomorrow.

Economic dependence on data further complicates privacy issues. Awareness that corporations monetize personal information through targeted advertising, behavioral tracking, and AI-driven analytics underscores the tension between convenience and control. Combining informed consumer choices, privacy tools, and advocacy for ethical corporate practices balances technological benefits with personal security. Regulatory frameworks that enforce consent, transparency, and accountability help maintain fairness in the digital economy. Understanding these economic drivers allows individuals to make empowered decisions about data sharing. Maintaining privacy safeguards economic autonomy alongside personal freedom.

Societal desensitization to privacy loss is an emerging concern. Awareness that normalized data collection can lead to complacency underscores the urgency of education and proactive behavior. Combining continuous learning, secure practices, and advocacy counters apathy and reinforces the value of privacy. Societies that recognize and resist gradual erosion of privacy can maintain control over personal information and digital rights. Promoting awareness, responsible behavior, and accountability cultivates resilience against encroaching surveillance. Vigilance and education are essential to prevent irreversible loss of privacy in the digital age.

The digital age has made personal data both a valuable resource and a potential weapon. Awareness that cybercriminals, corporations, and even governments can exploit information emphasizes the importance of proactive privacy measures. Combining secure practices, such as encryption and anonymization, with careful data sharing reduces vulnerability. Organizations must adopt privacy-by-design principles to safeguard users while leveraging data responsibly. Understanding the dual nature of data—its utility and its risk—guides safer digital behaviors. Vigilance, education, and policy enforcement create a framework where information can be used ethically without compromising privacy.

Data breaches and leaks have long-term societal consequences. Awareness that even minor security lapses can lead to identity theft, financial fraud, and reputational damage underscores the need for constant vigilance. Combining strong cybersecurity measures with regular monitoring and incident response ensures rapid mitigation of breaches. Governments and organizations have a responsibility to implement protective systems and notify affected parties promptly. Individuals, too, must remain proactive in monitoring accounts and securing sensitive information. Protecting privacy and preventing leaks safeguards both individual and societal trust in digital systems.

The rise of predictive analytics and AI intensifies privacy concerns. Awareness that algorithms can infer personal habits, beliefs, and vulnerabilities from minimal data illustrates the subtle but significant threats to autonomy. Combining privacy-conscious technologies, consent management, and transparency helps users retain control. Organizations must ensure that AI applications operate ethically, without bias, and with respect for individual privacy. Users who understand how predictive systems function can make informed choices about data sharing. Privacy protection in the age of AI requires both technical safeguards and awareness of systemic risks.

Digital surveillance can have chilling effects on free expression and civic engagement. Awareness that monitoring can alter behavior and reduce participation in social or political activities highlights broader societal risks. Combining secure communications, anonymity tools, and informed digital habits protects both personal freedom and collective voice. Advocacy for policies that limit unnecessary surveillance strengthens democratic values. Educating citizens on their rights and the implications of digital observation promotes a more engaged and resilient society. Protecting privacy is therefore foundational to preserving liberty in a connected world.

The long-term consequences of a world without privacy are profound and far-reaching. Awareness of potential identity theft, financial exploitation, psychological manipulation, and erosion of civil liberties emphasizes the urgency of protective action. Combining strong personal cybersecurity habits with advocacy for ethical corporate and governmental practices helps mitigate these risks. Society must prioritize privacy as a fundamental right, embedding it into technology, law, and culture. Continuous education, responsible data practices, and vigilance empower individuals to safeguard themselves and others. Understanding the stakes reinforces the need for proactive engagement in privacy protection.

Individuals must take ownership of their digital footprints. Awareness that every online interaction contributes to a permanent record highlights the importance of careful, deliberate behavior. Combining mindful online engagement with technical safeguards like encryption, secure passwords, and privacy settings preserves autonomy. Teaching digital literacy, critical thinking, and safe data habits empowers all users to navigate the online world securely. Responsible management of personal information strengthens both individual resilience and collective security. Digital self-discipline and awareness are foundational for thriving in a privacy-conscious society.

Organizations play a critical role in preserving trust through data stewardship. Awareness that breaches, misuse, or negligent handling of information erode confidence underscores the importance of ethical practices. Combining transparent policies, security measures, and regulatory compliance ensures users feel protected and respected. Organizations that prioritize privacy enhance loyalty, reputation, and overall societal trust. Leadership and corporate culture must emphasize privacy as an ongoing responsibility rather than a one-time effort. Protecting privacy is both a moral and strategic imperative for sustainable digital engagement.

Technology itself can be designed to reinforce privacy. Awareness of privacy-enhancing tools, such as end-to-end encryption, anonymization, and secure cloud storage, enables safer digital interaction. Combining technical safeguards with responsible usage habits maximizes protection. Developers and policymakers should prioritize privacy-by-design principles to ensure that convenience does not compromise security. Educating users on these tools empowers individuals to actively protect themselves. A proactive approach to technology design strengthens societal resilience against intrusion and exploitation.

CHAPTER .40

BUILDING A PERSONAL CYBERSECURITY STRATEGY: YOUR ROADMAP TO DIGITAL SAFETY

How to Create and Implement a Comprehensive Plan to Protect Your Data, Devices, and Identity

Building a personal cybersecurity strategy starts with awareness of the risks in your digital environment. Awareness of threats such as malware, phishing, identity theft, and social engineering allows you to anticipate vulnerabilities before they are exploited. Combining this awareness with a clear plan ensures that protective measures are systematic rather than reactive. Assessing your devices, accounts, and habits is the first step in identifying areas that need attention. A well-defined strategy provides structure for consistent application of cybersecurity practices. Taking control of your digital security empowers you to act proactively rather than reactively.

The next step is inventorying all your digital assets. Awareness of the devices, accounts, passwords, and personal data you possess highlights points of vulnerability. Combining this inventory with categorization of sensitive and non-sensitive information helps prioritize protective measures. Regularly updating and auditing this inventory ensures nothing is overlooked as your digital footprint grows. Maintaining a clear picture of your assets allows you to apply targeted security measures efficiently. Understanding what you need to protect is the foundation for a strong cybersecurity strategy.

Password management is a critical element of personal cybersecurity. Awareness that weak, reused, or predictable passwords are a primary vector for attacks underscores the importance of strong authentication. Combining unique, complex passwords with password managers ensures both security and convenience. Multi-factor authentication adds an additional layer of protection, reducing the likelihood of unauthorized access. Regularly reviewing and updating passwords minimizes the risk of compromise. Strong password practices form the first line of defense in protecting personal accounts and data.

Device security is equally important in a personal cybersecurity strategy. Awareness that smartphones, laptops, and IoT devices can be exploited highlights the need for comprehensive protection. Combining antivirus software, firewalls, regular updates, and secure configurations ensures devices remain resilient against threats. Physical security, such as screen locks and safe storage, complements digital safeguards. Routine monitoring for unusual behavior or potential intrusions helps catch issues early. Securing devices is not a one-time action—it requires consistent attention and vigilance.

Data backup and recovery planning are essential components of a robust cybersecurity strategy. Awareness that data loss can occur from malware, accidental deletion, or system failure underscores the importance of regular backups. Combining local, external, and cloud-based backups provides redundancy and peace of mind. Testing recovery procedures ensures that backups are reliable and accessible when needed. Documenting backup schedules and storage locations supports consistent implementation. A solid backup plan minimizes disruption and ensures continuity in the face of unexpected incidents.

Online behavior and awareness play a pivotal role in personal cybersecurity. Awareness that oversharing information on social media or interacting with suspicious links increases risk is critical. Combining cautious online behavior with privacy settings and content review helps minimize exposure. Being mindful of what you post, who you interact with, and what permissions apps request strengthens overall security. Educating yourself about common scams, phishing tactics, and social engineering techniques reduces the likelihood of falling victim. Conscious digital behavior complements technical safeguards to create a comprehensive defense.

Securing your communications is a key part of protecting personal information. Awareness that emails, messaging apps, and calls can be intercepted highlights the importance of encrypted channels. Combining secure email practices, encrypted messaging apps, and cautious sharing of sensitive information reduces vulnerabilities. Verifying the identity of contacts before sharing personal data prevents unauthorized access. Using tools like virtual private networks (VPNs) safeguards your online activity from prying eyes. Ensuring communication privacy strengthens overall digital security and protects your identity.

Monitoring and alert systems provide real-time defense against potential threats. Awareness of suspicious activity on accounts, devices, and networks allows for rapid intervention. Combining automated alerts, monitoring services, and manual checks ensures that anomalies are detected early. Regularly reviewing account activity and notifications helps identify breaches before serious damage occurs. Setting up alerts for unusual login locations, large transactions, or system changes enhances proactive protection. Continuous monitoring provides both security and peace of mind.

Education and continual learning are foundational to personal cybersecurity. Awareness that threats evolve constantly requires individuals to update their knowledge and skills. Combining online courses, webinars, blogs, and security news ensures you stay informed about new risks and mitigation strategies. Practicing safe habits and reviewing emerging threats strengthens resilience against cybercrime. Sharing knowledge with friends, family, or colleagues promotes a culture of collective security. Lifelong learning is essential for maintaining robust defenses in a rapidly changing digital landscape.

Incident response planning prepares you for the unexpected. Awareness that no system is completely immune to attacks underscores the importance of having a recovery plan. Combining step-by-step action plans, contact lists, and backup protocols ensures swift and effective responses. Regularly testing and updating your incident response plan minimizes downtime and data loss. Knowing how to respond reduces panic, mitigates damage, and accelerates recovery. Being prepared for potential breaches completes a comprehensive personal cybersecurity strategy.

Implementing multi-layered security strengthens your personal defenses. Awareness that relying on a single protective measure leaves vulnerabilities is crucial. Combining strong passwords, multi-factor authentication, device security, and network protection creates redundancy, making attacks more difficult to succeed. Each layer compensates for potential weaknesses in others, reinforcing overall resilience. Regularly reviewing and updating these layers ensures that defenses adapt to evolving threats. Multi-layered security transforms individual actions into a robust and reliable defense strategy.

Managing and limiting digital footprints is essential for long-term security. Awareness that every online interaction leaves traces highlights the importance of careful digital behavior. Combining privacy settings, cautious sharing, and data minimization reduces exposure to tracking, profiling, and potential exploitation. Regularly reviewing your online presence helps identify and correct vulnerabilities before they are exploited. Limiting unnecessary data collection and sharing protects both personal and sensitive information. Maintaining control over your digital footprint strengthens your cybersecurity strategy and personal autonomy.

Financial security is a critical component of personal cybersecurity. Awareness that banking, online purchases, and digital wallets are common targets for cybercrime emphasizes the need for protection. Combining secure passwords, two-factor authentication, and transaction monitoring safeguards your financial assets. Avoiding unsecured networks and suspicious links reduces the risk of fraud. Keeping track of financial activity and reporting anomalies promptly enhances security and mitigates potential damage. Integrating financial vigilance into your broader cybersecurity plan ensures comprehensive protection.

Regular software updates are essential to maintaining security. Awareness that outdated software exposes systems to known vulnerabilities underscores the importance of keeping devices current. Combining automatic updates with manual checks for critical patches ensures that security gaps are minimized. Updating operating systems, applications, and firmware maintains compatibility with protective measures and reduces exposure to malware. Continuous maintenance prevents attackers from exploiting overlooked weaknesses. Keeping software up to date is a simple yet powerful component of a personal cybersecurity strategy.

Cyber hygiene habits complete your personal security framework. Awareness that consistent, routine practices reduce risk highlights the importance of daily vigilance. Combining secure browsing, cautious email handling, device maintenance, and data management strengthens resilience. Practicing good cyber hygiene ensures that technical safeguards are reinforced by responsible behavior. Developing these habits fosters long-term security and reduces the likelihood of breaches. Cyber hygiene transforms knowledge and strategy into consistent protective action, making it the cornerstone of personal digital safety.

Creating a personal incident response plan is critical for minimizing damage in the event of a breach. Awareness that even with the best preventive measures, attacks can still occur highlights the importance of preparation. Combining step-by-step procedures, contact lists, and backup verification ensures that you can respond swiftly and effectively. Knowing whom to notify, what systems to isolate, and how to restore backups reduces panic and accelerates recovery. Periodic testing of your response plan ensures it remains practical and effective. Being prepared transforms potential crises into manageable situations, strengthening overall security confidence.

Regular monitoring of accounts and devices is essential for early threat detection. Awareness that unauthorized access can occur at any time underscores the need for vigilance. Combining automated alerts, manual checks, and anomaly reporting allows you to quickly identify suspicious activity. Keeping an eye on unusual login attempts, unexpected emails, and system performance anomalies increases your ability to respond before damage occurs. Monitoring complements preventive measures by providing real-time oversight of potential threats. Continuous attention reinforces your personal cybersecurity strategy and ensures ongoing protection.

Education and training enhance your ability to stay ahead of cyber threats. Awareness that new attack techniques evolve constantly emphasizes the importance of lifelong learning. Combining courses, webinars, and practical exercises with news on emerging threats ensures you remain informed and capable. Practicing simulated attacks and phishing awareness exercises reinforces theoretical knowledge in real-world contexts. Sharing knowledge with family and colleagues multiplies protective effects across your community. An educated user is a resilient user, capable of adapting to the dynamic landscape of cybersecurity.

Securing cloud storage and online accounts is a key aspect of personal cybersecurity. Awareness that cloud-based services are convenient but vulnerable underscores the need for careful account management. Combining strong authentication, encrypted storage, and selective data sharing ensures sensitive information remains protected. Regularly reviewing permissions, activity logs, and backup policies reduces risk of unauthorized access. Cloud security practices should be integrated into your overall strategy rather than treated as optional. Protecting data in the cloud preserves both convenience and security.

Reflecting on building a personal cybersecurity strategy, it is clear that knowledge, habits, and preparation are equally important.

Awareness of the risks, combined with structured protective measures, ensures that you maintain control over your digital life. Each layer of defense—passwords, device security, backups, education, and monitoring—works together to create a resilient system. Cultivating a proactive mindset allows you to anticipate threats rather than react to them after the fact. Cybersecurity is not solely a technical endeavor; it is a practice that integrates awareness, strategy, and consistent action. By committing to this approach, you take ownership of your safety, privacy, and digital identity.

Author reflection: I have come to understand that personal cybersecurity is both a responsibility and an empowering practice. Awareness alone does not suffice; action transforms knowledge into protection. Over time, I have observed that those who implement multi-layered strategies, remain vigilant, and continually educate themselves experience far fewer breaches and enjoy greater peace of mind. Cybersecurity is an ongoing journey that combines technology, psychology, and discipline. Embracing this responsibility equips you not only to protect yourself but also to model safe behavior for others in your network.

Practical implementation of a personal cybersecurity strategy requires discipline and adaptability. Awareness that threats evolve constantly highlights the need for continuous learning and adjustment of protective measures. Combining tools, habits, and education ensures your defenses remain effective even as cybercriminals develop new tactics. Regular review, updates, and testing of your systems create confidence in your ability to respond. Taking a structured and deliberate approach transforms digital security from a source of stress into a sustainable, manageable practice. Proactivity, persistence, and mindfulness are the keys to long-term protection.

EPILOGUE:

The digital landscape will continue to evolve, and so will the threats that inhabit it. Yet, the principles you've learned in this book—awareness, vigilance, layered security, and proactive habits—will remain your steadfast allies. Personal cybersecurity is not a one-time effort but a lifelong practice, requiring reflection, adaptation, and conscious choices. By integrating these strategies into daily life, you become both the protector and architect of your digital world.

Remember, the most secure systems are those guided by informed, mindful users. Technology is a tool, but your habits, knowledge, and decision-making are what truly safeguard your data and identity. The power to create a safe digital life is in your hands. Take it seriously, practice it consistently, and teach it to others. In doing so, you are not only protecting yourself but also contributing to a safer, more secure digital community for everyone.

ABOUT THE AUTHOR

Laura Lee is a writer, digital strategist, and advocate for personal empowerment in the modern world. She bridges the gap between technology and human experience, helping individuals and organizations navigate the digital landscape with clarity and confidence. Raised in a small town where curiosity and storytelling were celebrated, Laura developed a lifelong passion for learning and teaching.

As the founder of a digital design and strategy agency, Laura has helped countless clients safeguard their digital presence while building meaningful connections online. Her work reflects a commitment to intentionality, integrity, and human-centered solutions. Through writing, consulting, and digital education, she empowers others to understand technology, protect their data, and make informed decisions that honor their privacy and identity.

This book is an extension of Laura's mission: to provide practical guidance, foster awareness, and inspire proactive stewardship of one's digital life. It is a roadmap to personal empowerment in a world where privacy and security are increasingly fragile but always attainable.

www.ingramcontent.com/pod-product-compliance
Lightning Source LLC
LaVergne TN
LVHW052244200926
848481LV00002B/265
* 9 7 9 8 2 3 3 4 1 8 4 9 5 *